THE
COLLECTOR'S ENCYCLOPEDIA
OF
PATTERN GLASS

A Pattern Guide to Early American Pressed Glass

by Mollie Helen McCain

COLLECTOR BOOKS
P.O. BOX 3009
PADUCAH, KENTUCKY 42001

The current values in this book should be used only as a guide. They are not intended to set prices, which vary from one section of the country to another. Auction prices as well as dealer prices vary greatly and are affected by condition as well as demand. Neither the Author nor the Publisher assumes responsibility for any losses that might be incurred as a result of consulting this guide.

Additional copies of this book may be ordered from:

Collector Books
P.O. Box 3009
Paducah, KY 42002-3009

@12.95. Add $2.00 for postage and handling.

ACKNOWLEDGEMENTS

This revised and expanded EDITION reflects the requests and criticisms of readers, whose correspondence is always welcome. Most particularly I thank William Heacock, who shared his personal notes with me. Much information in this book was taken from Mr. Heacock's marvelous research.

Others who helped in various ways are Don Brown, Mrs. Douglas Garrison, Craig A. Younkman, Mrs. R. L. Windeknecht, the Jackson (Michigan) District Library, and Bill Schroeder of Collector Books.

-Mollie Helen McCain

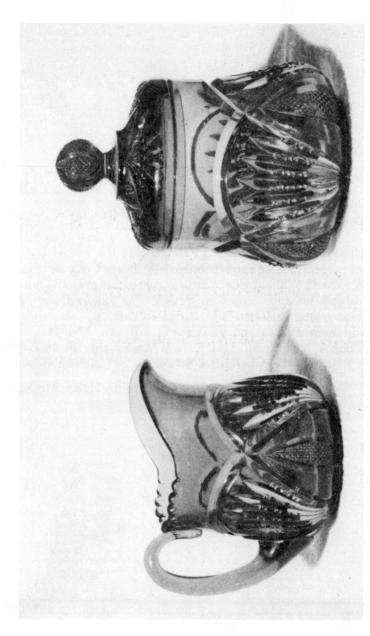

FRONTISPIECE: HEISEY'S PINEAPPLE AND FAN sugar and creamer. To classify this ornate pattern in this book, the diamondpoint indicates a place in the "Diamond" category. Information, a drawing of the syrup, and similar patterns appear on Plate 78.

Photo courtesy of Edwin Fitzpatrick, Charles Town, W. Va.

DEDICATION

To the Harrington Girls
— Margaret, Katharine,
Lillian, Fern, Helen, and
most of all, Doris.

INTRODUCTION

This guide is planned to allow easy identification of early American pressed glass patterns. Categories are used to group similar patterns together according to **molded characteristics**. Most patterns in this book were made in clear crystal glass; many came also in colors, staining, flashing, gilding, slag, or with painted decorations. They date from the middle 1800's to World War I.

Some patterns have more than one name — company names, researcher's names, local names — and these are included with the best-known designation. An abbreviated reference to the original researchers follows the pattern name. When known, the manufacturer and a known date (not necessarily the only date) of production is given; and a listing of known pieces available (but not necessarily all pieces made).

EXPLANATION OF TERMS USED:

The term **Basic Table Service** means sugar bowl, creamer, spoon holder, and butter dish. **Extended Table Service** means basic table service plus water and milk pitchers, bowls, syrups, salt shaker, celery vases, plates, and the many other pieces made in table sets. These are listed if known.

A **Price Key** is given to each pattern, and a price table follows the category listings. These prices reflect a general range of values as well as I can determine. Large, ornate pieces in a given category, such as high covered compotes or fancy fluted bowls, may be priced in the next higher key of a given pattern; while smaller pieces, such as jelly compotes or low, plain bowls, may fall to the next lower key. Pieces with fancy finials or fine etching have more value; and certain pieces in a pattern may be scarce or rare. Some patterns come in both flint glass and glass of lesser quality; values should be adjusted accordingly. **All prices are for crystal glass** unless color is designated; colored and opaque glass will be significantly higher in value than the keys listed.

All illustrations are original drawings by the author, and are intended to help identify patterns. As such, they have no consistency in size scale, either to the actual piece of glass or to each other.

Much pressed glass will soon be placed in the market from collections made in the 1930's and '40's; research in the field is on-going; and new information is surfacing almost daily. New collectors of pressed glass, as well as the old-timers, will find this to be an exciting time in a fascinating field of glass filled with beauty, history, and heritage.

REFERENCE ABBREVIATIONS (See also Bibliography at end of book)

Bond	- Bond, Marcelle *The Beauty of Albany Glass,* Publishers Printing House, Berne, Indiana
Bones	- Bones, Frances *The Book of Duncan Glass*
Boul	- Boultinghouse, Mark *Art and Colored Glass Toothpick Holders* (Author)
Gob I & Gob II	- Millard, Dr. S. T. *Goblets I* and *Goblets II*
H I-V	- Heacock, William *Encyclopedia of Victorian Colored Pattern Glass,* Volumes I, III, V
Her	- Herrick, Dr. Ruth *Greentown Glass*
HPV	- Heacock, William *Pattern Glass Preview,* Issues I-V
HTP	- Heacock, William *1000 Toothpick Holders*
K 1-8	- Kamm, Minnie Watson *Pattern Glass Books 1-8*
Lechler	- Lechler, Doris and O'Neill, Virginia *Children's Glass Dishes,* Thomas Nelson, Inc., New York, N.Y.
Metz 1 & 2	- Metz, Alice H. *Early American Pattern Glass* and *Much More Early American Pattern Glass,* Collector Books, Paducah, Kentucky
Mil	- Miller, Everett and Addie *The New Martinsville Glass Story,* Richardson Publishing Co., Marietta, Ohio
Miller	- Miller, Robert *Price Guide to Antiques - 7th Ed.*
MOP	- Millard, Dr. S. T. *Opaque Glass*
MU I & II	- Murray, Dean L. *Cruets Only* and *More Cruets Only,* Kilgore Graphics, Inc., Phoenix, Arizona
OMN	- Original manufacturer's name
PetSal	- Peterson, Arthur *Glass Salt Shakers*
PetPat	- Peterson, Arthur *Glass Patents and Patterns,* Celery City Printing, Sanford, Florida
SmFin	- Smith, Don E. *Findlay Pattern Glass,* Gray Printing Co., Fostoria, Ohio
Stout	- Stout, Sandra McPhee *The Complete Book of McKee Glass,* Trojan Press, Inc., Kansas City, Missouri
Taylor	- Taylor, Ardelle *Colored Glass Sugar Shakers and Syrup Pitchers* (Author)
W	- Warman, Edwin G. *Antiques and Their Current Prices*

9

Updated Values

	KEY A	KEY B	KEY C	KEY D	KEY E	KEY F
Bowl, Med. size	$ 12-20	$ 18-35	$ 25-45	$ 30-60	$ 50-75	$ 75+
Butter dish w/Lid	23-40	35-65	50-80	60-100	90-150	150+
Cake Stand	28-40	35-60	50-80	75-120	110-150	150+
Celery Vase	23-40	30-45	35-75	50-100	80-150	150+
Compote, Lge. w/Lid	30-55	40-60	50-90	80-150	120-180	180+
Compote, Jelly w/Lid	18-25	20-30	25-40	35-60	50-100	100+
Compote, Open	12-20	18-35	25-40	35-55	45-85	75+
Cordial	13-25	20-40	30-65	55-90	80-120	120+
Cracker Jar	20-38	35-50	40-60	45-70	60-100	100+
Creamer	18-35	30-50	40-65	50-100	85-160	160+
Cruet	25-40	30-55	40-60	50-85	80-110	110+
Cup	5-10	6-15	10-22	15-28	25-40	35+
Decanter/Bottle	35-55	45-70	60-110	80-140	125-200	200+
Egg Cup	15-25	20-40	25-45	30-70	60-100	100+
Goblet	15-30	25-45	32-55	45-90	70-150	150+
Jam Jar w/Lid	25-35	30-50	35-70	50-100	90-150	150+
Mug	15-25	20-35	25-45	35-60	50-80	80+
Pitcher	25-45	35-55	50-85	80-150	130-200	200+
Plate (Med. Size)	10-20	15-30	27-55	40-75	60-100	100+
Relish Dish	10-20	15-25	20-35	30-50	40-60	60+
Salt Shaker	9-20	16-30	25-50	28-55	40-75	60+
Salt, Master	10-22	18-40	23-50	40-75	55-90	80+
Sauce Dish	6-12	10-20	15-30	20-40	30-60	60+
Spill Holder	30-40	35-45	40-70	50-85	60-80	80+
Spoon Holder	15-30	20-40	25-50	35-60	50-90	80+
Sugar Bowl w/Lid	20-35	30-55	40-75	50-80	75-140	140+
Sugar Bowl, Open	15-25	20-30	25-35	30-40	35-60	60+
Sugar Shaker	30-40	35-50	45-65	60-90	80-125	125+
Syrup, Orig. Lid	30-50	40-70	60-85	70-120	105-160	160+
Toothpick Holder	15-25	20-40	25-45	40-75	50-100	100+
Tray/Platter	25-35	28-45	35-70	55-100	80-140	140+
Tumbler	15-25	20-38	28-48	38-68	60-100	100+
Vase, Med. Size	12-20	15-30	25-45	30-65	50-70	70+
Waste Jar	20-30	25-40	35-50	45-65	50-80	80+
Wine Goblet	15-25	20-35	30-60	40-70	60-120	120+

PLATE 1 ANIMALS

EGYPTIAN (PARTHENON), 8″ footed bowl.—*Ref. L111; K1-31*
Boston and Sandwich Glass Co., 1870's. Made in extended table
service (see explanation in introduction) including Cleopatra platter,
Salt Lake Temple platter, large pyramids plate, sauce, pickle dish,
bread tray, celery vase. Lots of this pattern can be found.
Crystal—**Key C**
This beautiful pattern could fit into several identifying categories
such as flowers, animals, plants, beads or people. Not all pieces depict
all of its motifs, but always present is the stippled, stylized-flower
rim.

PLATE 2 ANIMALS

Row 1

1. RACING DEER (DEER RACING), pitcher.—*Ref. K6-60* Dalzell, Gilmore and Leighton, 1890's. Crystal pitcher known. —**Key E**

2. THREE DEER, goblet.—*Ref. K8-69* Crystal goblet known.—**Key D**

3. DEER ALERT, pitcher.—*Ref. K4-124* —**Key D**

Row 2

1. DEER AND OAK TREE, pitcher.—*Ref. K3-122* Dalzell, Gilmore and Leighton; Indiana Tumbler and Goblet (National), c. 1880's; c. 1900. Pitcher known. Crystal, chocolate glass.—**Key D**

2. HORSEHEAD MEDALLION, spooner.—*Ref. LV pl. 29* c. 1885-95. Extended table service including toy table set. Crystal; milk-white glass.—**Key C**

3. WESTWARD HO! (PIONEER; TIPPECANOE), pitcher.—*Ref. L89; K1-16* Gillander and Sons, 1879. Made in extended table service including covered candy dish, celery vase, footed sauce, compotes, bread platter, jam jar, sherbet, relish, wine, rare champagne, individual creamer. Good availability. See Plate 180. Crystal, frosted.—**Key E**

Row 3

1. DEER AND PINE TREE (DEER AND DOE), mug.—*Ref. L119; K4-31* Belmont Glass Co., c. 1883. Extended table service including celery vase, cake stand, waste bowl, compotes, jam jar, platter, pickle dish, oblong plate, bread plate, sauces, tray, miniature mug. Fair availability. Crystal, blue, amber, lt. green, yellow.—**Key D**

2. DEER WITH LILY-OF-THE-VALLEY, goblet.—*Ref. L164#17; Gob I-36* Known in crystal goblet.—**Key E**

3. LOOP WITH ELK, goblet.—*Ref. Gob II-144* Crystal—**Key E**

PLATE 3 ANIMALS

Row 1

1. TINY LION (LION WITH CABLE), open sugar bowl.—*Ref. K2-35* 1880's. Made in extended table service including celery vase, compote, salt shaker (without lions). Fair availability but expensive. Crystal.—**Key C**
2. MONKEY, butter dish. See Row 3 #1.
3. GIRAFFE, goblet.—*Ref. Gob II-117* Novelty.

Row 2

1. JUMBO (ELEPHANT), compote.—*Ref. L-94; K5-14* Canton Glass Co., 1883; Aetna Glass Co. 1883. Extended table service including castor set, jam jar, covered bowl, two butter dishes, compote, cup and saucer, very rare spoon rack. Crystal.—**Key F**
2. OASIS, pitcher.—*Ref. K8-1* This design is acid etched. Extended table service including celery vase.—**Key D**

Row 3

1. MONKEY (MONKEY UNDER TREE), pitcher.—*Ref. K4-81* c. 1880's. Extended table service including finger bowl, toothpick holder, tumbler, mug, pickle jar, jam jar, celery vase, ash tray. No goblet was made. Crystal; opalescent.—**Key E**
2. LION AND BABOON, pitcher.—*Ref. K3-57* 1880's. Extended table service including covered compote, toy table set.—**Key E**

Row 4

1. LION, open salt.—*Ref. L-93; K1-44* Gillander and Sons, 1876. Extended table service including rare frosted cheese dish, celery vase, footed sauce, toy table set. When frosted is called "Frosted Lion". Crystal; milk glass.—**Key D**
2. CLEAR LION HEAD (ATLANTA), salt shaker.—*Ref. K5-83* Fostoria Glass Co., 1895. Extended table service including toothpick holder, berry set, cake stand, jam jar, pickle dish, sauce, toy table set. Crystal.—**Key D**

PLATE 4 ANIMALS

Row 1

1. BRINGING HOME THE COWS, pitcher.—*Ref. K4-125* Dalzell, Gilmore and Leighton, 1880's. Made in basic table service plus pitcher. Crystal.—**Key E (double)**
2. PIG AND CORN, goblet.—*Ref. K8-67; Gob I Pl. 36* c. 1875-85. Made in goblet only.—**Key F (double)**
3. DANCING GOAT, ale glass.—*Ref. K7-74* c. 1878. Novelty. See Goblet.—**Key D**

Row 2

1. CURRIER AND IVES (BALKY MULE), tray.—*Ref. K3-117; LV86* Bellaire Glass Co., 1890. Extended table service including syrup, salt shaker, wine, lamp, decanter, canoe-shaped bowls, cup and saucer, plate. See Plate 102. Crystal, canary (rare), amber, blue.—**Key C**
2. RABBIT IN TREE, salt shaker.—*Ref. PetSal 36K* Novelty.—**Key C**
3. BEAVER BAND, goblet—*Ref. Gob II-130* Goblet only. Made in Canada for a church celebration.—**Key E**

Row 3

1. SQUIRREL, pitcher.—*Ref. L100* Indiana Tumbler and Goblet Co., 1890's. Extended table service including rare goblet, sauce, toothpick holder. Crystal. Wide range in prices. Pitcher **Key E;** butter dish **Key F;** Toothpick holder **Key B;** sauce **Key C**
2. SQUIRREL-IN-BOWER, pitcher.—*Ref. K4-60* Portland Glass Co., c. 1870. Known in scarce water pitcher and very rare goblet.—**Key F**
3. SQUIRREL WITH NUT, pitcher.—*Ref. K5-128* —**Key F**

PLATE 5 ANIMALS

Row 1

1. FOX AND CROW, pitcher.—*Ref. K4-124* Indiana Tumbler and Goblet Co. (National), late 1890's. Pitcher known.—**Key F**
2. DEER AND DOG (DOG AND DEER; DEER, DOG AND HUNTER), pitcher—*Ref. K1-52; L101* 1880's. Made in extended table service including mug, celery vase, compotes, covered bowl. Pieces with finial and pitcher.—**Key F**; smaller pieces **Key D**
3. DEER AND DOG, finial detail. See Above.

Row 2

1. DOG HUNTING, Pitcher.—*Ref. K4-125* National Glass Co., c. 1902.—**Key F**
2. SHELL AND TASSEL (ROUND), sugar bowl.—*Ref. L157; K3-120* George Duncan and Sons, #555; 1880. Extended table service in both round and square forms including celery vase, sauce, cake stand, salt shaker, historical and plain platters, jelly compote, berry set. See Plates 217 and 245. Pieces with dog finial.—**Key F**; others **Key E**
3. OWL AND POSSUM, goblet.

Row 3

BUTTERFLY WITH FLOWERS, cup plate (3½"). (Author's name).

Row 4

1. POLAR BEAR (ICEBERG; ARCTIC; NORTH POLE), goblet.—*Ref. L91* Crystal Glass Co., 1880's. Extended table service including finger bowl, oval tray, sauce. Crystal, frosted.—**Key E**
2. FISH, salt shaker.—*Ref. PetSal 28T* Novelty.
3. GRASSHOPPER WITH INSECT (LOCUST; LONG SPEAR), spoon holder.—*Ref. K1-88* 1880's. Extended table service including celery vase, sauce, compote. Crystal. Check wings of insect for damage.—**Key C**

PLATE 6 ANIMALS, INSECTS & FISH

Row 1

1. BUTTERFLY HANDLES (BUTTERFLY), sugar bowl.—*Ref. LV27* Extended table service including celery vase, salt shaker. With handles— **Key C**

2. BUTTERFLY EARS (ALARIC), mustard pot.—*Ref. K8-131* Bryce, Higbee and Co., mid-1880's. Made in extended table service.—**Key A**

3. BUTTERFLY WITH SPRAY (ACME), mug.—*Ref. K8-130* Bryce, Higbee and Co., 1880's. Extended table service including compotes, tumbler, celery vase. Crystal.—**Key D**

Row 2

1. BUTTERFLY, pitcher.—*Ref. K2-123* U.S. Glass Co. #6406, 1908. Extended table service including celery vase, covered mustard jar, pickle dish, salt shaker, relish. Crystal; frosted handles. —**Key B**

2. STIPPLED LEAF, FLOWER AND MOTH (STIPPLED LEAF AND FLOWER), pitcher.—*Ref. K1-47* 1870's. Extended table service including tumbler, decanter, sauce, goblet. Crystal.—**Key C**

3. LATE BUTTERFLY (MIKADO), pitcher.—*Ref. Gob II-31; LV28* Indiana Tumbler and Goblet Co., 1907. Extended table service including salt shaker.—**Key C**

Row 3

1. GARDEN OF EDEN (LOTUS; TURTLE; FISH), pitcher.—*Ref. Gob II-8; K3-58* Made c. 1865 in extended table service including cake stand, mug, platter, bread tray. See Plate 199.—**Key C**

2. AQUARIUM, pitcher.—*Ref. K4-119* U.S. Glass Co. after 1909. Pitcher known. Crystal, amber, emerald green.—**Key D**

3. DOLPHIN, candlestick.—*Ref. L143* Boston and Sandwich; Bakewell, Pears; 1850's; 1868. Made in a number of dolphin-based pieces including compote.—**Key E**

PLATE 7 ANIMALS AND BIRDS

Row 1

1. PARROT (PARROT AND FAN; OWL AND FAN), goblet.—*Ref. K8-67; Gob I pl. 95* 1880's. Extended table service including bowl, celery vase, rare wine.—**Key C**

2. BIRD-IN-RING (GRACE), spoon holder.—*Ref. K2-16; K7-76* Part of the pattern "JAPANESE" by Duncan Glass, 1881. The "BIRD IN RING" appears on sugar bowl and spooner. A butterfly is on the goblet (called "BUTTERFLY AND FAN".) See Plate 180.—**Key D**

3. STRUTTING PEACOCK, creamer.—*Ref. K6-13* Imperial Glass, late 1880's. Extended table service including tumbler, decanter, mug, plates. Crystal, blue, purple, green, carnival.—**Key C**

Row 2

1. PEACOCK AT THE FOUNTAIN (PEACOCK AND PALM), creamer.—*Ref. K6-24* Northwood Glass Co. Extended table service including berry set, punch bowl and cups, footed orange bowl, tumbler. Carnival glass in many colors.

2. KITTENS, toy spoon holder and plate detail.—*Ref. Hartung* Fenton Art Glass Co., c. 1912. Toy table service including cup and saucer, vase, bowls, plate. Crystal, carnival.—**Key C**

Row 3

1. CHICK, sugar bowl finial.—*Ref. LV20* Extended table service including salt shaker. See Plate 166. Value is higher with chick finial.—**Key B**

2. DRAGON, open sugar bowl.—*Ref. Gob II-130* Extended table service including small compote. All pieces rare; goblet is most often seen. Crystal.—**Key F**

3. ST. BERNARD, sugar bowl. See Plate 68.

PLATE 8 BIRDS

Row 1

1. CARDINAL BIRD, spoon holder.—*Ref. L100; K1-31* Possibly Ohio Flint Glass Co., 1870's. Extended table service including sauce. There is a tiny caterpillar on the leaf of pictured piece. Crystal. —**Key C**
2. CARDINAL BIRD, covered sugar bowl. See above.
3. ROBIN, custard cup.—**Key C**
4. BIRD AND STRAWBERRY (BLUEBIRD), pitcher.—*Ref. K2-85* Beatty Glass Co.; Indiana Glass Co.; 1910-20. Extended table service including punch set, cake stand, compotes, heart-shaped relish, tumbler, wine. An abundant pattern. Crystal, colors, decorated.—**Key D**

Row 2

1. HUMMINGBIRD (FLYING ROBIN; BIRD AND FERN), pitcher.—*Ref. K4-25* 1888. Extended table service including tumbler, sauce, water tray, celery vase, compote, covered bowl, cheese plate, open salt. Crystal, canary, amber, blue.—**Key C**
2. FLYING BIRDS, goblet.—*Ref. L164-6* c. 1870. Known in goblet.—**Key C**
3. SINGING BIRDS, creamer—*Ref. K2-67* Northwood Glass Co., 1900. Extended table service including bowls, sherbet, tumbler, berry set, mug. Crystal, carnival, custard glass.—**Key C**

Row 3

PANELLED CARDINAL, goblet.—*Ref. Gob II-111* —**Key C**

Row 4

1. BIRD AND TREE, pitcher.—*Ref. L190* —**Key D**
2. BIRD HANDLED (ROBIN), salt shaker.—*Ref. PetSal 23A* 1882 Novelty. Very rare in color.—**Key C**
3. THRUSH, salt shaker.—*Ref. W-124* Dalzell, Gilmore and Leighton, c. 1890.—**Key C**

PLATE 9 BIRDS

Row 1

1. WADING HERON, pitcher.—*Ref. K6-61* U.S. Glass #6404, c. 1915. Crystal, green (rare)—**Key D**
2. BLUE HERON, creamer.—*Ref. K4-24* —**Key C**
3. MOON AND STORK (OSTRICH LOOKING AT THE MOON; STORK LOOKING AT THE MOON), goblet.—*Ref. K8-67* —**Key E**

Row 2

1. HERON, pitcher.—*Ref. Miller* Indiana Tumbler and Goblet Co., 1890's. Made in extended table service including water tray, celery vase.—**Key C**
2. FROSTED STORK (FLAMINGO; FROSTED CRANE), pitcher.—*Ref. L-100.* Has stork finial. Extended table service including jam jar, tray, finger bowl, 9″ plate, platter, pickle castor. All pieces scarce.—**Key D**

Row 3

1. FLYING STORK, perfume bottle. Whitall-Tatum Glass Co. A similar goblet is shown in *Gob II-117.*—**Key C**
2. OWL AND STUMP (OWL), toothpick holder.—*Ref. Lee; HTP-744* Central Glass Co., c. 1890. Novelty. Crystal, colors. —**Key B**

Row 4

1. OWL, pitcher.—*Ref. K1-56* Milk glass, blue slag in pitchers of various sizes.
2. LITTLE OWL, creamer.—*Ref. K1-56* U.S. Glass Co. (Challinor), 1891. Made in toy basic table service with "bear" sugar, "fish" spooner, "Turtle" butter; the set called "MENAGERIE". Crystal, opaque colors, amber.—**Key B**
3. CLEAR STORK (CRANE; STORK), pitcher.—*Ref. K3-64* 1890-91. Extended table service including tumbler, compote. —**Key C**

PLATE 10 BIRDS

Row 1

1. SWAN, pitcher.—*Ref. K1-63; L-177* 1880's. Made in extended table service including jam jar, sauce, covered dish. Crystal, amber, canary, cobalt blue.—**Key C;** Pitcher **Key E**

2. SWAN ON POND (SWAN TWO), pitcher.—*Ref. K3-36* 1880. Milk Glass.—**Key F**

3. SWAN WITH TREE, pitcher.—*Ref. K5-127* U.S. Glass Co. (Gas City factory), 1890's. Known in goblet and pitcher.—**Key C**

Row 2

1. FLYING SWAN, pitcher.—*Ref. K2-81* Westmoreland Specialty Co., 1890's. Extended table service including toothpick holder, celery vase. Crystal, slag.—**Key D**

2. LATE SWAN, creamer.—*Ref. K1-92* Westmoreland Specialty Co., 1891-1892. Known in sugar and creamer. Opaque white and turquoise.—**Key D**

3. PANELLED SWAN, goblet.—*Ref. Gob II-30* —**Key C**

Row 3

1. PARROT, pitcher.—*Ref. K5 pl. 16* Dalzell, Gilmore and Leighton, 1889.—**Key E**

Row 4

1. FROSTED EAGLE, compote.—*Ref. K6-62* Probably Crystal Glass Co., late 1870's. Extended table service including salt shaker, compote. See Plate 189.—**Key D**

2. BULLET EMBLEM (SHIELD IN RED, WHITE AND BLUE; EAGLE AND ARMS), butter dish. U.S. Glass Co., 1898. A Spanish-American War Commemorative. Made in basic table service.—**Key F**

PLATE 11 CIRCLES

ROMAN ROSETTE, creamer.—*Ref. K1-34; L-157* Bryce, Walker and Co.; U.S. Glass Co. #15030. 1875; 1891. Made in extended table service including cake stand, compotes, salt shaker, mug, toy mug, bread plate, pickle dish, celery vase, wine, tumbler, syrup, flat and footed sauces, bowls, plate. Being reproduced; the stippling should have a pebbled look, not a pitted appearance. Crystal; ruby-stained. (U.S. Glass produced the stained items.)—**Key D**

PLATE 12 CIRCLES, PLAIN

Row 1

1. CANNONBALL (BULLET), pitcher.—*Ref. K2-15* 1889.
—**Key C**
2. ATLAS (CRYSTAL BALL), jelly compote.—*Ref. K2-15; LV26*
Bryce Brothers; Adams and Co.; U.S. Glass Co.; 1882, 1891. Made
in extended table service including toothpick, open salt, cake stand,
wine, bowls. The water pitcher does not have "balls"; see Plate 189.
Good availability. Crystal, ruby-stained.—**Key B**
3. ELECTRIC, creamer.—*Ref. K3-78* U.S. Glass Co. #15038, 1891.
Extended table service including salt shaker, cracker jar, sauce.
Crystal, ruby-stained.—**Key B**

Row 2

1. EYEBROWS, pitcher.—*Ref. K5-11* U.S. Glass Co. (Doyle #11),
1891. Extended table service including salt shaker, tray, waste bowl,
tumbler, celery vase, pickle dish, wine. Crystal. See Plate 13.
—**Key A**
2. ANGELUS, creamer.—*Ref. K5-54* 1895. Extended table service
including wine.—**Key A**
3. PANELLED "S", goblet. 1880's. Extended table service
including plates, celery vase, compotes.—**Key B**
4. ATLAS, celery vase. See Row 1 #2.

Row 3

1. EYEWINKER (CRYSTAL BALL; WINKING EYE),
pitcher.—*Ref. K5-76* Dalzell, Gilmore and Leighton, 1889. Extended
table service including tall compote, salt shaker, banana boat. No
toothpick made originally. Crystal.—**Key D**
2. PILLAR BULLS-EYE (THISTLE), pitcher.—*Ref. L190* 1860's.
Extended table service including bowls, egg cup, wine, decanter.
Crystal.—**Key E**

Row 4

1. DOUBLE ARCH (INTERLOCKING CRESCENTS),
creamer.—*Ref. K5-73* King Glass Co.; U.S. Glass Co. #15024
(Columbia), 1892. Extended table service including salt shaker,
toothpick holder.—**Key B**
2. IMPERIAL'S CANDLEWICK, salt shaker.—*Ref. PetSal 156-G*
Imperial Glass Corp., 1889. Known in five types of shakers.
—**Key B**

PLATE 13 CIRCLES, PLAIN

Row 1

1. EYEBROWS, tumbler. See Plate 12.
2. BRYCE (RIBBON CANDY; FIGURE EIGHT; DOUBLE LOOP; CANDY RIBBON), creamer.—*Ref. K1-32; LV32* Bryce Brothers; U.S. Glass Co. #15010, 1880's; 1891. Made in very large extended table service including wine, cordial, claret, goblet, many sizes bowls and compotes, cruet, syrup, salt shaker, toothpick, tumbler. Crystal, green.—**Key B**
3. TEARDROP AND THUMBPRINT, pitcher.—*Ref. K3-32; LV69* U.S. Glass Co. #15032 (Ripley), 1896. Extended table service including salt shaker, cake stand, compote (open), wine, celery vase. Crystal, blue, decorated.—**Key B**

Row 2

1. ARCHED OVALS (CONCAVED ALMOND; OPTIC), creamer.—*Ref. K8-39; Gob II-80* U.S. Glass Co. #15091 (Ripley), 1905. Extended table service including toothpick holder, wine, salt shaker, tumbler. Crystal, ruby-stained, rose-flashed, emerald green.—**Key A**
2. CRYSTAL WEDDING (COLLINS; CRYSTAL ANNIVERSARY), pint tankard.—*Ref. K3-74; LV48* Adams and Co.; U.S. Glass Co., 1880's, 1891. Extended table service including footed fruit basket, syrup, cruet, salt shaker, tumbler, cake plate. Crystal, ruby-stained, cobalt blue (scarce).—**Key B**
3. LONG TEARDROP AND THUMBPRINT (TEARDROP AND THUMBPRINT VARIANT), pitcher.—*Ref. K3-103* Extended table service including lamp, tumbler, water tray. Lamp value: See **Key D** in syrup.—**Key B**

Row 3

1. FULTON (MARTHA'S TEARS), salt shaker.—*Ref. K8-166* Brilliant and Greensburg Glass Co., 1889. Extended table service including tray, cake stand, tumbler, finger bowl, wine, celery vase, bowls, sauce. See Plate 203.—**Key B**
2. TENNIS RACQUET, goblet.—*Ref. Gob II-97* U.S. Glass Co. #15102 (Ripley), 1907. Extended table service.—**Key B**
3. QUESTION MARK (OVAL LOOP), pitcher.—*Ref. K4-135* U.S. Glass Co. (Richards and Hartley), 1891. Extended table service including salt shaker, tumbler, wine, four size pitchers, oblong bowls, footed bowls, tall compotes. Crystal.—**Key B**

PLATE 14 CIRCLES, THUMBPRINTS

Row 1

1. RIBBED THUMBPRINT, pitcher.—*Ref. K8-190* Jefferson Glass Co. #221, 1907. Extended table service including toothpick holder, salt shaker, shot glass, mug, jelly compote, cruet, sauce, berry bowl.—**Key B**

2. ASHBURTON WITH CONNECTED OVALS (DOUBLE FLUTE), goblet.—*Ref. L-3* Boston and Sandwich; McKee and Brothers; New England Glass Co., 1850's. Made in very large table service including bitters bottle, ale glass, cordial, mug, lamp, egg cup, tumblers, rare covered toddy jar. Good availability.—**Key D**

3. BLOCKED THUMBPRINT BAND, syrup.—*Ref. HI-15* Duncan glass, c. 1900. Found in bar goods, shot glass, toothpick holder, toy mug, cruet. Crystal, Ruby-stained.—**Key A**

Row 2

1. DISC AND FERN (LOOP WITH DISC AND FERN BAND), goblet.—*Ref. Gob II-126* —**Key B**

2. ASHBURTON WITH DIVIDED OVALS (LARGE THUMBPRINTS), wine. Same as Row 1 #2.

3. OVAL THUMBPRINT BAND, pitcher.—*Ref. K5-28* c. 1850. Flint.—**Key D**

Row 3

1. FINDLAY BELLAIRE, toothpick holder.—*Ref. K5-114* Bellaire Goblet Co.; U.S. Glass Co.; 1885; 1890. Made in extended table service including salt shaker.—**Key A**

2. WILCOX, salt shaker.—*Ref. PetSal 177B* Has name etched on bottom.—**Key A**

PLATE 15 CIRCLES, THUMBPRINTS

Row 1

1. CAROLINA (INVERNESS), covered sugar bowl.—*Ref. K2-28; Gob II-53* U.S. Glass Co. #15083 (Bryce), 1903. A State Series pattern. Made in extended table service including sauce, salt shaker, tumbler, jelly compote, large compote, cake stand, bowls, individual creamer, wine. The row of thumbprints is pressed on **inside** of glass. Crystal, ruby-stained.—**Key A**

2. DAKOTA (BABY THUMBPRINT), spooner.—*Ref. K4-8; LV67* U.S. Glass Co. (Ripley), 1891; 1898. A State Series pattern. Extended table service including castor set, rare cake cover, salt shaker, cake plates, tray, tumbler, six sizes pitchers.—**Key C**

3. BAR AND FLUTE (RUBY BAR AND FLUTE), pitcher.—*Ref. K2-106* 1893. Extended table service including syrup. See Plate 209. Crystal, ruby-stained.—**Key B**

Row 2

1. U.S. THUMBPRINT, pitcher.—*Ref. K5-5* U.S. Glass Co. #15013 (Nickle Plate), 1891. Extended table service. Crystal.—**Key A**

2. DOUBLE THUMBPRINT BAND, syrup.—*Ref. HIII-23* c. 1880. Only syrup known.—**Key B**

Row 3

1. DAKOTA, salt shaker. See Above.

2. COLONIAL, creamer.—*Ref. K8-9* Boston and Sandwich, 1850-60. Extended table service. See Plate 20.—Flint—**Key C**

Row 4

1. CELTIC, creamer.—*Ref. K3-116* McKee and Brothers, 1894. Extended table service.—**Key A**

2. CAT'S-EYE (THUMBPRINT ON SPEARHEAD), goblet.—*Ref. PetSal 175P; Gob II-141* Extended table service including salt shaker.—**Key B**

3. THUMBPRINT ON SPEARPOINT (TEARDROP AND CRACKED ICE), salt shaker.—*Ref. PetSal 175Q* Cambridge Glass Co.; Dalzell, Gilmore and Leighton.—**Key B**

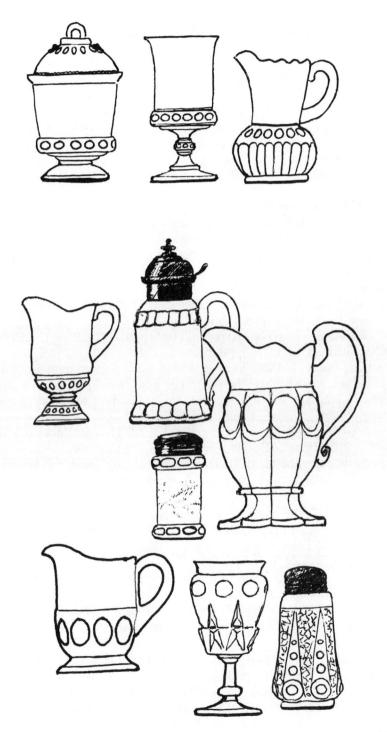

PLATE 16 CIRCLES, THUMBPRINTS

Row 1

1. LATE WASHINGTON, pitcher. U.S. Glass Co. #15074 (Ripley; King), 1901. A State Series pattern. Extended table service including flat and footed sauces, flat and footed bowls, cake stands, tumblers, rectangular bowl, 8″ covered bowl, celery tray, claret, wine, champagne, cordial, toothpick holder, cruet, plates. Finials are beaded acorns. Limited availability. Very desirable with rose flashing and painted flowers. Crystal, ruby-stained, rose-flashed.—Plain **Key A**

2. APOLLO, creamer.—*Ref. K3-6* Adams and Co., 1875; U.S. Glass Co., 1891. Extended table service including cheese dish, high and low compotes, rare cake stand, bowls, syrup, salt shaker, cruet, celery vase, sugar shaker, egg cup, sauces, tray, tumbler. Good availability. See Plate 223. Crystal, ruby-stained.—**Key C**

Row 2

1. MADISON, spill holder.—*Ref. K6-75* Flint glass. Extended table service including covered compote.—**Key E**

2. KING'S CROWN (RUBY THUMBPRINT; RUBY CROWN; EXCELSIOR; "XLCR"), pitcher.—*Ref. K1-104; L162* U.S. Glass Co. (Adams factory), 1891. Very extended table service including pickle castor set, fruit basket, footed orange bowl, toothpick holder, square honey dish, cup and saucer, mustard, individual open salt. Crystal, ruby-stained, amber-stained.—**Key B**

3. PUNTY BAND, creamer.—*Ref. K7-132* Heisey Glass Co. #1220, 1897-1910. Extended table service including toothpick holder, syrup, candy dishes, spoon tray, banana compote, mug, tumbler, salt shaker, salt dip, cake basket, cake stand, wine.—**Key C**

Row 3

1. EYELET (NEARCUT #2508), creamer. (Author's name).—*Ref. K7 Pl. 73* Cambridge Glass Co., 1906. Extended table service including tumbler, compote, bowls.—**Key A**

2. TARENTUM THUMBPRINT, creamer.—*Ref. K5-83* Tarentum Glass Co., 1904. Extended table service including toothpick holder, salt shaker.—**Key A**

3. OVAL THUMBPRINT, creamer.—*Ref. K2-26* Central Glass Co. #610, c. 1880. Extended table service.—**Key A**

Row 4

1. MARIO, salt shaker.—*Ref. K6-31; LV43* U.S. Glass Co. (Hobbs #341), 1891. Extended table service including syrup. May be etched. See Plate 205. Crystal, amber-stained; ruby-stained.—**Key C**

2. FOUR THUMBPRINTS, creamer. —*Ref. K5-57* U.S. Glass Co.

#05012 (Richards & Hartley), 1892. Extended table service.
—**Key B**
3. THUMBPRINT AND DIAMOND, goblet. —*Ref. K7-70*
—**Key A**
4. THUMBPRINT WINDOWS, creamer. —*Ref. K2-14.* c. 1890's.
Basic table service. Crystal, slag. —**Key B**

PLATE 17 CIRCLES

Row 1

1. ARGUS (THUMBPRINT), tumbler.—*Ref. L11* Bakewell, Pears and Co., 1870. Made in extended table service including ale glass, champagne, wine, cordial, handled whiskey (scarce), mug, celery vase, egg cup, decanters. See Plate 29.—**Key C**

2. BIGLER, tumbler.—*Ref. L10* Boston and Sandwich, 1850's. Extended table service including cordial, decanter, champagne, tumbler, wine, bowl, celery vase, mug.—**Key C**

3. ALLIGATOR SCALES, goblet.—*Ref. Gob II-12* c. 1870's. Flint glass.—**Key D**

Row 2

MICHIGAN, salt shaker. See Plate 214.

Row 3

1. FRISCO, creamer.—*Ref. K7-39* Fostoria Glass Co. #1229, 1904. Extended table service including bar tumbler, bitters bottle, cruet, olive dish, sauces, bowls, flared-rim bowls, compotes, toothpick holder, vases, salt shaker, cake stand; 33 items in all.—**Key B**

2. LOWER MANHATTAN, toothpick holder.—*Ref. HTP-75* Crystal, colored eyes.—**Key B**

3. MANHATTAN, pitcher.—*Ref. K6-44* U.S. Glass Co. #15078 (Glassport), 1902-10. Extended table service including tall covered jar, cracker jar, sauce, fruit compote, lamp, cake stand, bowls, toothpick, cruet, plate, berry set. Being reproduced. See Plate 92. Crystal, rose-flashed, green-flashed.—**Key A**

Row 4

1. SPEARHEADS (ALLIGATOR SCALE WITH SPEARPOINT), pitcher.—*Ref. K1-112* McKee Glass Co., 1880's. Extended table service.—**Key A**

2. CONCAVED ARROWHEADS, creamer. —*Ref. K8-10* King Glass Co., 1875. Extended table service.—**Key B**

3. BULLS-EYE AND ROSETTE, tumbler. Extended table service including spill holder.—**Key C**

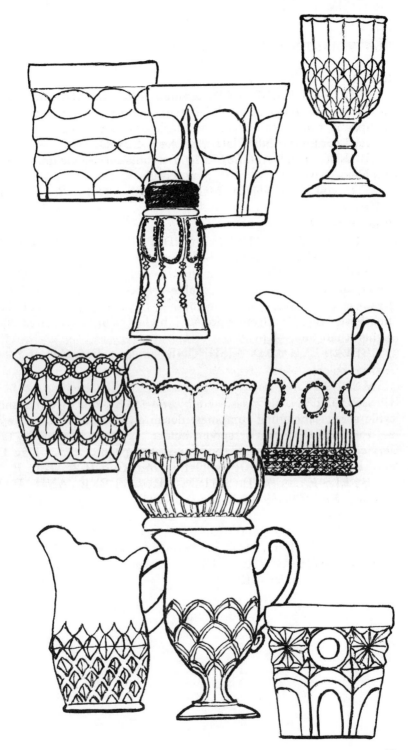

PLATE 18 CIRCLES, BULLS-EYE

Row 1

1. BULLS-EYE AND BAR, covered egg cup.—*Ref. Gob II-144*
Pieces known include bitters bottle, bar tumbler, goblet.—Flint
Key C
2. BULLS-EYE AND LOOP, goblet.—**Key C**
3. BAND, goblet—*Ref. L61* Extended table service including footed tumbler.—**Key B**
4. COLONIAL WITH DIAMOND BAND, goblet.—*Ref. Gob II-29*
—**Key D**

Row 2

1. BULLS-EYE WITH DIAMOND POINTS, goblet.—*Ref. L27*
Extended table service including tumbler, sauce.—**Key E**
2. YORK COLONIAL, sugar base.—*Ref. Miller* 1850's; Central Glass Co., c. 1870's. Extended table service including tumbler, ale glass, celery vase, covered compote. Crystal (flint), opalescent, amethyst, blue. Flint prices are 50% higher than key; colored 200% higher than key.—**Key B**
3. BULLS-EYE AND WISHBONE, goblet.—*Ref. Gob II-F*
—**Key D**

Row 3

1. BROOKLYN, ale glass.—*Ref. L154-12; K7-3* c. 1870. Extended table service including compotes, decanter. See plate 32. —**Key C**
2. PANELLED OVAL, spoon holder. c. 1860. Extended table service including egg cup, compotes, champagne, wine.—**Key C**
3. MIRROR AND LOOP, goblet. —*Ref. Gob II-2* —**Key B**
4. BULLS-EYE AND PRISM (BULLS-EYE AND BAR), goblet.—*Ref. Gob II-152* c. 1860.—**Key E**

PLATE 19 CIRCLES, BULLS-EYE

Row 1

1. BULLS-EYE AND BROKEN COLUMN, goblet.—*Ref. Gob II-30* —**Key E**

2. EXCELSIOR, EARLY, goblet.—*Ref. L-4* Boston and Sandwich, 1850's; Ihmsen & Co., 1851; McKee and Brothers, 1868; Bryce Brothers. Made in extended table service including decanters, ale glass, compote, bitters bottle, tumbler, egg cups, footed tumbler, wine, cordial, claret.—**Key E**

3. HOURGLASS (EXCELSIOR WITH DOUBLE-RINGED STEM; EGG AND DART; EXCELSIOR VARIANT), spoon holder.—*Ref. Gob II-2; K2-8* 1868; 1880's. Extended table service including sauce, goblet. See Plate 64. Crystal, canary, amber, blue.—**Key C**

Row 2

1. EYE BAND, salt shaker.—*Ref. PetSal 160L* —**Key A**

2. BARREL EXCELSIOR, spoon holder. Boston and Sandwich; McKee; 1850's and '60's. Extended table service including ale glass, decanters, mugs, tumblers, wine, bottle, celery vase.—**Key C**

3. TULIP AND OVAL, creamer.—*Ref. K7-4* c. 1865. Known in creamer and celery vase.—**Key D**

Row 3

1. FRAMED CIRCLES, wine.—*Ref. Miller* Flint, c. 1840's. Known in goblet and wine.—**Key D**

2. BULLS-EYE AND SPEARHEAD, wine.—*Ref. Miller* Dalzell, Gilmore and Leighton, 1870's. Extended table service including castor set, compotes, decanter, lamp. Crystal.—**Key C**

3. TONG, creamer.—*Ref. K5-24; LV pl. 25* c. 1860's. Extended table service.—**Key E**

Row 4

1. COMET, goblet.—*Ref. L-49* Extended table service including whiskey tumbler.—**Key D**

2. REVERSE TORPEDO (BULLS-EYE BAND; BULLS-EYE WITH DIAMOND POINT), celery vase.—*Ref. K3-100; Gob II-76* Dalzell, Gilmore and Leighton, 1891. Extended table service including banana dish, cake stand, fruit basket, berry bowl, compote, salt shaker, sauce.—**Key B**

3. BEADED CIRCLE, goblet.—*Ref. LV-34* Extended table service including egg cup, bud vase, jelly compote. Fairly abundant. —**Key E**

PLATE 20 CIRCLES

Row 1

1. TEXAS BULLS-EYE (BULLS-EYE VARIANT; FILLEY), goblet.—*Ref. L50; K7-72* U.S. Glass Co. (Bryce factory); 1875; 1891. Made in extended table service including wine, tumblers, castor set.—**Key B**

2. HAMMOND, goblet.—*Ref. Gob II-39* —**Key D**

3. LINCOLN DRAPE, spoon holder.—*Ref. L-46* Boston and Sandwich, 1860's. Extended table service including celery vase, compotes, wine, egg cup, decanter, tumbler, plate, syrup, footed salt, lamp, sauce, spill holder. Crystal, milk glass, sapphire blue. —**Key D**

Row 2

1. HALEY'S COMET, goblet. This is a crude drawing as I had only a quick sketch to work from. An abundant pattern made in extended table service.—**Key D**

2. COLONIAL, ale glass. See Plate 15.

3. BULLS-EYE (LAWRENCE), goblet.—*Ref. L49* New England Glass Co.; Boston and Sandwich. An early pattern. Very extended table service including bitters bottle, castor bottle, champagne, water bottle, decanter, compotes, cologne bottle, cruet, rare covered egg cup, lamp, open salt, pomade jar. Crystal, milk glass; colors are rare.—**Key D**

Row 3

CIRCLE AND SWAG, cup.—*Ref. HPV 4-p. 6* Ohio Flint Glass Co., 1904. Extended table service.—**Key A**

Row 4

1. LINCOLN DRAPE WITH TASSEL, goblet.—*Ref. L-46* 1860's. Extended table service including tall lamp, miniature lamp, compote, egg cup.—Flint **Key E**

2. BULLS-EYE WITH FLEUR-DE-LIS, goblet.—*Ref. L51* Boston and Sandwich, 1860's. Extended table service including rare ale glass, compotes, decanter, lamp, rare pitcher, mug, footed master salt, wine, cordial. Crystal, amber.—**Key E**

3. ALABAMA (BEADED BULLS-EYE AND DRAPE), pitcher.—*Ref. K1-81* The first State Series pattern by U.S. Glass Co. (#15062) in 1892 and 1899 (Glassport). Extended table service including tray, cake stand, celery vase, syrup, relish, salt shaker, compotes, tumbler, covered honey dish, handled sauce, cruet, toothpick holder. Crystal, ruby-stained, green.—**Key C**

PLATE 21 CIRCLES

Row 1

1. MCKEE'S VIRGINIA, pitcher.—*Ref. K4-85* McKee and Brothers, 1900-1915. Made in extended table service including relish dish, sauces.—**Key A**

2. BLOCKED THUMBPRINT, creamer.—*Ref. K8-9* c. 1870. Extended table service.—**Key C**

Row 2

1. DICKINSON, goblet.—*Ref. Gob II-6* Sandwich glass, 1860's. Extended table service including wine, open and covered compotes, sauce, open salt.—**Key C**

2. BLOCK WITH THUMBPRINT LATE, goblet.—*Ref. L-101* Extended table service.—**Key B**

3. WASHINGTON EARLY, decanter.—*Ref. L-10* New England Glass Co., 1869. Extended table service including tumbler, wine, syrup, egg cup, high compote, pedestalled butter dish, celery vase. All pieces are scarce.—**Key F**

Row 3

1. PRISM AND CRESCENT, cup. Extended table service. —**Key B**

2. ELLIPSES, toothpick holder.—*Ref. Boul. Pl. 93; HI-21* Beaumont Glass Co. #106, 1901. Extended table service. Crystal, cranberry-flashed.—**Key B**

3. BEADED THUMBPRINT BLOCK, salt shaker.—*Ref. PetSal 154-R* —**Key B**

Row 4

1. THUMBPRINT ROW, salt shaker.—*Ref. PetSal 175T* —**Key A**

2. EYEBROWS, salt shaker. The shaker has a more ornate pattern than the rest of the set. See Plate 12.

3. BROKEN BAR AND THUMBPRINT, salt shaker.—*Ref. PetSal 155Q* —**Key B**

53

PLATE 22 CIRCLES

Row 1

1. NAIL, pitcher (etched).—*Ref. K2-87* Bryce Brothers; U.S. Glass Co. #15002, 1890-96. Made in extended table service including finger bowl, water tray, vases, wine, cruet, salt shaker. Crystal, ruby-stained.—**Key B**

2. JAM JAR, creamer.—*Ref. K8-28* Jenkins Glass Co., c. 1920. Extended table service.—**Key A**

3. BLOCK AND CIRCLE, pitcher.—*Ref. Miller* Extended table service including miniature lamp, tumbler.—**Key B**

Row 2

1. NORTHWOOD-DUGAN BEADED CIRCLE, cruet.—*Ref. PetSal 154J* Northwood Glass Co., 1904; Dugan Glass Co. Extended table service including tumbler, berry set, salt shaker, jelly compote. Crystal, apple green, blue, amethyst (rare), custard (rare).—**Key B**

2. DUCHESS, cruet.—*Ref. HIII-55* Riverside Glass Co., 1899. Extended table service. Crystal, emerald green, amethyst-flashed, opalescent.—**Key C**

3. DUCHESS, toothpick holder. See Above.

Row 3

1. MELLOR, spoon holder. Basic table service.—**Key B**

2. MIRROR-KAMM'S, salt shaker.—*Ref. K6 pl. 98* McKee Glass Co., 1894. Part of castor set.—**Key A**

3. TOKYO, toothpick holder.—*Ref. K7-147* Jefferson Glass Co. #212, c. 1904. Extended table service including donut stand, salt shaker. Crystal, opalescent colors.—**Key B**

Row 4

1. OVAL LENS, salt shaker.—*Ref. PetSal 154J* **Key A**

2. TOKYO, creamer. See Row 3 #2.

3. ROMOLA, pitcher.—*Ref. K8 pl. 38* Robinson Glass Co. 1894; Model Flint Glass, 1901. Extended table service including compote, cruet, salt shaker, tray, berry bowl, sugar shaker.—**Key B**

PLATE 23 CIRCLES

Row 1

1. BEADED OVAL AND SCROLL (DOT), pitcher.—*Ref. L77; K1-61* Bryce Brothers, 1870's. Made in extended table service including cordial, compotes, cake stand, salt shaker. Crystal. —**Key B**

2. LENS AND STAR (STAR AND OVAL), creamer.—*Ref. K2-36; LV75* U.S. Glass Co. (O'Hara), 1891. Extended table service including compote, tumbler, celery vase, salt shaker, bowl, sauce. Crystal, frosted.—**Key B**

3. IMPERIAL #261, creamer.—*Ref. K7-10* Imperial Glass Co., 1901. Extended table service including wine, sauces, berry bowl, celery tray, jelly compote, tumbler.—**Key A**

Row 2

1. SNAKESKIN WITH DOT, pitcher.—*Ref. K3-69; L74* 1870's. Extended table service including plates, celery vase, salt shaker. Crystal, amber, cobalt blue.—**Key A**

2. EIGHT-O-EIGHT, creamer.—*Ref. K4-78* c. 1890. Extended table service including celery vase, lamp, berry bowl, plates. —**Key B**

3. MONROE, spill holder.—*Ref. K6-75* 1850's. Extended table service including rare lamp. Crystal, cobalt blue.—**Key E**

Row 3

1. BEADED ELLIPSE (ALDINE), pitcher.—*Ref. K3-106* McKee Glass Co., c. 1900; possibly Cambridge Glass also. Extended table service including compotes, wine, salt shaker.—**Key B**

2. JEWEL WITH DEWDROP (KANSAS), pitcher.—*Ref. K1-77; L75* Cooperative Flint Glass Co., 1870's; U.S. Glass Co. #15072 (King), 1901. A State Series pattern. Extended table service including salt shaker, berry bowl, cake stand, compotes, rare goblet, syrup, wine, sauce, relish, rare toothpick holder, cordial, jelly compote, bread plate. Good availability. Crystal, color-stained.—**Key B**

Row 4

1. BEADED OVALS IN SAND, cruet.—*Ref. HI-14* Dugan Glass Co., 1905. Extended table service including toothpick holder, mug, tumbler, sauce.—**Key B**

2. TARGET, cruet.—*Ref. HV-117* U.S. Glass Co. (Richards and Hartley), 1891. Made in wine set; crystal, ruby-stained.—**Key B**

3. BEADED OVAL BAND, syrup.—*Ref. PetSal 154P* U.S. Glass Co. (Nickel Plate #2), 1891. Extended table service including salt shaker, bitters bottle, bowls. Crystal.—**Key B**

PLATE 24 CIRCLES

Row 1

1. LEE, goblet. Named in honor of Ruth Webb Lee. Extended table service including whiskey tumbler, celery vase, decanter, wine. —**Key E**

2. OVAL PANEL (OVAL SETT), creamer.—*Ref. K2-120* U.S. Glass Co. (Challinor #23), c. 1870's; 1891. Extended table service including celery vase; no spoon holder known. Crystal, purple slag, opaque white.—**Key B**

3. DUNCAN PANEL, creamer.—*Ref. K3-110* George Duncan and Sons, 1890's. Extended table service including celery vase, rare covered honey dish with handles. Has cross-hatched bottom. May be etched. Clear, canary, amber, blue.—**Key A**

Row 2

1. PANEL, RIB AND SHELL, pitcher.—*Ref. K4-118* General Glass Co., 1885. Extended table service including salt shaker. Has been found with Daisy and Button design in large oval. Crystal.—**Key B**

2. TOOTHED MEDALLION, creamer (etched).—*Ref. K7-6* —**Key B**

Row 3

1. RAYED WITH LOOP, plate.—*Ref. L37* Sandwich-type glass. Extended table service.—Flint **Key D**

2. NOTCHED OVAL, salt shaker.—*Ref. PetSal 34G* —**Key A**

3. OVAL MEDALLION (ARGYLE), goblet.—*Ref. K2-39* U.S. Glass Co., 1891. Extended table service.—**Key A**

Row 4

1. DIVIDED HEARTS, goblet.—*Ref. Gob II-68* Boston and Sandwich Glass Co., 1860's. Extended table service including compote, syrup, lamp.—**Key D**

2. PEACOCK FEATHER (PEACOCK EYE; GEORGIA), pitcher.—*Ref. L-106; K1-77* U.S. Glass Co. #15076 (Richards and Hartley), 1902 (also produced earlier). A State Series pattern. Made in extended table service including cruet, bowls, mug, tumbler cake stand, salt shaker, jelly compote, syrup, large compote, 7″ and 9″ lamps, plate, sauces, relish. U.S. Glass pieces are abundant. Crystal, blue (scarce).—**Key B**

PLATE 25 CIRCLES

Row 1

1. FROST CRYSTAL, plate.—*Ref. K6 pl. 51* Tarentum Glass Co., 1906. Made in extended table service including celery boat, custard cup, salt shaker, bowls. Crystal, ruby-stained.—**Key B**
2. MELTON, spoon holder.—**Key B**
3. BELFAST, goblet.—*Ref. Gob II-60* —**Key B**

Row 2

1. DOUBLE CIRCLE, salt shaker.—*Ref. K7-155* Jefferson Glass Co. #231, c. 1905. Made in cruet, toothpick holder, salt shaker, and tray. Apple green, "electric" blue.—**Key D**
2. GOTHIC (CATHEDRAL), pitcher.—*Ref. L55* McKee and Brothers, 1860's. Extended table service including compote, egg cup, sauce, compotes, fruit bowl, relish, wine, champagne, cordial, castor bottle.—**Key D**
3. BLOCKED ARCHES (BERKELEY), pitcher.—*Ref. K6-25* U.S. Glass Co. #15020 (Bryce; Gas City), 1891. Extended table service including finger bowl, syrup, salt shaker, tumbler, wine, salt shaker, cup and saucer. Crystal, ruby-stained, frosted.—**Key B**

Row 3

1. TWO-HANDLE, creamer.—*Ref. K5-150* Basic table service. Crystal, blue.—**Key C**
2. EUGENIE, celery holder.—*Ref. L5* McKee and Brothers, c. 1850's. Extended table service including egg cup, cordial, wine, champagne, covered bowls, covered sugar bowl with dolphin finial (rare), tumbler. Crystal.—Flint **Key E**
3. EUGENIE, goblet. See Above.

PLATE 26 CIRCLES

Row 1

1. GIANT BULLS-EYE (EXCELSIOR), pitcher.—*Ref. K2-101* U. S. Glass Co. #157, 1898; Bellaire Goblet Co. Made in extended table service including celery vase. Crystal.—**Key B**

2. SPECIALTY, pitcher.—*Ref. K5-80* Specialty Glass Co. #100, 1891. Basic table service.—**Key A**

3. BUTTON BAND (WYANDOTTE; UMBILICATED HOB-NAIL), pitcher.—*Ref. K3-111* Ripley and Co., 1880s; U.S. Glass Co., 1890's. Extended table service including castor sets, cake stand, open compote, tumbler, wine. Crystal. See Plate 150.—**Key B**

Row 2

1. FLOWERED OVAL, egg cup and detail. Extended table service.—**Key B**

2. BEAD AND SCROLL, pitcher.—*Ref. K2-112* Extended table service including jelly compote, toothpick holder, salt shaker, tumbler, toy table set (rare). Crystal, frosted, ruby-stained, cobalt blue, green.—**Key B**

3. BULLS-EYE AND DAISY, goblet.—*Ref. Metz #2443* U.S. Glass Co. #15117, 1909. Extended table service including tumbler, wine, salt shaker, toothpick holder. See Plate 135. Crystal, ruby-stained, emerald green, decorated.—**Key B**

Row 3

1. FLOWERED OVAL, goblet. See Row 2 #1.

2. CO-OP'S ROYAL, toothpick holder.—*Ref. K6-23* Cooperative Flint Glass Co., 1894-1915. Extended table service including wine, salt shaker.—**Key B**

3. CORRIGAN, salt shaker.—*Ref. Gob II-39* Extended table service.—**Key B**

Row 4

1. ART (JOB'S TEARS; TEARDROPS AND DIAMOND BLOCK), fruit basket.—*Ref. K3-77* Adams and Co.; U.S. Glass Co.; 1870's; 1891. Extended table service including cracker jar, banana dish, tumbler, compotes. Very good availability. See Plates 56 and 58. Crystal, ruby-stained.—**Key C**

2. U.S.#156, cruet.—*Ref. HIII-88* U.S. Glass Co., 1909.—**Key B**

PLATE 27 CIRCLES

Row 1

1. INVERTED THUMBPRINT (COIN SPOT; POLKA DOT), cruet.—*Ref. LV283* Hobbs, Brockunier and Co., 1885-1890. A blown pattern. Made in extended table service including biscuit jar, syrup, finger bowls, sauce, several types of goblets, toothpick holder, salt shaker, mustard jar, bitters bottle. Crystal, colors.—**Key B**

2. INVERTED THUMBPRINT OVAL, creamer.—*Ref. K1-87* King, Son and Co. Made in water set and odd pieces.—**Key B**

3. ROPE AND THUMBPRINT (INVERTED ROUND), syrup.—*Ref. K1-119* Central Glass Co. # 796, 1885. Extended table service — no cruet or toothpick —*(Ref. HIII-59).* Crystal, amber, blue, canary.—**Key C**

Row 2.

1. ORION THUMBPRINT, goblet. Canton Glass Co., 1894. Extended table service including celery vase, compotes, footed sauce. Crystal, milk glass, black glass, colors.—**Key C**

2. PILLAR, goblet.—*Ref. L28* Bakewell, Pears and Co., c. 1850's. Extended table service including ale glass, decanter, bar bottle, cordial (scarce), sauce.—Flint **Key D**

3. PANNIER, goblet.—*Ref. Gob II-103* —**Key A**

Row 3

1. DOT, creamer.—*Ref. K8-99* U.S. Glass Co. (Doyle), 1891. Extended table service. See also "Raindrop", plate 148.—**Key B**

2. ALMOND THUMBPRINT (POINTED THUMBPRINT; FINGERPRINT), pitcher.—*Ref. L154 #14* Bakewell, Pears and Co.; Bryce Brothers. Extended table service including celery vase, compotes, tumbler, cruet.—**Key B**

3. ARGUS (THUMBPRINT), pitcher. See Plate 17.

Row 4

1. THOUSAND HEXAGONS, bowl.—*Ref. HPV#2, p.5* Duncan glass, c. 1890. Extended table service including two sizes butter dish, sauce.—**Key B**

2. MIRROR, goblet.—*Ref. L2* McKee Brothers, 1870's. Primarily made in drinking pieces — ale glass, champagne, cordial, tumbler, wine; and compote, spooner, pickle jar.—**Key C**

3. LONG OPTIC (TYCOON), creamer.—*Ref. K4-66* Columbia Glass Co.; U.S. Glass Co., 1891. Extended table service including mug, cup. Crystal.—**Key B**

PLATE 28 CIRCLES

Row 1

1. MIDGET THUMBPRINT, goblet.—*Ref. Gob II-95* Made in extended table service.—**Key A**
2. COIN AND DEW DROP, goblet.—*Ref. Gob II-62* —**Key B**
3. HUNDRED EYE, goblet.—*Ref. PetSal 31M* Extended table service including salt shaker.—**Key B**
4. THOUSAND EYE (DAISY), pitcher.—*Ref. L137; K1-18* Richards and Hartley Flint Glass Co.; New Brighton Glass Co.; Adams and Co. #11; U.S. Glass Co. (1891), 1888. Very extended table service including salt shaker and plate. Crystal, many colors. —**Key B**

Row 2

1. THREE PANEL, pitcher.—*Ref. K3-115; L96-159* Richards and Hartley Glass Co. #25, 1888; U.S. Glass Co., 1891. Extended table service including celery vase, cruet, mug, tumbler, compotes, bowls, sauce. Crystal, amber, yellow, blue.—**Key B**
2. PANELLED THOUSAND EYE (DAISY SQUARE), pitcher.—*Ref. K2-66* Richards and Hartley. Extended table service with a woman's face modelled as a finial.—**Key B**

Row 3

BARRELLED THUMBPRINT (CHALLINOR THUMB-PRINT), pitcher.—*Ref. K1-103; LV58* Challinor, Taylor and Co. #312; U.S. Glass Co., c. 1891. Extended table service including wine, square bowls, celery vase, tankard pitcher. Crystal.—**Key B**

Row 4

1. PRINTED HOBNAIL, goblet.—*Ref. L72* 1880's-1890's. Extended table service including celery vase, mug, water tray, tumbler, wine, sauce. Crystal, green, amethyst, amber, canary, blue.—**Key C**
2. THOUSAND EYE, twine holder. See Row 1, #4.

PLATE 29 CIRCLES

Row 1

1. NIAGARA, creamer.—*Ref. K8-195* Fostoria Glass Co. #793, 1900. Made in extended table service including tankard pitcher, tumbler, berry set, salt shaker, syrup, cruet, sauce, bowls, celery vase.—**Key B**

2. YALE (CROWFOOT), spooner.—*Ref. LV19; K3-126; Gob I-68* McKee and Brothers, 1894. Extended table service including cake stand, compotes, cordial, tumbler, syrup, celery vase, sauces, salt shaker.—**Key B**

3. BANDED RAINDROPS (CANDLEWICK), pitcher.—*Ref. K2-31* Extended table service including small compote, plates, wine, salt shaker. See Plate 150. Crystal, amber, milk glass, opalescent blue.—**Key B**

Row 2

1. CRYSTAL #12, rose bowl.—*Ref. K6 pl. 42* Crystal Glass Co., 1891-92. Extended table service.—**Key B**

2. VICTORIA, footed bowl.—*Ref. L18* Bakewell, Pears and Co., 1870's. Extended table service including cake stand, compotes, scarce sugar bowl. Crystal, canary.—**Key B**

3. SHUTTLE (HEARTS OF LOCH LAVEN), mug.—*Ref. K8-24* Indiana Tumbler and Goblet Co., 1900. Extended table service including punch cups, salt shaker, wine, tumbler, cordial, syrup, sauce. See Plate 232. Crystal, chocolate, caramel (high prices). —**Key B**

Row 3

1. SAWTOOTHED HONEYCOMB (CHICKENWIRE), creamer —*Ref. K1-115* Steiner Glass Co.; Union Stopper Co, c. 1906-08. Extended table service including celery vase, toothpick holder, salt shaker. Crystal, ruby-stained.—**Key B**

2. BEADED ARCH PANELS, mug. Only goblet and mug known.—**Key B**

3. JEWELLED MOON AND STAR (MOON AND STAR VARIATION; MOON AND STAR WITH WAFFLED STEM), syrup.—*Ref. K1-131; Metz 2-211* Cooperative Flint Glass Co.; Wilson Glass Co., c. 1890. Extended table service including egg cup, bread tray, cake salvers, individual open salt, salt shaker, celery vase. See Plates 146 and 232. Crystal, frosted, decorated.—**Key B**

Row 4

1. HEXAGONAL BULLS-EYE (CREASED HEXAGON BLOCK; DOUBLE RED BLOCK), pitcher.—*Ref. K1-114* Dalzell, Gilmore and Leighton, 1890's. Extended table service including celery vase,

tumbler, wine.—**Key B**

2. HEXAGONAL BULLS-EYE, goblet. See above.

3. HONEYCOMB WITH STAR, pitcher.—*Ref. L102* Fostoria Glass Co., c. 1905. Extended table service including cake stand, flat sauce, tumbler, compote, cruet.—**Key B**

PLATE 30 CIRCLES

Row 1

1. DUNCAN #77, tumbler.—*Ref. Bones* George Duncan and Sons, c. 1900.—**Key A**
2. HONEYCOMB (VERNON; THOUSAND FACES), decanter.—*Ref. L60* Bakewell, Pears and other glass companies, 1869; 1895. Made in extended table service including salt shaker, spill holder, compotes, celery vase, custard cup, finger bowl, egg cups.—Flint **Key C;** Non-flint **Key B**
3. OVAL MITRE, goblet—*Ref. L12* McKee Brothers, c. 1865. Extended table service including compotes, bowl, sauce, open and covered sugar bowls.—**Key C**

Row 2

1. LOOP AND HONEYCOMB, goblet.—*Ref. Gob II-2* —**Key B**
2. FRONTIER (COLONIAL AND MITRE), sugar bowl. See Martinsville Glass Co., c. 1917. Extended table service. See Plate 163.—**Key A**
3. BEVELLED WINDOWS (ST. REGIS), syrup.—*Ref. HV-146* U.S. Glass Co. (Glassport) #15107; 1907. Extended table service including toothpick holder. Crystal.—**Key A**

Row 3

1. U.S. #341, syrup.—*Ref. HIII-80* U.S. Glass Co., c. 1908 —**Key B**
2. BLOCK AND HONEYCOMB, pitcher.—*Ref. K5-38* McKee and Brothers, 1860's. Known in goblet, butter dish, sugar bowl and pitcher.—**Key B**
3. HEXAGON BLOCK, celery vase.—*Ref. PetSal 30T* U.S. Glass Co. (Hobbs #335), c. 1891. Extended table service including syrup, custard cup, salt shaker. Crystal, ruby-stained, amber.—**Key C**

Row 4

1. NEW YORK HONEYCOMB, open salt dish.—*Ref. L60* New England Glass Co., 1869; U.S. Glass Co., 1895. A State Series pattern for New York; always has three rows of honeycomb. Extended table service including cordial, footed tumbler, wines. Crystal, ruby-stained.—**Key B**
2. HONEYCOMB OBI, salt shaker.—*Ref. PetSal 163N* —**Key A**
3. HONEYCOMB AND ZIPPER, salt shaker.—*Ref. PetSal 163L* —**Key A**

PLATE 31 CIRCLES

Row 1

1. ROMAN ROSETTE, spooner. See Plate 11.
2. DAISY WHORL (DAISY WHORL WITH DIAMOND BAND), goblet.—*Ref. Gob II-121* 1870's. Made in extended table service including open and covered compotes.—**Key B**
3. BANDED BUCKLE, spoon holder.—*Ref. K4-9* Doyle and Co., 1870; King, Son and Co., 1875-80. Extended table service including high and low compotes, cordial, egg cup, tumbler, wine.—**Key C**
4. BUCKLE, goblet—*Ref. L102* Boston and Sandwich; Gillander and Sons; 1870's. Extended table service including compote, cordial, egg cup, open salt, tumbler, champagne, wine, sauce, relish. Fair availability.—**Key B**

Row 2

FINECUT AND FAN, sauce.—*Ref. HPV #1 & #2* Bryce, Higbee and Co., c. 1905. Extended table service including toy service. —**Key B**

Row 3

1. MIRROR AND FAN, goblet—*Ref. HV-73* U.S. Glass Co. (Bryce), 1891. Wine set including decanter, tray. Crystal, emerald green, ruby-stained.—**Key B**
2. ELLIPSE ONE, creamer.—*Ref. K7-17* —**Key A**
3. BEADED OVAL, pitcher.—*Ref. K7-32* Imperial Glass Co., 1904. Extended table service.—**Key B**

Row 4

1. EGG BAND, goblet—*Ref. K7-71* c. 1880's.—**Key B**
2. EGG IN SAND (BEAN), pitcher.—*Ref. K3-71; LV-67* Extended table service including tray, tumbler, cake stand, cordial, wine, sauce, compote, salt shaker, bread platter, jam jar, relish. Crystal, amber.—**Key B**
3. OVAL WINDOWS, salt shaker—*Ref. PetSal 34-0* —**Key A**

Row 5

1. HEART IN SAND (VINCENT'S VALENTINE), toothpick holder.—*Ref. Mil 18* New Martinsville Glass Co., c. 1910. Toothpick is rare. Crystal, decorated, ruby-stained (rare).—**Key B**
2. WYOMING (ENIGMA), pitcher.—*Ref. K2-49* U.S. Glass Co. #15081 (Richards and Hartley; Gas City), 1903. A State Series pattern. Extended table service including compotes, cake stand, bowls, tumbler, wine, open and covered compotes, open and covered sugar bowls, salt shaker. Limited availability. Crystal.—**Key C**
3. OVALS AND FINE PLEAT, goblet.—*Ref. Gob II-152* —**Key B**

PLATE 32 CIRCLES

Row 1

1. BOW TIE, spoon holder.—*Ref. K6-50; Gob II-5* Thompson Glass Co., 1889. Made in extended table service including 10″ footed fruit bowl, 10″ flat bowl, salt shaker, compotes, cake stand, punch bowl.—**Key C**
2. BEADED RAINDROP, pitcher.—*Ref. K3-108* U.S. Glass Co., c. 1906. Extended table service.—**Key B**
3. ONE-HUNDRED-AND-ONE (ONE-O-ONE), goblet.—*Ref. K1-71* 1870's. Extended table service including lamp, sauces, platter, celery vase, salt shaker, 5″-7″-8″ plates. Crystal, opaque white. —**Key C**
4. JASPER (ELEANOR; LATE BUCKLE), creamer.—*Ref. K2-13; L72* U.S. Glass Co., 1891. Extended table service including open salt, footed sauce, pickle dish, salt shaker. Called "Eleanor" in blue glass.—**Key B**

Row 2

1. CO-OP COLUMBIA, creamer.—*Ref. K5-115* Cooperative Flint Glass Co. Extended table service including salt shaker. Crystal, decorated.—**Key B**
2. PIONEER #21, pitcher.—*Ref. K3-81* Pioneer Glass Co. Extended table service including celery vase, bowl, tumbler, cruets, castor set, cracker jar, sauces.—**Key B**
3. BULLS-EYE AND FAN (DAISIES IN OVAL PANELS), pitcher.—*Ref. K1-58; Gob II-115* U.S. Glass Co. #15090, c. 1900's. Extended table service including mug, toothpick holder, cake stand, tumbler. Crystal, green, sapphire blue.—**Key B**

Row 3

1. PARACHUTE, pitcher.—*Ref. K4-130* —**Key B**
2. BUTTRESSED LOOP, creamer.—*Ref. K2-114* Adams and Co. #16, 1874. Crystal, yellow, amber, blue, green.—**Key B**
3. CAT'S-EYE AND FAN (ROMAN), creamer.—*Ref. K1-25* George Duncan and Sons, early 1880's. Extended table service including compotes, bowls, large footed bowl, sauce.—**Key B**

Row 4

1. ELLIPSE TWO, pitcher.—*Ref. K6-20* —**Key A**
2. BROOKLYN, pitcher. See Plate 18.

PLATE 33 CIRCLES

Row 1

1. PAISLEY (PAISLEY WITH PURPLE DOTS), goblet.—*Ref. Gob II-83* Made in extended table service including tumbler, sauce, punch cup, toothpick holder.—**Key A**
2. TWIN LADDERS, creamer.—*Ref. K7-30* Cambridge Glass Co. #2503, 1903. Extended table service.—**Key A**

Row 2

1. TRIPLE THUMBPRINTS, creamer.—*Ref. K8-34* Extended table service including salt shaker.—**Key A**
2. ENGLISH HOBNAIL AND THUMBPRINT, bowl.—*Ref. L14* Extended table service including sauce, flared fruit bowl.—**Key B**
3. WAFFLE AND THUMBPRINT, pitcher.—*Ref. L26; K3-29* James B. Lyon and Co., Pittsburgh, 1861. Extended table service including cordial, decanters, egg cup, rectangular bowl. See Plate 226.—Flint **Key E**

Row 3

1. HORN OF PLENTY (COMET; PEACOCK TAIL), egg cup.—*Ref. L47* Boston and Sandwich; Bryce Brothers; McKee and Brothers; 1830's, 1850's. Extended table service including lamp, wine, decanters, whiskey tumbler, handled mug, bowls, plates, sauce, spill holder.—**Key E**
2. PUNTY AND DIAMOND POINT, bitters bottle.—*Ref. K7-138* A. H. Heisey Glass Co. #305, 1889-1907. Extended table service including toothpick holder, salt shaker, tumbler, sauce, bowls, cruet, decanter, syrup, water bottle, vase, sugar shaker.—**Key C**
3. FAMOUS (PANELLED THUMBPRINT; THUMBPRINT PANEL), creamer.—*Ref. K1-114; PetSal 175R* Cooperative Flint Glass Co., 1899. Extended table service including toothpick holder, salt shaker, scarce syrup.—**Key B**

Row 4

1. RAY, celery vase.—*Ref. K1-110; L14* McKee Brothers, 1894. Extended table service including sauce, 6″ plate, bowls, salt shaker. Crystal, ruby-stained.—**Key B**
2. PEACOCK FEATHER (GEORGIA), salt shaker. See Plate 24.
3. HEART WITH THUMBPRINT (BULLS-EYE IN HEART), creamer.—*Ref. K2-103; LV23* Tarentum Glass Co., 1898. Extended table service including berry set, celery vase, tumbler, vases, sauce, cruet, wine, salt shaker, 8″ lamp, finger lamp. Crystal, custard, green custard.—**Key D**

PLATE 34 CIRCLES

Row 1

1. WASHINGTON CENTENNIAL (CHAIN WITH DIAMONDS), spoon holder.—*Ref. Gob II-20; K2-124* Gillander and Sons, 1876-1889. Made in extended table service including bowls, salt shaker, oval relish, compotes, fish-shaped pickle dish, syrup, platters with various motifs, champagne, wine, celery vase. See Plate 179. Crystal, milk glass.—**Key E**
2. CHAIN AND SHIELD, pitcher.—*Ref. K1-21* 1870's. Extended table service including platter, sauce.—**Key B**
3. LARGE STIPPLED CHAIN, pitcher.—*Ref. Gob II-63* Extended table service.—**Key B**

Row 2

1. BEADED CHAIN (LOOPED CORD), goblet.—*Ref. Gob II-102, 134* c. 1870's. Extended table service including plate, sauce, celery vase, open sugar.—Flint **Key E**
2. LOOP AND CHAIN BAND, goblet.—*Ref. Gob II-122*—**Key A**
3. BELLAIRE (BELLAIRE #2), pitcher.—*Ref. K7-14* c. 1879.—**Key A**

Row 3

1. ABERDEEN, egg cup. c. early 1870's. Extended table service including compote, sauce, open and covered sugar bowls. Crystal.—**Key B**
2. STIPPLED CHAIN, open salt.—*Ref. K8-74; L190; LV pl. 22* Gillander and Sons, 1870's. Extended table service including sauce, relish, footed salt, tumbler, pickle dish.—**Key A**
3. YOKE AND CIRCLE (ERA), goblet.—*Ref. Gob II-124* J. B. Higbee Co. Extended table service including salt shaker.—**Key B**

Row 4.

1. SCROLL (STIPPLED SCROLL), goblet.—*Ref. K7-71; L140* Duncan Glass Co., c. 1880's. Extended table service including egg cup, wine, celery vase, compotes, cordial, salt shaker.—**Key A**
2. TAPE-MEASURE (SHIELDS), pitcher.—*Ref. K5-9* Portland Glass Co., early 1870's. Extended table service including sauce.— **Key C**
3. TWO BAND, creamer—*Ref. K1-64* c. 1890. Extended table service including toy table set, salt shaker. Crystal, ruby-stained.—**Key A**

PLATE 35 CIRCLES

Row 1

1. CHAIN WITH STAR (FROSTED CHAIN), goblet.—*Ref. L132; K8-12* U.S. Glass Co. (Bryce #79), 1890's. Made in extended table service including cake stand, footed bowls, pickle dish, plates, sauce, relish, wine, salt shaker.—**Key B**

2. CHAIN, goblet.—*Ref. L132* c. 1880's. Extended table service including wine, cordial, covered compote. Crystal.—**Key B**

3. DOUBLE GREEK KEY, pitcher. Nickel Plate Glass Co., 1890's. Extended table service including tumbler, compotes, syrup. Crystal, stippled, opaque white, opalescent blue.—**Key D**

Row 2

1. WEDDING RING, syrup. 1870's. Extended table service including champagne, wine, decanter, syrup. No toothpick holder originally made.—Flint **Key E**; Non-flint **Key C**

2. SCROLL WITH STAR (WYCLIFF), cup.—*Ref. LV28; Gob II-6* U.S. Glass Co. (Challinor), 1891. Extended table service including sauce, plate, bowls, cup and saucer.—**Key B**

3. TENNESSEE (JEWELLED ROSETTES; JEWEL AND CRESCENT), salt shaker.—*Ref. K3-62* U.S. Glass Co. (King) #15064, 1899. A State Series pattern. Extended table service including syrup, tall celery vase, toothpick holder, mug, cake stand, compote, bread plate, jelly compote, jam jar, oval relish, tumbler. Moderately limited availability. Crystal.—**Key B**

Row 3

1. CHAIN, EARLY, pitcher. Boston and Sandwich. Extended table service including platter and wine.—**Key D**

2. CHAIN, FT. PITT, pitcher. Ft. Pitt Glass Works, 1830's. Extended table service.—**Key D**

PLATE 36 CIRCLES

Row 1

1. DRAPERY (LACE), pitcher.—*Ref. L108; K5-9; Gob I-133* Boston and Sandwich, c. 1865; Doyle and Co. #7, 1870's. Made in extended table service including sauce, plate, covered compote, egg cup, 6″ plate. Has pine cone finial.—**Key B**

2. TEARDROP AND TASSEL (SAMPSON), pitcher.—*Ref. L78; K1-95* Indiana Tumbler and Goblet, 1890's. Extended table service including wine, tumbler, relish tray, salt shaker, open compote, sauce. Crystal, blue, amber; opaque white, green and yellow.—**Key C**

3. DRAPED JEWEL, tumbler.—*Ref. L137* c. 1900. Extended table service including salt shaker.—**Key B**

Row 2

1. HEAVY JEWEL, tumbler.—*Ref. L137* Fostoria Glass Co. #1225, c. 1900. Extended table service including celery vase, compotes.—**Key B**

2. LOCKET ON CHAIN (STIPPLED BEADED SHIELD), cruet.—*Ref. K8-186* A. H. Heisey #160, 1897. Extended table service including rare toothpick holder, tumbler, salt shaker, rare cruet, celery vase, rare wine, pickle tray, bowls, compote, cake stand. No syrup known. Crystal, ruby-stained, colors.—**Key F**

3. LOOP AND DART - ROUND ORNAMENT (LOOP AND JEWEL), goblet. See Plate 81.—*Ref. L149* Boston and Sandwich; Richards and Hartley; Portland Glass Co., c. 1869. Extended table service including egg cup, butter pat, covered compote, footed tumbler, cordial, celery vase.—Non-Flint **Key C**

Row 3

1. FESTOON, plate.—*Ref. L166* Portland Glass Co., 1860's. Extended table service including cake stand, tumbler, high compote, pickle jar, wine, berry set, finger bowl, plates, celery vase, cake plate.—**Key B**

2. FESTOON, pitcher. See above.

Row 4

1. LEAF AND DART, pitcher.—*Ref. L149* Extended table service including finger lamp, wine, celery vase, master salt, rare cruet, footed sauce. See Plate 81.—**Key C**

2. JEWELLED HEART (SWEETHEART), salt shaker.—*Ref. K5-41* Dugan Glass Co., 1898-1905. Extended table service including toothpick holder, salt shaker, cruet, syrup, tumbler, lamp. Crystal, green, blue, carnival, opalescent.—**Key A**

3. LACY DEWDROP (BEADED JEWEL), creamer.—*Ref. K3-108; L-151* Cooperative Flint Glass Co., c. 1890. Extended table service

including mug, berry set, tumbler, sauce, salt shaker, compotes, covered berry bowls. Crystal, milk glass.—**Key A**

PLATE 37 CIRCLES

Row 1

1. HOOK, creamer—*K6-18* —**Key B**
2. SCROLL WITH ACANTHUS, creamer.—*Ref. K5-41* Central Glass Co.; Northwood in slag, 1904. Made in extended table service including jelly compote, open sugar, salt shaker, toothpick holder. No goblet originally made. See Plate 200. Crystal, apple green, amber, blue, slag.—**Key B**
3. FLEUR-DE-LIS (FROSTED FLEUR-DE-LIS), pitcher.—*Ref. K1-84* Indiana Tumbler and Goblet Co. Extended table service including toothpick holder, sauce, berry bowl, compote, plate, cake stand. Crystal, amber, blue, green, milk glass.—**Key B**

Row 2

1. SCROLL IN SCROLL, salt shaker.—*Ref. PetSal 171R* Milk Glass.—**Key B**
2. VICTORIAN JUBILEE, pitcher.—*Ref. K3-59* c. 1897. Extended table service including cup and saucer, plate. The open compote bears a medallion portrait of Queen Victoria.—**Key A**
3. MULTIPLE SCROLL, pitcher.—*Ref. K5-77* Canton Glass Co., 1893. Extended table service.—**Key B**

Row 3

1. FOSTORIA'S ROCOCO, spoon holder.—*Ref. K6-p. 59* Fostoria Glass Co. #234, 1891. Basic table service.—**Key B**
2. WHEEL IN BAND (CORCORAN), pitcher.—*Ref. K2-45* 1870's. Extended table service including jam jar, celery vase, wine. Crystal.—**Key B**
3. LOOP WITH FISH-EYE, goblet.—**Key B**
4. CONVENTIONAL BAND, creamer.—*Ref. K1-17* Extended table service.—**Key C**

Row 4

1. NET AND SCROLL, salt shaker.—*Ref. PetSal 34D* Opaque glass.—**Key C**
2. TRELLIS SCROLL, salt shaker.—*Ref. PetSal 38V* —**Key A**
3. TASSEL AND BEAD, salt shaker.—*Ref. PetSal 175C* Bryce Brothers.—**Key A**
4. STIPPLED ACANTHUS (AZTEC MEDALLION), salt shaker.—*Ref. PetSal 153-B* Mold-blown. Known in limited pieces in condiment set including rare syrup.—**Key C**

PLATE 38 CIRCLES

Row 1

1. ROCOCO, creamer.—*Ref. K3-105* Central Glass Co., 1891; Imperial Glass Co., 1906. Made in extended table service.—**Key B**
2. TOSSED SCROLLS, creamer.—*Ref. K8-39* Milk Glass—**Key C**
3. BAROQUE, creamer.—*Ref. K3-31* c. 1850's.—**Key D**

Row 2

1. FOSTORIA'S #1008, syrup.—*Ref. HIII-49* Fostoria Glass Co. Painted milk glass.—**Key D**
2. EAGLE'S FLEUR-DE-LIS (author's name), syrup.—*Ref. HIII-85* Eagle Glass and Mfg. Co., 1901.—**Key B**
3. ESTHER (TOOTH AND CLAW), cruet.—*Ref. K5-54; LV40* Riverside Glass Works, 1896. Extended table service including toothpick holder, berry set, salt shaker, castor set, jelly compote, jam jar, celery vase, lamp, rare syrup. Crystal, ruby & amber stained, emerald green.—**Key B**

Row 3

1. CROESUS, salt shaker.—*Ref. K4-112* Riverside Glass Co. #484; McKee and Sons, c. 1897-1901. Extended table service including tumbler, toothpick holder, cruet, celery vase, berry set, pickle dish, bowls, cake stand, compotes. Crystal, emerald green, amethyst. —**Key C**
2. TIEBACK, salt shaker.—*Ref. PetSal 176D* Milk Glass.—**Key C**
3. TOP AND BOTTOM SCROLL, salt shaker.—*Ref. PetSal 171T* Opaque glass.—**Key B**
4. CAPITAL, toothpick holder.—*Ref. Hartung; HTP-73* Novelty items. Crystal, color flashed, iridized.—**Key B**

Row 4

1. BELMONT'S ROYAL, salt shaker.—*Ref. K6 pl. 90* Belmont Glass Co., 1881. Extended table service including celery vase with handles, salt shaker. See Plate 179.—**Key C**
2. CHRYSANTHEMUM LEAF, toothpick holder.—*Ref. LV52* Boston and Sandwich, late 1880's; later c. 1900-1903, probably National Glass Co.—*(Ref. Hi-17).* Extended table service. Crystal, chocolate.—**Key C**
3. SCROLL AND CHAIN, salt shaker.—*Ref. PetSal 171P* Milk glass.—**Key C**
4. MOSAIC SCROLL, salt shaker.—*Ref. PetSal 171S* Milk glass.—**Key C**

PLATE 39 CIRCLES

Row 1

1. LACY MEDALLION, tumbler.—*Ref. K1-106* U.S. Glass Co., 1905. Souvenir ware including mugs, salt shaker, toothpick holder, wine, toy table set. Crystal, green, ruby-stained, cobalt blue (rare).—**Key A**

2. COLORADO, salt shaker. See Plate 154.

3. TIDY (STAYMAN; DRAPERY VARIANT; RUSTIC), creamer.—*Ref. Gob II-68; K4-22* McKee and Brothers, 1880. Extended table service including compote.—**Key A**

4. PRINCESS FEATHER (ROCHELLE; LACY MEDALLION), spooner.—*Ref. L-19* Boston and Sandwich; Bakewell, Pears; U.S. Glass, 1890's. Extended table service including egg cup, compotes, plates, celery vase. Crystal, opaque white.—**Key B**

Row 2

1. GYRO, covered jar. National Glass Co. (McKee), 1901. Opalescent novelty.

2. SHIELD AND SPIKE, goblet. —*Ref. Gob II-22* —**Key A**

3. BEAD AND BAR MEDALLION (AEGIS), creamer.—*Ref. K1-60; Gob II-82* McKee and Brothers, c. 1880. Extended table service.—**Key B**

Row 3

1. STIPPLED MEDALLION, goblet.—*Ref. L28* Union Glass Co., 1860's. Extended table service including egg cup, plates, cake plate, honey dish.—**Key B**

2. DOUBLE SCROLL, salt shaker.—*Ref. K6 Pl. 58* Fostoria Glass Co. #233, 1891. Extended table service. See Plate 242.—**Key B**

3. IDYLL, creamer.—*Ref. K7-46* Jefferson Glass Co. #251, 1904. Extended table service including toothpick holder, salt shaker, half-gallon jug, berry set, cruet, condiment set, tumbler. Crystal, colors, opalescent.—**Key A**

4. ARCHED FLEUR-DE-LIS, salt shaker.—*Ref. PetSal 161D* Bryce Higbee and Co., 1898. Extended table service including cruet. See Plate 116. Crystal; ruby-stained.—**Key B**

Row 4

1. BANDED FLEUR-DE-LIS, pitcher.—*Ref. K2-44; Gob II-164* Imperial Glass Co., 1890's. Extended table service including salt shaker.—**Key B**

2. RIBBED ELLIPSE (ADMIRAL), creamer.—*Ref. K5-70* J.B. Higbee Co., c. 1905. Extended table service including cake plate, handled mug, tumbler, plate, bowls, compote.—**Key B**

3. PRINCE OF WALES PLUMES (FLAMBEAUX), creamer.

—Ref. K1-115; K8-185 A. H. Heisey Glass Co. #335, 1900. Extended table service of 60 items including toothpick holder, salt shaker, sauce, bowls.—**Key E**

PLATE 40 CIRCLES

Row 1

1. ROBIN HOOD, creamer.—*Ref. K7-7* Fostoria Glass Co., 1898. Extended table service including salt shaker, compotes, scarce syrup, celery vase, tumbler.—**Key A**

2. FROSTED CIRCLE (HORN OF PLENTY), goblet.—*Ref. K4-19* Bryce Brothers, 1876; U.S. Glass Co. #15007 (Columbia; Nickel Plate), 1891. Made in extended table service including salt shaker, plates, tumblers, wine, celery vase, bowl, cake stand, pickle jar, compotes, bowls. A fairly abundant pattern.—**Key C**

Row 2

1. SNAIL (IDAHO; COMPACT), butter dish.—*Ref. K7-123; LV-46* George Duncan and Sons, 1880's; U.S. Glass Co., 1898. A State Series pattern. Extended table service including syrup, cruet, salt shaker, compotes, individual salt and sugar, rose bowl, plate, relish, celery vase, tumbler, scarce goblet, cake stand, punch cup, covered cheese dish, banana stand, berry set. A fairly abundant pattern. See Plate 242. Crystal, ruby-stained (scarce).—**Key C**

2. MOON AND STAR (STAR AND PUNTY; BULLS-EYE AND STAR; PALACE), pitcher.—*Ref. L69 & 103; K1-80* Boston and Sandwich, 1870; Pioneer Glass Co.; Wilson Glass Co.; Cooperative Flint Glass Co.; Adams and Co.; U.S. Glass Co., 1891. Made in very large extended table service including egg cup, cruet, salt shaker, salt dish, cake stand, claret. No toothpick holder made originally. Many reproductions. See Plate 232. Crystal, ruby-stained.—**Key C**

Row 3

1. BLOCK AND ROSETTE, sugar bowl.—*Ref. Gob II-91* Duncan glass, c. 1902. Extended table service including toy table service (rare), toothpick holder, tumbler. Crystal, ruby-stained.—**Key B**

2. CHILSON, goblet.—*Ref. Gob II-4* —**Key D**

3. STAR-IN-BULLS-EYE, creamer.—*Ref. K1 -100; Gob I-99* U.S. Glass Co. #15092 (Glassport factory), 1905. Made in extended table service including tumbler, toothpick holder, salt shaker, relish, punch cup. Crystal, rose-flashed.—**Key B**

Row 4

1. KNOBBY BULLS-EYE (CROMWELL), creamer.—*Ref. Gob I-214* U.S. Glass Co. #15155 (Glassport), 1915. Extended table service including toothpick holder, two types salt shaker, bowls, celery tray, wine, decanter. Crystal, decorated.—**Key A**

2. THE STATES (CANE AND STAR MEDALLION), spoon holder—*Ref. K5-142; Gob II-69* U.S. Glass Co. #15093, 1908. Extended table service including plate, relish, punch bowl and cup,

syrup, two kinds of toothpick holders, salt shaker, compotes. Crystal, emerald green.—**Key B**

PLATE 41 DIAMONDS

Row 1

1. CZARINA, pitcher.—*Ref. K5-91* Fostoria Glass Co. #444, 1895. Made in extended table service including tumbler, celery tray, syrup, cruet, salt shaker, berry bowl, cake stand, jelly compote, vases, handled relish, bowls.—**Key B**

2. BANDED DIAMOND POINT, spoon holder.—**Key B**

Row 2

1. SAWTOOTH, celery vase.—*Ref. L40* Boston and Sandwich; Union Glass Co.; U.S. Glass Co. (Bryce; Gillander), 1891. Extended table service including several sizes sauce dishes, spill, tumbler, wine, champagne, goblet, toy table service.—Toy set **Key C;** Flint **Key D;** Non-flint **Key B**

2. CORAL GABLES, goblet.—*Gob II-15* —**Key A**

3. DIAMOND BAND, goblet.—*Ref. K4-137* Indiana Glass Co., after 1910. Extended table service including celery vase, wine, small footed compote, shallow dish.—**Key B**

Row 3

1. LATE DIAMOND POINT BAND (SCALLOPED DIAMOND POINT; PANEL WITH DIAMOND POINT BAND), pitcher.—*Ref. K1-36* Central Glass Co., 1870's. Extended table service including cake stand, covered cheese dish, bowl, mustard dish.—**Key A**

2. DIAMOND POINT, spill holder.—*Ref. L43* Sandwich glass; Bryce, Richards and Co., and others, 1830; 1890's. Extended table service including celery vase, egg cup, compotes, tumblers, plates.—Flint **Key D**

PLATE 42 DIAMONDS

Row 1

1. SERRATED RIB AND FINE CUT, goblet.—*Ref. Gob II-153*
—**Key B**
2. DIAMOND ROSETTES, goblet. 1870's-1900's. Made in extended table service including covered compote, tumbler, celery vase. Crystal, yellow, blue, light green.—**Key B**
3. BUCKLE AND SHIELD, goblet.—*Ref. Gob II-64* —**Key B**
4. HARTFORD, spoon holder.—*Ref. K8-193* Fostoria Glass Co., 1900's. Extended table service including salt shaker, syrup, celery vase, tumbler, bowls, sauce. Crystal, canary, amber.—**Key B**

Row 2

1. OVAL DIAMOND PANEL (OVAL PANEL), goblet.—*Ref. L62*
—**Key B**
2. BULLS-EYE AND DIAMOND QUILTED, goblet.—*Ref. Gob II-118* —**Key B**
3. KENTUCKY, salt shaker. See Plate 43.
4. TEASEL, goblet.—*Ref. L96* Bryce Brothers, 1870's. Extended table service including celery vase, compotes, cruet, footed sauce, salt shaker, cake stand. See plate on Plate 132.—**Key B**

Row 3

1. DIAMOND POINT AND PUNTY, salt shaker.—*Ref. PetSal 27L* Do not confuse with PUNTY AND DIAMOND POINT, Plate 33.—**Key A**
2. IMPERIAL'S #80, pitcher.—*Ref. K7-66* Imperial Glass Co., 1901.—**Key A**
3. DIAMOND IN POINTS, creamer.—*Ref. K4-81* c. 1860. The diamond-point is depressed rather than raised.—**Key D**

Row 4

1. FLAT DIAMOND AND PANEL (LATTICE AND OVAL PANELS), egg cup. Sandwich glass. Extended table service including tumbler, decanter, claret, wine, lamp. Crystal, opaque.—Flint **Key F**
2. RICHMOND, pitcher.—*Ref. LV61* Richards and Hartley #190, 1888; U.S. Glass Co., 1891. Extended table service including half-gallon and quart pitchers, tumbler, wine, salt shaker. Crystal.—**Key B**
3. CRISS-CROSS BAND, goblet.—*Ref. Gob II-85* Extended table service including toy set.—**Key A**

PLATE 43 DIAMONDS

Row 1

1. PANELLED DIAMOND POINT, spoon holder.—*Ref. L-104*
1860's. Made in extended table service including compote, sauce,
celery vase, spill holder.—**Key B**

2. HINOTO (DIAMONDPOINT WITH PANELS), spill
holder.—*Ref. L-153-11* Boston and Sandwich, 1850's. Extended table
service including champagne, rare covered sweetmeat, celery vase,
open salt.—Flint **Key C**

3. NEW ENGLAND PINEAPPLE, tumbler.—*Ref. L53* New
England Glass Co.; Boston and Sandwich; c. 1860's. Extended table
service including decanter, tumbler, compote, sauce.—Flint **Key D**

Row 2

1. KENTUCKY, goblet.—*Ref. K4-68; LV39* U.S. Glass Co. #15051
(King), 1897. A State Series pattern. Extended table service including
salt shaker, cruet, cup, toothpick holder. Similar pattern:
"MILLARD". Limited availability. Crystal, emerald green, cobalt
blue (scarce).—**Key B**

2. SWIRL AND DIAMOND (AMERICA; SWIRL AND
DIAMOND WITH OVALS), spoon holder.—*Ref. K6 Pl. 11* American
Glass Co., 1890; Riverside Glass Works, 1890. Extended table service
including salt shaker, open and covered sugar bowls, sauce, carafe,
tumbler, bowl, pickle tray, berry bowl. See Plate 241. Crystal.
—**Key B**

3. DIAMOND PANELS, toothpick holder.—*Ref. HTP-30* c. 1895.
Toy basic table service. Crystal, green, blue.—**Key B**

Row 3

1. FLAT DIAMOND (LIPPMAN), goblet.—*Ref. Gob II-59*
Richards and Hartley, 1885-93. Extended table service including
tumbler.—**Key B**

2. TULIP WITH SAWTOOTH, pitcher.—*Ref. L-53* Extended
table service including decanter, celery vase, powder jar, footed salt,
cordial, cruets.—**Key D**

3. TULIP, decanter.—*Ref. L53* Bryce, Richards and Co., c. 1854.
Extended table service including celery vase, high and low compotes,
several sizes decanters, pint and quart jugs, tumbler, wine.—Flint
Key D

PLATE 44 DIAMONDS

Row 1

1. DIAMOND SWAG, creamer. See Plate 112.
2. PINEAPPLE AND FAN (SHEPHERD'S PLAID; CUBE WITH FAN; HOLBROOK; CZARINA; PSEUDO-CZARINA; CUBE AND DIAMOND; DIAMOND BLOCK AND FAN; MILTON CUBE AND FAN), salt shaker.—*Ref. K3-79; Gob II-84* U.S. Glass Co. #15041 (Gillander; Adams), 1891. Extended table service including water bottle, celery vase, celery tray. Crystal, ruby-stained, emerald green.—**Key A**
3. CARMEN (PANELLED DIAMONDS AND FINECUT), pitcher.—*Ref. K5-121; LV-37* Fostoria Glass #575, 1896. Extended table service including toothpick holder, salt shaker, syrup, candy dish. Crystal, yellow-flashed.—**Key C**

Row 2

1. DIAMOND WITH DIAMOND POINT (ENGLISH), creamer.—*Ref. K2-109* Westmoreland Glass Co., 1894. Extended table service including celery vase, compote, tumbler, salt shaker. Crystal, opalescent.—**Key B**
2. HAMILTON (CAPE COD), tumbler.—*Ref. L-56* Sandwich glass, 1860's. Extended table service including castor set, decanter, egg cup, sauce, syrup, compotes, celery vase, whiskey (scarce), wine.—Flint **Key D**
3. PINEAPPLE AND FAN, cruet. See Row 1 #2.

Row 3

DIAMOND POINT WITH FAN, creamer.—*Ref. K1-99* Extended table service including toothpick holder.—**Key A**

Row 4

1. QUILTED FAN TOP, goblet.—*Ref. Gob II-56* —**Key A**
2. DIAMOND WITH DUAL FAN, salt shaker.—*Ref. PetSal 27Q* Extended table service including 10″ plate.—**Key B**
3. HARVARD YARD (CRYSTAL), salt shaker.—*Ref. PetSal 162S* Tarentum Glass Co., 1896. Extended table service including cake stand, wine, cordial, egg cup.—**Key A**

PLATE 45 DIAMONDS

Row 1

1. AUSTRIAN (FINE CUT MEDALLION; PANELLED OVAL FINE CUT), pitcher.—*Ref. Gob II-8; K2-43* Indiana Tumbler and Goblet, 1897-98. Made in extended table service including toothpick holder, jelly compote, vase, handled sauce, toy basic service, berry set, banana dish, compote, punch cup, rose bowls, tumbler. Crystal, canary, green, chocolate, opaque white.—**Key B**

2. CHALLINOR #314, creamer.—*Ref. K4-84* Challinor, Taylor and Co.; U.S. Glass Co., 1891. Basic table service. Milk glass.—**Key D**

Row 2

1. LOOP AND BLOCK WITH WAFFLE BAND, goblet.—*Ref. Gob II-83* —**Key A**

2. DIAMOND CRYSTAL, creamer.—*Ref. K5-60* George Duncan and Sons, 1900. Made in extended table service including sauce, berry bowls.—**Key A**

Row 3

1. DIAMOND QUILTED IMPERIAL, sugar bowl. Imperial Glass Co., 1920's/30's. Extended table service.—**Key A**

2. ENGLISH HOBNAIL, pepper shaker.—*Ref. L85* Extended table service including bowls, open salt, toy condiment set.—**Key A**

3. THOUSAND DIAMONDS, syrup.—*Ref. HIII-44* George Duncan and Sons, c. 1890. Has raised quilting. Known in water set and syrup.—**Key C**

Row 4

1. ACORN DIAMONDS, syrup.—*Ref. HIII-51* U.S. Glass Co. (Bryce), 1891. Syrup only known.—**Key B**

2. DIAMOND QUILTED, celery vase.—*Ref. L104; Gob I-151* c. 1880's. Extended table service including water tray, footed tumbler, footed sauce, salt shaker. Crystal, canary, amber, blue, amethyst, purple.—**Key A**

3. PANEL WITH DIAMOND POINT BAND, creamer.—*Ref. K1-35* Central Glass Co. #439; Crystal Glass Co; 1881. Extended table service including compotes, plates, bowls.—**Key B**

PLATE 46 DIAMONDS

Row 1

1. STEPPED DIAMOND POINT, pitcher.—*Ref. K7-5* 1860's.—**Key D**
2. GIANT SAWTOOTH, lamp.—*Ref. Gob II-103* 1830. Known in lamp, spill, tumbler.—Flint **Key E**

Row 2

1. HEAVY DIAMOND (DIAMOND BLOCK), pitcher.—*Ref. K1-99* Imperial Glass Co., c. 1925-35.—**Key A**
2. ROANOKE (SAWTOOTH), creamer.—*Ref. K2-99; K8-168* Gillander and Sons, 1885; U.S. Glass Co. (Ripley), 1891. Made in extended table service including cake stand, wine, tumbler, celery vase, flat and footed creamers. See Plate 48. Crystal, green, ruby-stained.—**Key C**

Row 3

1. GIANT SAWTOOTH, tumbler. See Row 1 #3.
2. PRISM AND FLATTENED SAWTOOTH (RIBBED PINEAP-PLE), spill.—*Ref. Gob II-19* 1850's. Extended table service including lamp.—**Key E**

Row 4

1. ENGLISH COLONIAL, creamer.—*Ref. K3-138* McKee Glass Co. #75, c. 1900. Extended table service of forty-six pieces including toothpick holder, tumbler, syrup, salt shaker, cruet, bowls, punch bowl, compotes, berry, wine, cordial, claret, sauce.—**Key A**
2. SUPERIOR, creamer (engraved).—*Ref. HV-172* U.S. Glass Co. #15031 (Ripley), 1896. Crystal.—**Key B**

PLATE 47 DIAMONDS

Row 1

1. PAVONIA (PINEAPPLE STEM), spoon holder.—*Ref. K4-142* Ripley and Co., 1885; U.S. Glass Co., 1891. Made in extended table service including tray, salt shaker, cake stand, wine, tumbler, finger bowl, footed sauce, bowls, compotes. Crystal, ruby-stained.—**Key C**

2. AMAZON (SAWTOOTH BAND), creamer.—*Ref. K3-9; LV42* U.S. Glass Co. (Bryce), c. 1890. Huge table service including waste bowl, cake stands, champagne, wine, cordial, claret, flared bowls, toy table set, compote, syrup, sauce, flat and footed celery vases, individual and master salts, lion-head handled bowls, covered bowls. Good availability. Crystal, amber, vaseline, blue.—**Key B**

Row 2

1. O'HARA DIAMOND, pitcher. See Plate 60.

2. ADAMS DIAMOND, creamer.—*Ref. K7-8* Adams and Co., c. 1880's.—**Key B**

Row 3

1. AMAZON, salt shaker. See Row 1 #2.

2. BAR AND DIAMOND (KOKOMO; R & H SWIRL; ZIPPERED SWIRL), salt shaker.—*Ref. LV62; PetSal 174R; Gob I-142* U.S. Glass Co. (Richards and Hartley), 1891. Made in extended table service including sugar shaker, compotes, two types salt shaker, decanter, trays, cruet, hand lamp, toy table set, wine, celery vase. On some pieces the swirls reverse. Good availability. See Plate 241. Crystal, ruby-stained.—**Key B**

Row 4

1. SAWTOOTH AND WINDOW, salt shaker.—*Ref. PetSal 171M* —**Key A**

2. SAWTOOTH, salt shaker. See Plate 41.

PLATE 48 DIAMONDS

Row 1

1. STRATFORD, pitcher.—*Ref. K7-65* Cambridge Glass Co., 1906. Made in extended table service including 20 vases, 12 bowls, pickle jar, mustard jar, compote, 15 open sugar bowls with varying rims.—**Key B**

2. ROANOKE, rose bowl. This rose bowl was fitted with a wire bail and chain to hang it. See Plate 46.

Row 2

1. Three piece castor set by Doyle and Co., c. 1891.—*Ref. K8-107*

2. FLATTENED SAWTOOTH, pitcher.—*Ref. L65* George Duncan and Sons, c. 1880. Extended table service including finger bowl, wine, celery vase, covered compote, bowl.—**Key B**

Row 3

1. HOME (SQUARE AND DIAMOND BANDS), creamer.—*Ref. K1-59* Pioneer Glass Co.; McKee Brothers, 1880's; 1894. Extended table service including celery vase, tumbler. Crystal, ruby-stained.—**Key B**

2. AUSTRIAN, rose bowl. See Plate 45.

Row 4

1. HARVARD (QUIXOTE), salt shaker.—*Ref. K6-51* Tarentum Glass Co., 1898-1912. Extended table service including wine, punch cup, plate, finger bowl, toothpick holder, compote, individual creamer, footed bowl. Crystal, green, ruby-stained, custard.—**Key B**

2. BEAUMONT'S COLUMBIA, salt shaker.—*Ref. K7-168* Beaumont Glass Co. #100, 1898. Extended table service including jelly compote, bowls, celery vase, toothpick holder, cruet, syrup, pickle jar, tumbler.—**Key B**

3. FLATTENED SAWTOOTH, salt dish. See Row 2 #2.

PLATE 49 DIAMONDS

Row 1
1. AURORA, bread plate. See Plate 80.
2. MIRROR STAR (OLD GLORY), pitcher.—*Ref. K4-138* New Martinsville Glass Co., c. 1910-15.—**Key B**

Row 2
1. DIAMOND THUMBPRINT (DIAMOND AND CONCAVE), pitcher.—*Ref. L25* Boston and Sandwich; McKee and Brothers; Union Glass Co., 1850's. Made in extended table service including decanter, wine, wine jug, very rare goblet, cake stands, celery vase. All pieces rare. Crystal, amethyst, yellow.—Flint **Key E**
2. HECK (DOUBLE PRISM; TEARDROP ROW), creamer.—*Ref. K1-97; PetSal 41Q* Model Flint Glass Co., c. 1890. Extended table service including celery vases, salt shaker.—**Key B**

Row 3
1. STAR AND DIAMOND POINT, salt shaker.—*Ref. PetSal 173-E* —**Key B**
2. OPPOSING PYRAMIDS (GREENBURG'S FLORA; TRUNCATED PRISMS; FLORA), salt shaker.—*Ref. K8-31; Gob II-82* Greensburg Glass Co., 1889. Extended table service including celery vase, cake stands, bowls, compotes, wine, tumbler. See Plate 203.—**Key B**

PLATE 50 DIAMONDS

Row 1

1. PANELLED SAWTOOTH (FLUTED DIAMOND POINT), pitcher.—*Ref. K1-37* Made by Duncan, c. 1880's in extended table service including cake stand, wine, celery vase.—**Key B**

2. ENGLISH QUILTING, creamer.—*Ref. K2-5* —**Key C**

Row 2

1. PRISM AND SAWTOOTH, goblet.—*Ref. Gob II-152* An early flint pattern, made in extended table service including celery vase.—**Key D**

2. PANELLED HONEYCOMB, pitcher.—*Ref. K3-55* Bryce, Walker and Co., c. 1885-90. Extended table service including compote, celery vase.—**Key B**

Row 3

1. HOBNAIL-IN-SQUARE, pitcher.—*Ref. K5 pl. 24* Aetna Glass and Mfg. Co., 1887. Extended table service including salt shaker. Crystal, opalescent, colors.—**Key B**

2. HECK, salt shaker. See Plate 49.

3. ZIG-ZAG BLOCK (AMERICAN), salt shaker.—*Ref. Gob II-106* Fostoria Glass Co., c. 1898-1915. Being produced in the 1960's. Extended table service including toothpick holder.—**Key A**

PLATE 51 DIAMONDS

Row 1

1. WARD'S NEW ERA, pitcher.—*Ref. K5-80* Cooperative Flint Glass Co., 1901. Was sold by Montgomery Ward in 1901 and 1903. Extended table service including tumbler, compote, cake plate, bowls, cruet, jelly compote.—**Key A**

2. SMOCKING, spill holder.—*Ref. K6-12* Boston and Sandwich, 1840's. Extended table service including compote, 9″ lamp, rare creamer, egg cup, water and whiskey tumblers, 10″ vase, wine, bar bottle, berry set.—Flint **Key D**

3. ALL-OVER DIAMOND, cruet.—*Ref. K3-134* U.S. Glass #15011 (Gillander; Duncan), 1891. Extended table service including condensed milk jar, syrup, salt shaker, egg cup. Crystal.—**Key B**

Row 2

1. NAILHEAD (GEM), pitcher.—*Ref. K4-41; L108/158* Boston and Sandwich; Bryce, Higbee and Co., c. 1880's. Extended table service including cordial, tumbler, wine, sauce, compotes, cake stand, celery vase, round and square plates, salt shaker, berry bowl. Crystal, aquamarine, decorated.—Non-Flint **Key B**

2. NICKEL PLATE'S RICHMOND (BLOCK AND DOUBLE BAR; BAR AND BLOCK; BARS AND BUTTONS; AKRON BLOCK), creamer.—*Ref. K1-76; K6 pl. 16* U.S. Glass Co. (Nickel Plate), 1891. Extended table service including celery vase, finger bowl, tumbler. See Plate 226 for example of this pattern in a vertical block design; salt shaker on Plate 91; and tankard pitcher, called "BAR AND BLOCK" on Plate 227.—**Key B**

Row 3

1. BEVELLED DIAGONAL BLOCK (CROSSBAR), creamer. —*Ref. LV59* U.S. Glass Co. (Challinor #311), 1891. Extended table service including jam jar, cake stand, cordial, plate, tumbler, wine, salt shaker. Crystal, ruby-stained.—**Key A**

2. DIVIDED DIAMONDS, goblet.—*Ref. Gob II-6* —**Key B**

Row 4

1. DIAMOND WEB, salt shaker.—*Ref. PetSal 27P* —**Key A**

2. ARTICHOKE (VALENCIA), creamer.—*Ref. K7-78.* Fostoria Glass Co., 1891. Extended table service including tumbler, punch cup, syrup, salt shaker. No goblet originally made. See Plate 199. Crystal, opalescent, satin, colors.—**Key C**

PLATE 52 DIAMONDS

Row 1

1. MISS AMERICA, creamer. Hocking Glass Co., 1933-37. This is "Depression" glass. Extended table service.

2. RUBY DIAMOND, pitcher.—*Ref. K2-93* c. 1893. Extended table service. Crystal, ruby-stained.—**Key A**

Row 2

1. HICKMAN (LA CLEDE), cruet.—*Ref. Gob I-57; 112* McKee and Brothers, 1897. Extended table service including three types salt shaker, jelly compote, toy condiment set, sauce, toothpick holder.—**Key B**

2. DIAMONDPOINT THUMBPRINT, plate. (Author's name).—**Key A**

Row 3

1. HUNGARIAN, salt shaker.—*Ref. PetSal 163S* —**Key A**

2. CADMUS, goblet.—*Ref. Gob II-83* Beaumont Glass Co. —**Key A**

3. OVERALL DIAMOND (SYLVAN; ENGLISH HOBNAIL VARIANT), creamer.—*Ref. K7-32; K4-100* Fostoria Glass Co. #1119, 1902. Made in extended table service including bowls, punch set, lemonade, toothpick holder, individual sugar and creamer, rose bowls, tumblers, celery vase, jelly compote, carafe, syrup, salt shaker, cologne bottle, celery tray.—**Key B**

Row 4

1. OVERALL DIAMOND, salt shaker, See Above.

2. FLAT DIAMOND BOX, creamer.—*Ref. K3-94* Fostoria Glass Co. #301, 1892. Extended table service including salt shaker. —**Key B**

PLATE 53 DIAMONDS

Row 1

1. TARENTUM'S MANHATTAN, butter dish. Tarentum Glass Co., 1895. Made in extended table service including cake stand, wine, celery vase. Crystal.—**Key B**

2. PATTERN F, goblet.—*Ref. K8-180* Specialty Glass Co., 1892. Known in goblet and wine.—**Key B**

Row 2

1. STAR IN DIAMOND, creamer.—*Ref. K1-62* U.S. Glass #414, 1891.—**Key B**

2. DIAMOND LATTICE (CHESTERFIELD), creamer.—*Ref. K2-77* Cambridge Glass Co. #2500, c. 1903. Extended table service including sauce, berry set, plate.—**Key A**

Row 3

1. DIAMOND IN SPACE, salt shaker.—*Ref. PetSal 158R* —**Key A**

2. BLOCK AND PANEL, salt shaker.—*Ref. LV60* Extended table service.—**Key B**

3. MASCOTTE (MINOR BLOCK), salt shaker.—*Ref. LV42; K1-17; Gob II-132* U.S. Glass Co. (Ripley), 1891. Extended table service including several sizes tall compotes, celery vase, jelly compote, wine, sauce, cookie stand. Often etched. See Plate 88. Good availability.—**Key B**

PLATE 54 DIAMONDS

Row 1

1. INDIANA, butter dish. See Plates 218, 221.

2. GRAND (NEW GRAND; DIAMOND MEDALLION), pitcher.—*Ref. K8-119; LV31* Bryce, Higbee and Co., 1885. Extended table service including cake stand, celery vase, footed sauce, finger bowl, compote, tumbler, wine, salt shaker. Fair availability. —**Key B**

Row 2

1. DEEP STAR (DIAMOND WALL), creamer.—*Ref. K4-77* Model Flint Glass Co., c. 1890. Extended table service including salt shaker, toy table service.—**Key A**

2. FANCY DIAMONDS, pitcher. Extended table service including wine, bowl.—**Key A**

Row 3

1. DEEP STAR, salt shaker. See above.

2. STAR AND DIAMOND, salt shaker.—*Ref. PetSal 173D* —**Key A**

3. TACOMA, cruet.—*Ref. K6 pl. 46* Greensburg Glass Co., 1894; Model Flint Glass Co., 1900; McKee. Extended table service including toothpick holder, salt shaker, jam jar, tumbler, sauce, decanter.—**Key C**

PLATE 55 DIAMONDS

Row 1

1. DIAMOND BAR AND BLOCK, pitcher—*Ref. K2-68* c. 1900.—**Key B**

2. CROSSED BLOCK (ROMAN CROSS), goblet.—*Ref. Gob II-31* Late 1800's. Extended table service. See Plate 219.—**Key B**

Row 2

1. U.S. SHELL (KNIGHT), creamer.—*Ref. K3-76* U.S. Glass Co., 1892. Made in extended table service. Crystal.—**Key B**

2. CROSS IN DIAMOND (CRUSADER CROSS; STAR; DIAMOND), tray.—*Ref. K5-51; Gob II-44* U.S. Glass Co. (Challinor #9), 1891. Extended table service including bowls, compote. Crystal.—**Key B**

Row 3

1. CROSS IN DIAMOND, pitcher. See above.

2. NONPARIEL, spoon holder.—**Key B**

Row 4

1. GLADIATOR, tumbler.—*Ref. K6 pl. 60* McKee Brothers, 1897. Extended table service.—**Key A**

2. SUNBURST AND BAR, tumbler.—**Key B**

3. HOLLIS, tumbler.—**Key A**

PLATE 56 DIAMONDS

Row 1

1. UNIQUE, syrup.—*Ref. K7-38* Cooperative Flint Glass Co., 1898. Made in extended table service including tumbler, celery vase. —**Key B**

2. PEQUOT, compote.—*Ref. Gob II-127* Extended table service including jam jar, castor set.—**Key C**

Row 2

1. HEISEY #150, creamer.—*Ref. K4-90* A. H. Heisey Co., 1897. Extended table service including bowls.—**Key B**

2. HIGH HOB, creamer.—*Ref. K3-147* Westmoreland Glass Co., 1915. Extended table service including tumbler.—**Key A**

3. SUNK PRISM (PITCAIRN), pitcher.—*Ref. K3-36; Gob II-52* King, Son and Co., c. 1880. Extended table service including compote.—**Key B**

Row 3

1. LADY HAMILTON (PEERLESS), tumbler.—*Ref. K7-64* Richards and Hartley, 1875. Extended table service including mustard jar, tumbler, bread plate, celery vase, two creamers, sauce, castor set, twenty-two compotes, berry bowl, pickle jar, cruet, cake stand, individual salt.—**Key B**

2. AMBOY, goblet.—*Ref. Gob II-27* —**Key A**

3. DIAMOND POINT DISCS, creamer.—*Ref. K3-90* J. B. Higbee; later New Martinsville; c. 1905. Extended table service including compotes, cake stand, salt shaker, celery vase, bowls, individual salt.—**Key A**

Row 4

1. BULLS-EYE AND BUTTONS, syrup.—*Ref. MUR-2* c. 1895-1900. Known in syrup, cruet, toothpick holder. Green, crystal.—**Key B**

2. TIPTOE (RAMONA; HOGAN'S SALT SHAKER), salt shaker.—*Ref. PetSal 42H* McKee Glass Co., after 1900. Extended table service including toothpick holder.—**Key A**

Row 5

1. ART, pitcher. See Plates 26 and 58.

2. SEELY (FOSTORIA), creamer.—*Ref. K8-35; K6-76; Gob II-27* U.S. Glass Co. (Nickel Plate), 1891. Extended table service including berry bowl. Crystal.—**Key A**

PLATE 57 DIAMONDS

Row 1

1. WORLDS PATTERN, pitcher.—*Ref. K8-145* Bryce, Walker and Co., 1880's. Made in extended table service including salt shaker, cake stand, tumbler, bowls, sauce, celery vase, open and covered compotes.—**Key B**

2. WESTMORELAND (SWIRLED BLOCK), cruet.—*Ref. K1-117; LV49* Gillander and Sons, 1888; U.S. Glass Co. #15011, 1892. Extended table service of seventy-five pieces including toy table set, sauce, honey jar, salt shaker, punch bowl, nut bowl, ice tub, decanter, covered cheese plate. Good availability.—**Key B**

Row 2

1. TARENTUM'S ATLANTA (ROYAL CRYSTAL; DIAMOND AND TEARDROP), pitcher.—*Ref. K6-31; LV57* Tarentum Glass Co., 1894. Extended table service including toothpick holder, celery vase, sauce, salt shaker, open compote, cologne bottle, syrup. Crystal, ruby-flashed.—**Key B**

2. COOP #190, creamer.—*Ref. K6 pl. 47* Cooperative Flint Glass Co., 1892. Extended table service including tumbler, celery vase, syrup, wine, bowls, sauce, salt shaker, compotes, berry bowls, individual sugar and creamer.—**Key A**

Row 3

1. SANDWICH PLAID, plate. 1835-45. Made in extended table service but not common.—**Key E**

2. PRESSED DIAMOND, syrup.—*Ref. K8-33; LV70* Central Glass Co. #775 c. 1885; U.S. Glass Co., 1891. Extended table service including cruet, tumbler, open compote, salt shaker, pickle castor. Crystal, amber, blue (scarce), vaseline.—**Key C**

Row 4

1. BAKEWELL BLOCK, spoon holder. Bakewell, Pears and Co., c. 1850's. Extended table service including champagne, bar tumbler, decanter, celery vase.—**Key E**

2. WESTMORELAND, toy pitcher. See Row 1 #2.

125

PLATE 58 DIAMONDS

Row 1
1. RIBS AND DIAMONDS, goblet.—*Ref. Gob II-101* —**Key A**
2. BROOCH BAND, goblet.—*Ref. Gob II-120* —**Key A**
3. FLAT IRON, pitcher.—*Ref. K4-101* c. 1890.—**Key A**

Row 2
1. PANTAGRAPH BAND, goblet.—*Ref. Gob II-24* —**Key A**
2. REGAL BLOCK, goblet.—*Ref. Gob II-97* —**Key A**
3. PIONEER'S VICTORIA, pitcher.—*Ref. K3-83* Pioneer Glass Co., 1885. Made in extended table service including salt shaker, egg cup, celery vase, compotes. Crystal, ruby-stained.—**Key B**

Row 3
1. KING'S #500, creamer.—*Ref. K8-72* King Glass Co.; U.S. Glass Co.; 1890-1900. Extended table service including cruet, rare oil lamp, rare salt shaker, cup, bowls, berry set, cologne bottle. See Plate 242. Crystal, cobalt blue.—**Key B**
2. PAVONIA, tumbler. See Plate 47.
3. VICTORIA, compote. See Plate 29.

Row 4
1. LENS AND BLOCK, creamer.—*Ref. K6-8* c. 1870.—**Key C**
2. ART, creamer. See Plates 26 and 56.

PLATE 59 DIAMONDS

Row 1

QUILT AND FLUTE, creamer.—*Ref. K1-71* Known in creamer, mustard jar and sugar bowl.—**Key A**

Row 2

1. PRISM WITH BLOCK (ESTHER), creamer.—*Ref. K1-109* Westmoreland Glass Co., 1896. Extended table service including tumbler, berry set.—**Key A**

2. PRISM AND DIAMOND, creamer.—*Ref. K6-9* Extended table service including compote, sauce.—**Key C**

Row 3

1. PRISM WITH BALL AND BUTTON, creamer.—*Ref. K1-111*—**Key B**

2. DROPPED DIAMONDS, pitcher.—*Ref. K7-186* Imperial Glass Co. #75, c. 1902.—**Key A**

Row 4

1. BALL AND BAR, pitcher.—*Ref. K7-20* Probably Westmoreland Glass Co., 1896—*(Ref. Kamm).* Made in extended table service including tumbler.—**Key A**

2. PRISM WITH DIAMOND POINTS, goblet.—*Ref. K3-28* Bryce Brothers; U.S. Glass Co. Extended table service including wine, cordial, two types goblet, tumbler, covered compote.—**Key C**

3. BEAUTY, pitcher.—*Ref. K8-176* Pioneer Glass Co., 1891. Extended table service including salt shaker, syrup. Crystal, ruby-stained.—**Key B**

129

PLATE 60 DIAMONDS

Row 1

1. SPECIALTY #6, creamer.—*Ref. K8-181* Specialty Glass Co., 1892. This piece was used as a container for condiments.
2. SPECIALTY'S PATTERN E, wine.—*Ref. K8-180* Specialty Glass Co., 1892. Made in extended table service.—**Key A**
3. PANELLED SMOCKING, creamer.—*Ref. K2-88* U.S. Glass Co.; Bartlett-Collins in the late 1920's. Made in basic table service. Crystal, decorated.—**Key A**

Row 2

1. DIAMOND BRIDGES, creamer.—*Ref. HV-51* U.S. Glass Co. #15040, 1896. Extended table service. Crystal, emerald green. —**Key B**
2. INVERTED PRISM AND DIAMOND BAND, creamer.—*Ref. K2-4* Extended table service including individual creamer. Kamm believed this to be of English origin, c. 1855.—**Key C**

Row 3

1. LAKEWOOD, goblet.—*Ref. Gob II-75* Extended table service.—**Key A**
2. SISTER KATE, pitcher.—*Ref. K2-46* Found as ruby-stained souvenir, c. 1890.—**Key B**
3. STIPPLED DIAMONDS, toy spoon holder (toothpick holder).—*Ref. Lechler 167* c. 1891. Toy table service.—**Key C**

Row 4

1. HERO (RUBY ROSETTE), hand lamp.—*Ref. K5-59* West Virginia Glass Co. #700, 1894. Extended table service including salt shaker, tumbler, cruet, bowls. See Plate 66.—**Key B**
2. O'HARA DIAMOND (SAWTOOTH AND STAR; RUBY STAR), syrup.—*Ref. LV57; K5 pl. 32* O'Hara Glass Co.; U.S. Glass Co. #15001, 1885-96. Extended table service including banana stand, salt shaker, tray (plain), finger bowl, cup and saucer, bowl, sauce. See Plate 47. Crystal, ruby-stained.—**Key B**

PLATE 61 DIAMONDS

Row 1

1. CONNECTICUT, covered compote.—*Ref. K4-65* U.S. Glass #15068 (King factory), 1898. A State Series pattern. Made in extended table service including belled bowls, low and high compotes, handled relish, cruet, salt shaker, tumbler, cup, skillet, wine, cake stand, celery vase, celery tray. See Plate 190. Crystal.—**Key A**

2. ZIG-ZAG BAND, pitcher.—*Ref. K4-10* c. 1870's. Extended table service including celery vase, tumbler.—**Key B**

3. BROKEN BANDS, creamer.—*Ref. K3-48* U.S. Glass Co. (Doyle #65), 1892. Extended table service. Crystal, amber, blue.—**Key B**

Row 2

1. LATTICE (DIAMOND BAR), pitcher.—*Ref. K4-40; L78* King, Son and Co., 1880; U.S. Glass Co., 1891. Made in extended table service including plate, platter, cake stand, celery vase, egg cup, sauce, wine, cordial, salt shaker, tumbler.—**Key B**

2. PANEL AND CANE, pitcher.—*Ref. K4-12* c. 1890. Extended table service including celery vase.—**Key A**

3. ANGORA, goblet.—*Ref. Gob II-27* c. 1890. Extended table service. Crystal.—**Key A**

Row 3

1. FLORAL DIAMOND BAND, syrup.—*Ref. HIII-24* Bryce Brothers #900, c. 1900. Only syrup made. Crystal, blue.—**Key E**

2. SPIREA BAND (SQUARE AND DOT; SQUARED DOT; EARL), goblet.—*Ref. K4-34; K8-17* Bryce, Higbee and Co., 1891. Extended table service including compotes, tumbler, wine, platter, celery vase, salt shaker, cake stand, sugar shaker. Crystal, amber, blue.—**Key B**

3. LEAFLETS, pitcher.—*Ref. K3-46* Central Glass Co. #585, 1881. Extended table service including champagne, tumbler, bread tray with tree and birds, compote, handled spooner, celery vase. Has dog finial.—**Key B**

PLATE 62 DIAMONDS

Row 1
1. PRISMATIC, creamer.—*Ref. K3-13* —**Key A**
2. CROSS BANDS, creamer.—*Ref. K4-36* c. 1878.—**Key A**
3. BUTTERFLY EARS, mustard pot. See Plate 6.

Row 2
1. POINTED ARCHES, toy pitcher.—**Key A**
2. ALBANY, butter dish.—*Ref. K8-138* Bryce Brothers, mid 1880's; U. S. Glass Co., c. 1890's.—**Key B**

Row 3
1. WAVERLY, individual creamer.—*Ref. K4-107* U.S. Glass Co. (Bryce #140), 1891. Made in extended table service including bowl. Crystal.—**Key A**
2. GALLOWAY (VIRGINIA; MIRROR), cruet.—*Ref. K3-89; Gob I-218* U.S. Glass Co. #15086 (Gas City; Glassport), 1904. Extended table service including toothpick holder, syrup, punch bowl, salt shaker, cup, toy set, plate, compote, decanter, handled relish, tumbler, lemonade, cracker jar, tall vase, bowls, water bottle, cake stand. See Plate 170. **Note:** GALLOWAY should never be called "Virginia" because the State Series pattern for Virginia is "Banded Portland." Good availability. Crystal, rose-flashed, ruby-stained.—**Key B**
3. FAN AND STAR, celery vase.—*Ref. LV66* Challinor, Taylor and Co. #304, 1880's; U.S. Glass Co., 1891. Extended table service including bowls, sauce. Crystal, purple slag, milk glass.—**Key B**

PLATE 63 DIAMONDS

Row 1

1. FOSTORIA'S #226, creamer.—*Ref. K6 pl. 58* Fostoria Glass Co., 1891. Made in extended table service. Crystal, opaque colors. —**Key A**

2. RUBY, creamer.—*Ref. K3-102* LaBelle Glass Co., 1878. Extended table service including compote. Crystal.—**Key A**

3. DART, creamer.—*Ref. K3-4* c. 1880. Extended table service including sauce.—**Key A**

Row 2

1. CENTRAL #438, creamer.—*Ref. K3-50* Central Glass Co., 1881. Extended table service including salt shaker, eight covered compotes, three low compotes, bowls, celery vase, pickle dish.—**Key A**

2. CORD DRAPERY (INDIANA), salt shaker.—*Ref. K1-79* National Glass Co. (Greentown), 1899-1903; Indiana Glass after 1907. Extended table service including toothpick holder, sauce, syrup (scarce), berry set, bowls, cake plate, compotes, tumbler. Crystal, amber, blue, green, opal, chocolate.—**Key C**

3. DIAMOND RIDGE, salt shaker.—*Ref. PetSal 158W* George Duncan and Sons, (#48), 1901. Extended table service including toothpick holder, toy table set, carafe, bar tumbler, cup, bowls, jelly compote, pickle jar. Fair availability.—**Key B**

Row 3

1. DIAMONDS AND DEWDROPS, goblet.—*Ref. Gob II-68* —**Key B**

2. STAR BAND (BOSWORTH), creamer.—*Ref. K1-13* Extended table service including sauce, celery vase, open footed salt. Crystal, opalescent.—**Key A**

3. BOX PLEAT (O'HARA'S CRYSTAL WEDDING), creamer.—*Ref. K8-110* Adams and Co., 1875. Extended table service including celery vase, cake stand. All pieces have three "feet". —**Key A**

PLATE 64 DIAMONDS

Row 1

1. ARCHED TRIPOD (TRIPOD STEM), creamer.—*Ref. Gob II-17; K3-6* c. 1885. Made in extended table service including lamp.—**Key B**

2. PHYTOLACCA, goblet.—*Ref. Gob II-105* —**Key A**

Row 2

1. ICICLE WITH CHAIN BAND, goblet.—*Ref. Gob II-52* —**Key A**

2. DIAMOND PRISMS, goblet.—*Ref. Gob II-58*—**Key A**

Row 3

1. SMOOTH DIAMOND (DOUBLE ICICLE; EARLY DIAMOND) goblet.—*Ref. Gob II-74* Indiana Tumbler and Goblet, c. 1900. Extended table service including compote, tumbler.—**Key A**

2. HERRINGBONE, goblet.—*Ref. L115; K7-75* c. 1890's. Extended table service including celery vase.—**Key B**

PLATE 65 DIAMONDS

Row 1

1. FOUR PETAL, sugar bowl.—*Ref. L12* McKee and Brothers, c. 1850's. Made in extended table service including compote.—**Key D**
2. PILLOWS, creamer.—*Ref. K2-96* A. H. Heisey Co. #325, c. 1900-1912. Extended table service of 45 pieces including toothpick holder, salt shaker.—**Key B**
3. HOURGLASS, pitcher. See Plate 19.

Row 2

1. BIG DIAMOND, creamer.—*Ref. K6-30* Dalzell, Gilmore and Leighton, 1885. Made in extended table service but scarce.—**Key C**
2. HELENE, spoon holder. Cooperative Flint Glass Co.—**Key B**
3. BEVELLED DIAMOND AND STAR (DIAMOND PRISMS; ALBANY), creamer.—*Ref. K2-74* Tarentum Glass Co., c. 1898—*(Ref. Heacock).* Extended table service including salt shaker, tumbler, syrup, cruet, bread plate. Crystal, ruby-stained.—**Key B**

Row 3

1. BEADED DIAMOND, creamer.—*Ref. K7-37* —**Key A**
2. IMPERIAL #9, creamer.—*Ref. K7-182* Imperial Glass Co., 1902. Extended table service including salt shaker, celery vase, wine, sugar shaker, rosebowl, lamps, trays, decanter, syrup, egg cup, cruet, cup, toothpick holder, sherbet, compote, carafe, tumbler, cracker jar, pickle jar. Crystal.—**Key B**
3. IMPERIAL #7, pitcher.—*Ref. K7-184* Imperial Glass Co., 1904. Extended table service including salt shaker, toothpick holder, cruet, wine, cracker jar, jelly compote, pickle jar, compote, cup, wine, celery vase, bottle, tumbler, sauce, sugar shaker, egg cup.—**Key A**

Row 4

1. PILLOW-IN-OVAL, creamer.—*Ref. K8-37* —**Key B**
2. HOURGLASS (EGG AND DART), creamer. See Plate 19.
3. DIAMOND MIRROR, spooner.—*Ref. Gob II-53* 1880's. Extended table service including celery vase, open and covered sugar bowls. Crystal.—**Key A**

PLATE 66 DIAMONDS

Row 1

1. CORNELL, pitcher.—*Ref. K7-37* Tarentum Glass Co., 1898. Made in extended table service including toothpick holder, salt shaker, rose bowl.—**Key B**

2. PILLOW AND SUNBURST (ELITE), pitcher.—*Ref. K1-100* Westmoreland Glass Co., 1891, 1896, 1917. Extended table service including toothpick holder, compotes, celery vase.—**Key B**

3. PATTEE CROSS (GEORGIA; BROUGHTON), goblet.—*Ref. K2-121; Gob II-79* U.S. Glass Co. (Richards and Hartley; Bryce) #15112, 1909. Made in very extended table service including toy set, crimped vase, jelly compote, tumbler, wine, syrup, straight vase, handled olive dish, relish dishes, cake stand, compote, ruffled bowl. Crystal, emerald green, rose-flashed.—**Key B**

Row 2

1. HERO, creamer (etched). See Plate 60.

2. PILLOW ENCIRCLED (MIDWAY), creamer (etched).—*Ref. K2-129* Model Flint Glass Co., 1894; National Glass Co., 1901. Extended table service including celery vase, compote, cruet, tray, tumbler. Crystal.—**Key B**

Row 3

1. CIRCLE X, open sugar bowl. (Author's name)—**Key A**

2. TWIN TEARDROPS, creamer.—*Ref. K4-76* Bryce, Higbee and Co., c. 1905. Extended table service including handled relish, bowls, cup, footed sauce.—**Key A**

Row 4

1. BEAUTIFUL LADY, creamer.—*Ref. K2-47* Bryce, Higbee and Co., c. 1905. Extended table service including cake stand, wine, toy cake stand, compotes.—**Key B**

2. SYDNEY, pitcher.—*Ref. K7-38* Fostoria Glass Co. #1333, 1905. Extended table service including syrup, bowls, 6″ plate, sauce, cup, decanter, compotes, celery vase, salt shaker, pickle dish, carafe. Crystal.—**Key B**

143

PLATE 67 DIAMONDS

Row 1

1. CAVITT, pitcher—*Ref. K5-143* Jones, Cavitt and Co. #128, 1887. Made in extended table service including compotes, bowls, tumbler, salt shaker, tray, pickle jar.—**Key B**

2. DOUBLE FAN, pitcher—*Ref. K1-39* Dalzell, Gilmore and Leighton, c. 1890. Extended table service including celery vase. —**Key A**

3. GEM STAR, cruet.—*Ref. K6-38* West Virginia Glass Co., 1894. Extended table service including celery vase, berry bowl. See Plate 230.—**Key B**

4. MARYLAND (LOOP AND DIAMOND; LOOP AND FAN; INVERTED LOOPS AND FAN), spoon holder.—*Ref. K1-60* U.S. Glass Co. #15049 (Bryce), 1897. A State Series pattern made in extended table service including bowls, compotes, tumbler, wine, cup, toothpick holder, bread plate, sauce, two types salt shaker, jelly compote, plate, celery vase. Good availability. Crystal, ruby-stained.—**Key B**

Row 2

1. BELMONT'S REFLECTING FANS (BLOCKADE), cruet.—*Ref. HIII-54* McKee; Belmont; c. 1885. Only cruet known.—**Key C**

2. CHALLINOR DOUBLE FAN, creamer.—*Ref. LV57* U.S. Glass Co. (Challinor #305), 1891. Made in extended table service. —**Key B**

3. KING'S CURTAIN, pitcher 1880's. Extended table service including cake stand, plate, sauce, salt shaker.—**Key B**

Row 3

1. BOLING, goblet.—*Ref. Gob II-138* U.S. Glass Co. (Bryce), 1891. Extended table service including bowls.—**Key B**

2. BELMONT DIAMOND, cruet.—*Ref. HIII-54* Belmont Glass Co., c. 1885. Only cruet known.—**Key D**

3. RIVERSIDE (DARBY), pitcher.—*Ref. K8-35; LV37* Riverside Glass Co., c. 1897. Extended table service including toothpick holder, tumbler, compotes, cruet, berry set. Crystal, vaseline.—**Key B**

PLATE 68 DIAMONDS

Row 1

1. ILEX, goblet.—*Ref. Gob II-104* —**Key A**
2. DIAMOND AND SUNBURST, creamer.—*Ref. K1-12* Bryce, Walker and Co., 1894. Made in extended table service including master salt, compote, sauce, cake stand, pickle dish.—**Key B**

Row 2

1. DIAMOND SUNBURST, pitcher.—*Ref. L78* c. 1860's. Extended table service including celery vase, lamp, cake stand, covered compote, wine, tumbler, egg cup, decanter.—**Key C**
2. DIAMOND AND SUNBURST ZIPPERS (DIAMOND AND SUNBURST VARIANT), creamer.—*Ref. K6 pl 30* U.S. Glass #15018, 1893. Extended table service including square bowl, salt shaker. Crystal, ruby-stained.—**Key B**

Row 3

1. DIAMOND SUNBURST, plate. See above.
2. ST. BERNARD, creamer.—*Ref. K4 pl. 8; K5-61* Fostoria Glass Co., 1895. Extended table service including relish, berry set, covered compote, jam jar, salt shaker. Has reclining dog as finial on covered pieces. See Plate 7.—**Key D**

PLATE 69 DIAMONDS

Row 1

1. EDGERTON, goblet.—*Ref. Gob II-67* —**Key A**

2. MELROSE, creamer (etched).—*Ref. K8-164* Greensburg Glass Co., 1887. Made in extended table service including salt shaker, tray, finger bowl, cake stand, jelly compote, cake plate, compotes, tumbler. Crystal, chocolate glass.—**Key B**

Row 2

1. HOBBS DIAMOND AND SUNBURST, pitcher.—*Ref. K3-22* Hobbs, Brockunier, 1880. Extended table service including tumbler, egg cup, cake stand, sauce, compote. Crystal.—**Key B**

2. CHAMPION (SEAGIRT; FAN WITH CROSSBARS; GREENTOWN #11; DIAMOND AND LONG SUNBURST), goblet.—*Ref. K1-106; Gob II-113* McKee Glass Co.; Indiana Tumbler and Goblet; 1894-1917. Made in extended table service including toothpick holder, decanter, salt shaker, cruet, carafe, tray, wine.—**Key B**

Row 3

1. DIAMONDS WITH DOUBLE FANS, goblet.—*Ref. Gob II-88* —**Key A**

2. DIAMOND AND SUNBURST-EARLY, plate.—*Ref. L12* c. 1864. Extended table service including celery vase, egg cup, wine.—**Key C**

PLATE 70 DIAMONDS

Row 1

1.   DIAMOND FAN, toy creamer. Made in extended table service including punch cup in milk glass.—**Key C**

2.   SUNBURST - DIAMOND, goblet.—**Key A**

Row 2

BOLING, 7″ dish. See Plate 67.

Row 3

1.   TARENTUM'S VIRGINIA, compote.—*Ref. K6 pl. 73* Tarentum Glass Co., 1895. Made in extended table service including salt shaker — forty-four pieces in all. Crystal, green.—**Key B**

2.   PANELLED DIAMOND BLOCKS (QUARTERED BLOCK), creamer.—*Ref. K3-96; Gob II-146* George Duncan and Sons #24, 1894. Extended table service including bowl, toothpick holder, wine, cake plates, cake stands, compotes, syrups, ice tub.—**Key B**

Row 4

1.   SHEAF AND DIAMOND, bowl.—*Ref. Metz 2-172* Bryce, Higbee and Co., c. 1905. Extended table service.—**Key B**

2.   MODEL PEERLESS (PEERLESS), toothpick holder.—*Ref. K3-91* Model Flint Glass Works (Albany, Ind.), 1893-1901. Made in extended table service including cruet.—**Key C**

PLATE 71 DIAMONDS

Row 1

1. MAJESTIC (DIVIDED BLOCK WITH SUNBURST; PURITAN), pitcher.—*Ref. K6-pl. 70* U.S. Glass Co., 1891. Made in extended table service including salt shaker, tumbler, celery vase, compotes, bowls, toothpick holder. Crystal, purple slag.—**Key B**

2. GRATED DIAMOND AND SUNBURST, creamer.—*Ref. K1-103* George Duncan and Sons #20, c. 1895. Extended table service including toothpick holder, salt shaker, punch cup, individual salt dip, water bottle.—**Key B**

Row 2

1. ANTWERP, goblet.—*Ref. Gob II-118* —**Key A**

2. SHEAF AND BLOCK (FICKLE BLOCK), goblet.—*Ref. Gob II-88; K6-16* Cooperative Flint Glass Co., 1893. Extended table service including celery vase.—**Key B**

Row 3

1. SHOSHONE (BLAZING PINWHEELS; FLORAL DIAMOND; VICTOR), syrup.—*Ref. K4-71* U.S. Glass Co., 1896 (#15046) (King; Glassport factories). Made in extended table service including salt shaker, tumbler, celery tray, cake stand, syrups, claret jug, bowls, salt dip, mustard jar, handled jelly, ice tub, cup and saucer, punch bowl. Crystal, ruby-stained, emerald green.—**Key B**

2. STERLING (PINWHEELS; BLAZING STAR), creamer.—*Ref. K1-102* Westmoreland Glass Co., 1891; 1917. Extended table service including toy set, punch bowl, cups.—**Key B**

PLATE 72 DIAMONDS

Row 1

1. FLATTENED DIAMOND AND SUNBURST, creamer,—*Ref.*
K2-54 c. 1885. Made in extended table service including sauce, celery
vase, toy table set, cordial, pickle dish.—**Key A**

2. BEADED FAN (DEWDROP AND FAN), pitcher.—*Ref. K1-65*
1875-1880. Extended table service including compote, celery
vase.—**Key B**

Row 2

1. PITTSBURGH FAN, goblet.—*Ref. Gob II-47* Extended table
service including cake stand.—**Key A**

2. DIAMOND FLUTE (FLAMBOYANT), individual creamer.
—*Ref. K4-93* McKee and Brothers, 1885. Made in extended table
service. Crystal; very rare in emerald green.—**Key B**

Row 3

1. DIAMOND FLUTE, goblet. See above.

2. FAN WITH SPLIT DIAMOND, creamer.—*Ref. K2-80* c. 1890.
Extended table service.—**Key A**

PLATE 73 DIAMONDS

Row 1

1. DOUBLE DIAMOND PANELS, goblet.—*Ref. Gob II-14* —**Key A**

2. NATIONAL'S EUREKA, toothpick holder.—*Ref. K5-69* National Glass Co., 1901. Made in extended table service including salt shaker.—**Key B**

3. CHECKERS, goblet.—*Ref. Gob II-12* Note: Millard named this "Checkerboard", but as there is already a pattern by that name I suggest shortening it to "Checkers".—**Key A**

Row 2

1. NATIONAL'S EUREKA, creamer. See Row 1 #2.

2. BLOCK BAND DIAMOND, syrup.—*Ref. K3-132* George Duncan and Sons #27, 1890's. Extended table service including wine, celery vase, tumbler; at least 52 pieces.—**Key B**

3. DIAMOND IN DIAMOND (DIAMOND), creamer.—*Ref. K3-14* Extended table service including compotes.—**Key A**

Row 3

1. SWIRL-ATOP-DIAMOND, salt shaker.—*Ref. PetSal 174P* —**Key A**

2. THREE-IN-ONE, compote.—*Ref. K4-74* Imperial Glass Co., late 1880's. Extended table service including tumbler, syrup, bowl, wine, covered bisquit jar. Crystal.—**Key B**

3. PETTICOAT, syrup (scarce).—*Ref. PetSal 35J* Riverside Glass Co., c. 1901. Known in novelties; toothpick holder, salt shaker. —**Key D**

Row 4

1. DIAMOND SIDE, salt shaker.—*Ref. PetSal 159A* —**Key A**

2. THREE-PLY PANEL, salt shaker.—*Ref. K4 pl. 10; PetSal 42E* McKee glass, made in condiment set.—**Key B**

3. TRIPLE X, salt shaker.—*Ref. PetSal 176-i* —**Key B**

PLATE 74 DIAMONDS

Row 1

1. KING'S #29 (ADAMS), bowl.—*Ref. K5-74; LV54* King Glass Co., 1890. Made in extended table service including salt shaker.—**Key A**

2. MITRED DIAMOND (CELTIC), goblet.—*Ref. Gob II-15* —**Key A**

3. MT. VERNON (PRISM), sugar bowl. McKee brothers, 1868. Made in extended table service.—**Key C**

4. PITTMAN, goblet.—*Ref. Gob II-20* —**Key A**

Row 2

1. BLOCK AND TRIPLE BARS, goblet.—*Ref. Gob II-88* —**Key B**

2. DICE AND BLOCK, cruet.—*Ref. MU I; HIII-55* Belmont Glass Co., c. 1885. Only the cruet was made.—**Key D**

3. PANELLED LATTICE, goblet.—*Ref. Gob II-85* —**Key A**

Row 3

1. WESTON, tumbler.—**Key A**

2. MAJESTIC KIN, salt shaker.—*Ref. PetSal 165S*—**Key A**

3. WIMPOLE, sugar bowl.—*Ref. HPV#2, 14* Extended table service including ketchup jug, celery vase.—**Key C**

PLATE 75 DIAMONDS

Row 1

1. PANAMA (FINE CUT BAR; VIKING), pitcher.—*Ref. K2-49* U.S. Glass Co. #15088, 1904. Made in extended table service including toothpick holder, salt shaker, celery vase, bowl.—**Key A**

2. PLEATED OVAL, creamer.—*Ref. K8-34* New Martinsville Glass Co. #700, c. 1910. Extended table service including toothpick holder.—**Key B**

Row 2

1. NAPOLEON, bowl.—*Ref. K6 pl. 61* McKee Brothers, 1896. Extended table service.—**Key B**

2. SUNK DIAMOND AND LATTICE, pitcher.—*Ref. K2-126* c. 1885-1890. Extended table service including celery vase, compotes, salt shaker, tumbler, plate.—**Key B**

Row 3

1. JABOT, pitcher.—*Ref. K8-27* —**Key A**

2. ADA, creamer.—*Ref. K7-199* Cambridge Glass Co.; Ohio Flint Glass Co., 1898. Extended table service of over 100 pieces including salt shaker, compotes. See Plate 111.—**Key B**

Row 4

1. TEPEE (NEMESIS; WIGWAM), spoon holder.—*Ref. K2-78; Gob II-128* George Duncan and Sons #28; U.S. Glass Co., 1897. Extended table service including wine, syrup, handled jelly, jelly compote, tumbler, salt shaker, rare green toothpick holder, rare covered cheese dish, cup, berry bowl.—**Key B**

2. TEPEE, salt shaker. See above.

3. FAN AND FEATHER, salt shaker.—*Ref. PetSal 160M* —**Key A**

PLATE 76 DIAMONDS

Row 1

1. SUNBEAM, pitcher.—*Ref. K4-76* McKee and Brothers, 1898-1902. Made in extended table service including toothpick holder, carafe, celery vase, cruet, syrup, tumbler, berry set, celery tray, bowls, jelly compote, sauce, salt shaker, pickle dish, carafe. Crystal, emerald green.—**Key B**

2. SCALLOPED SIX-POINT, cup.—*Ref. K7-125* George Duncan and Sons #30, c. 1900. Extended table service including two types toothpick holder, wine, tumbler, carafe, bowls, salt shaker.—**Key A**

Row 2

1. I H C, pitcher.—*Ref. K3-133* McKee Glass Co., 1894. Extended table service including compotes, bowls, tumbler, sauce. Crystal.—**Key A**

2. ZIPPERED DIAMOND, salt shaker.—*Ref. PetSal 43V*—**Key A**

3. MAGNA, creamer.—*Ref. K7-36* 1898. Made in extended table service.—**Key A**

Row 3

1. PENNSYLVANIA, toy creamer. See Plate 112.

2. PERSIAN (CROWN AND SHIELD; THREE STORIES), salt shaker.—*Ref. K7-35; Gob II-85* Fostoria Glass Co. #576, 1897. Made in extended table service including cruet, syrup, toothpick holder, claret, sauce, bowls, salt shaker, salt dip, cheese dish, tumblers, carafe, celery vase, celery dish, cup, jelly compote, finger bowl. —**Key B**

3. MAGNA, salt shaker. See Row 2 #3.

Row 4

1. PALMETTE, footed salt.—*Ref. K4-20; L95* c. 1870's. Extended table service including compotes, rare creamer, 10″ lamp, footed tumbler, wine, relish with scoop, sauce, compotes, celery vase, salt shaker. Clear, colors.—**Key C**

2. LONG STAR (TEUTONIC), salt shaker.—*Ref. K7-43; PetSal 175G* McKee glass, 1898 and made in extended table service. —**Key B**

3. MERRIMAC, salt shaker.—*Ref. K6 pl. 96* McKee and Brothers, 1898. Extended table service.—**Key B**

PLATE 77 DIAMONDS

Row 1

1. IVANHOE, pitcher.—*Ref. LV108* Dalzell, Gilmore and Leighton, c. 1890. Made in extended table service including toothpick holder (scarce), plate.—**Key B**

2. COARSE ZIG ZAG, pitcher.—*Ref. K2-28* Bryce, Higbee and Co., c. 1905. Extended table service including wine, plate, salt shaker, bowls, berry set.—**Key A**

Row 2

1. LATTICE AND LENS, creamer.—*Ref. K8-24* c. 1880.—**Key A**

2. HEARTS AND ARCHES, butter dish. A rare and old museum piece.

Row 3

1. SLEWED DIAMOND, pitcher.—*Ref. K4-119* —**Key B**

2. MEDALLION (SPADES; HEARTS AND SPADES), pitcher.—*Ref. L102* c. 1891. Extended table service including cake stand, celery vase, covered compote, tumbler, wine, mug, sauce. Crystal, blue, vaseline, amber.—**Key B**

3. BULLS-EYE IN DIAMOND, salt shaker.—*Ref. PetSal 156C* —**Key B**

Row 4

1. SPIRALLED TRIANGLE, creamer.—*Ref. K4-70* Beatty-Brady Glass Co. #106, 1898. Extended table service.—**Key A**

2. HEART PLUME (MARLBORO), salt shaker.—*Ref. PetSal 30-0* U.S. Glass Co. #15105 (Bryce), 1907. Extended table service. See Plate 115. Crystal, rose-flashed.—**Key B**

3. BEACON LIGHT, salt shaker.—*Ref. PetSal 22B* Beatty-Brady Glass Co., c. 1904. Extended table service including bowl.—**Key A**

PLATE 78 DIAMONDS

Row 1

1. PANELLED FLATTENED SAWTOOTH, tumbler.—*Ref. Gob II-143.* —**Key A**

2. TARENTUM'S LADDER WITH DIAMOND (FINE CUT AND RIBBED BARS), goblet.—*Ref. K8-42* Tarentum Glass Co., 1903. Made in extended table service including toothpick holder, salt shaker.—**Key B**

3. LADDER WITH DIAMONDS (FINE CUT AND RIBBED BARS), goblet.—*Ref. PetSal 32C* Duncan and Miller Glass Co. #52, 1904. Extended table service including celery vase, decanter, cup, wine, toothpick holder, salt shaker, tumbler, bud vase.—**Key A**

Row 2

1. STARS AND STRIPES (BRILLIANT), creamer.—*Ref. K2-70* Kokomo and Jenkins Glass Co., 1899. Extended table service including tumbler, cup, toy table service, salt shaker, sauce, berry bowl, vase, bowls. Crystal, milk glass.—**Key A**

2. REWARD, creamer.—*Ref. K5-109* National Glass Co. (Riverside), 1901. Extended table service including toothpick holder, salt shaker, tumbler, cruet, jelly compote, bowls, sauce.—**Key A**

Row 3

1. DIAMOND WITH FAN, salt shaker.—*Ref. PetSal 159E* —**Key A**

2. LADDER-TO-THE-STARS, salt shaker.—*Ref. PetSal 164Q* c. 1900. Known in toothpick holder, salt shaker.—**Key A**

3. MARDI GRAS, salt shaker.—*Ref. K3-77* George Duncan and Sons #42, 1894. Extended table service including champagne, wine, toothpick holder, cake stand, salt shaker, tumbler, flared-rim sherry, handled jelly, bowls, cordial, punch cup, bitters bottle. Very good availability. See Plate 214. **Note:** Some pieces have a row of thumbprints around the top.—**Key B**

Row 4

1. FANCY ARCH, salt shaker.—*Ref. PetSal 21H* McKee glass.—**Key A**

2. HEISEY'S PINEAPPLE AND FAN, syrup.—*Ref. K2-93; K7-136* A. H. Heisey Glass Co. #1255, c. 1897. Extended table service including toothpick holder, salt shaker, cruet, tumbler, mug, oval berry bowl, water jug, rose bowl. Crystal, green.—**Key C**

PLATE 79 DIAMONDS

Row 1

1. SNOWSHOE, creamer.—*Ref. K4-48* Basic table service known.—**Key A**

2. KAYAK, pitcher—*Ref. K2-95* Imperial Glass Co. Extended table service including cake stand, compotes, tray.—**Key B**

3. MAYPOLE (SILVER SHEEN), pitcher.—*Ref. K2-162* National Glass Co. (McKee factory). Made in extended table service including salt shaker, cruet, sauce, berry bowl.—**Key B**

Row 2

1. DOTS AND DASHES, goblet.—*Ref. Gob II-123* Made in extended table service.—**Key B**

2. RIVERSIDE'S VICTORIA (DRAPED RED TOP; DRAPED TOP), pitcher.—*Ref. K6 pl. 63.* Made by Riverside Glass Co., c. 1900 in extended table service including toothpick holder, jelly compote, salt shaker, individual creamer, cruet, celery vase, syrup, tall compote, berry set, tumbler, sauce.—**Key B**

3. LOOP AND BLOCK (DRAPED RED BLOCK), creamer.—*Ref. K8-178* Pioneer Glass Co. #23, 1890's. Extended table service including tumbler, celery vase, decanter, wine, tray, berry set, sauce, bowls, jelly compote.—**Key B**

Row 3

1. IMPERIAL #79, pitcher.—*Ref. K7-187* Imperial Glass Co., c. 1902.—**Key A**

2. THUMBPRINT AND DIAMOND, goblet.—*Ref. K7-70* —**Key A**

Row 4

1. CROSSED SHIELD, pitcher.—*Ref. K5-100* Fostoria Glass Co. #1303, 1890's. Extended table service including tumbler, cordial.—**Key B**

2. FAGOT (VERA), creamer.—*Ref. K4-74; K6 pl. 37; LV62* Robinson Glass Co., 1893. Extended table service including berry bowl, sauce.—**Key C**

3. FEATHERED OVALS, creamer.—*Ref. K7-13*—**Key A**

PLATE 80 DIAMONDS

Row 1

1. TANDEM DIAMONDS AND THUMBPRINT, goblet.—*Ref. Gob II-4* —**Key A**

2. JACOB'S LADDER (MALTESE), goblet.—*Ref. K1-20* Bryce Brothers, 1870's; U.S. Glass Co., 1891. Extended table service including syrup, compote, mug, tumbler, footed sauce, wine, open salt, pickle dish. Crystal; rare in amber, blue, vaseline.—**Key C**

3. AURORA (DIAMOND HORSESHOE), pitcher.—*Ref. K8-160* Brilliant Glass Co.; Greensburg Glass Co., c. 1888. Made in extended table service including cake stand, compotes, cordial, wine, salt shaker. See Plate 49.—**Key B**

Row 2

FAN WITH DIAMOND (SHELL), pitcher.—*Ref. K3-18* McKee and Brothers, 1880. Extended table service including wine, egg cup, compotes, cordial, sauce.—**Key B**

Row 3

1. LOZENGES, spooner.—*Ref. K8-74* c. 1880's.—**Key A**

2. PANELLED DIAMONDS AND ROSETTES, goblet.—*Ref. Gob II-61* —**Key A**

3. BUCKLE AND DIAMOND. pitcher.—*Ref. K1-51; L154-18* McKee and Brothers, c. 1880. Extended table service.—**Key B**

Row 4

1. DOUBLE SPEAR, pitcher.—*Ref. K1-21* McKee and Brothers, 1880's. Extended table service including compote, celery vase, sauce, pickle dish.—**Key A**

2. STIPPLED DIAMOND BAND, goblet.—*Ref. L164-8*—**Key B**

3. GARLAND, goblet.—*Ref. Gob II-131*—**Key A**

PLATE 81 DIAMONDS

Row 1

1. BEADED DART BAND, goblet.—*Ref. Gob II-7* George Duncan and Sons #600, 1880's. Made in extended table service including pickle castor, compote.—**Key A**

2. ARABESQUE, pitcher.—*Ref. L155* Bakewell, Pears and Co., 1860's. Extended table service including compotes, sauce, celery vase. Crystal.—**Key B**

3. JACOB'S COAT, creamer.—*Ref. L115* Extended table service including pickle dish, berry set, sauce. Crystal, amber.—**Key A**

Row 2

1. BEADED DIAMOND BAND, creamer.—*Ref. K2-37* George Duncan and Sons, 1890.—**Key A**

2. LOOP AND DART WITH DIAMOND ORNAMENT, goblet.—*Ref. L148* Boston and Sandwich; Richards and Hartley; Portland; 1860's. Made in extended table service including plate.—**Key C**

3. STIPPLED DART AND BALLS, pitcher.—*Ref. K8-38; Gob II-33* c. 1890. Extended table service including tumbler, wine. —**Key A**

Row 3

1. DOUBLE LOOP (STIPPLED DOUBLE LOOP), creamer.—*Ref. L101; Metz 2034* 1880's. Extended table service including wine, salt shaker.—**Key B**

2. DOUBLE LOOP AND DART, goblet.—*Ref. L148* —**Key A**

3. LEAF AND DART, celery vase. See Plate 36.

Row 4

1. LOOP AND DART WITH DIAMOND ORNAMENT, tumbler. See Row 2 # 2.

2. LOOP AND DART WITH ROUND ORNAMENT, footed tumbler. See Plate 36.

3. LOOP AND DART, goblet.—*Ref. L148* Boston and Sandwich; Richards and Hartley; Portland; 1860's. Extended table service including tumbler, sauce, celery vase, egg cup, rare 6″ plate, wine, footed tumbler, cordial, low compote.—**Key C**

PLATE 82 DIAMONDS

Row 1

1. PYRAMIDS, goblet—*Ref. Gob II-35*—**Key A**
2. RIBBON BAND WITH PENDANTS, goblet.—*Ref. Gob II-60*—**Key A**
3. WIGWAM (TEEPEE), pitcher.—*Ref. K8-11; Gob I-23* Iowa Glass Co.; late 1880's. Made in extended table service. Crystal.—**Key C**

Row 2

1. SHERATON (IDA), pitcher.—*Ref. K8-17* Bryce, Higbee, 1880's. Extended table service including tumbler, wine, berry set, compote, sauce, bread tray, celery vase. Crystal, amber, blue, green.—**Key A**
2. TRIPLE TRIANGLE, cup.—*Ref. K8-104* U.S. Glass Co. (Doyle #76), 1891. Extended table service including mug, wine. Crystal, ruby-stained.—**Key C**
3. TRIPLE TRIANGLE, pitcher. See above.

Row 3

1. X-LOGS (PRISM ARC; DIAMONDS IN OVAL), goblet.—*Ref. K5-134; Gob II-47* Extended table service including cake stand, bowl, mug, wine, salt shaker, sauce, pickle dish. Crystal, opaque white, colors.—**Key A**
2. SANBORN (IRON KETTLE), creamer.—*Ref. LV62* U.S. Glass Co. (Challinor #83), 1891. Extended table service including covered bowls. Crystal.—**Key B**

Row 4

1. U.S. COMET (DRAPED FAN), pitcher.—*Ref. K3-82; K7-113* Doyle and Co., c. 1880's; U.S. Glass Co., 1895. Extended table service including cake stand, compotes. Crystal, amber, vaseline.—**Key A**
2. AIDA, creamer (etched).—*Ref. K5 pl. 1* Belmont Glassworks, 1883. Extended table service.—**Key D**

175

PLATE 83 FACETS - DAISY AND BUTTON

Row 1

1. DAISY AND BUTTON WITH PRISMS, pitcher.—*Ref. K7-22* Made in extended table service.—**Key B**

2. DAISY AND BUTTON OVAL MEDALLION (OVAL PANELLED DAISY AND BUTTON; PANELLED DAISY), spoon holder.—*Ref. L154-3; K4-44* Made in extended table service including sauce.—**Key A**

3. PANELLED DAISY AND BUTTON (ELLROSE), salt shaker.—*Ref. K1-80* U.S. Glass Co. (Richards and Hartley), 1891. Extended table service including covered bowls, berry set. Crystal, amber & blue stained, amber, vaseline, blue.—**Key A**

Row 2

1. PANELLED DAISY AND BUTTON, spooner. See above.

2. CLOVER (R & H), spooner.—*Ref. K4-98* Richards and Hartley Glass Co., 1880's; U.S. Glass Co., 1891. Extended table service including berry bowls, sauces. See Duncan's "Clover" on Plate 93. Crystal, emerald green.—**Key A**

3. DAISY AND BUTTON WITH CROSSBAR-POINTED, tumbler.—*Ref. L168* Extended table service.—**Key B**

Row 3

1. DAISY AND BUTTON WITH CROSSBAR (MIKADO), cruet (rare).—*Ref. K3-53; L167* Made by Richards and Hartley, 1888; U.S. Glass Co., 1891. Extended table service including lamps, mug, wine, open and covered sugar bowls, tray, syrup, salt shaker. Crystal, amber, blue, yellow.—**Key B**

2. DAISY AND BUTTON, mustard bottle.—*Ref. L169; K8-13* Hobbs, Brockunier; Gillander; U.S. Glass Co.; 1888; c. 1891. Made in extended table service including many novelties. Crystal, red dots.—**Key B**

3. DAISY AND BUTTON WITH THIN BARS, pitcher.—*Ref. HV-124* U.S. Glass Co. (Gillander), 1891. Note: tumblers lack the thin bars. Crystal, vaseline.—**Key C**

Row 4

1. DAISY AND BUTTON, cup. See above.

2. DAISY AND BUTTON WITH THUMBPRINT, tumbler.—*Ref. K3-73; L161* Adams and Co., 1885; U.S. Glass Co., 1890's. Extended table service including covered compotes, berry bowl, two sizes frosted square bowls. All colors.—**Key B**

3. DAISY AND BUTTON "V", tumbler.—*Ref. Gob II-73; L161* Beatty and Sons, 1885; U.S. Glass Co., 1892. Extended table service including toothpick holder.—**Key B**

PLATE 84 FACETS - DAISY AND BUTTON

Row 1

1. GREENSBURG'S PILLAR, pickle jar.—*Ref. K8-75* Greensburg Glass Co. #42, 1880's. Made in extended table service. Crystal, colors.—**Key B**

2. ROSETTE AND PALMS, goblet.—*Ref. LV21* J. B. Higbee Co., c. 1910. Extended table service including tumbler, wine, salt shaker, relish, 9" plate, cake stand, celery vase, banana stand, sauce. —**Key B**

3. GLOBE AND STAR, creamer (engraved).—*Ref. K2-23* c. 1890. Made in extended table service including covered compote, sauce, cake stand, jelly compote. Crystal, colors.—**Key C**

Row 2

DAISY BAND, sauce. Novelty

Row 3

1. BELMONT, sugar bowl.—*Ref. K6 pl. 17* Belmont Glass Works #100, 1886.—**Key C**

2. QUEEN (SUNK; POINTED PANEL; PANELLED DAISY AND BUTTON), pitcher.—*Ref. K3-38* McKee and Brothers, 1894; and others. Made in extended table service including celery vase, cruet, sauce, compote, tumbler, relish boat. Crystal, canary, amber, apple green, blue.—**Key C**

Row 4

ROSETTE AND PALMS, salt shaker. See Row 1, #2.

Row 5

1. DAISY AND BUTTON BAND, salt shaker.—*Ref. K6-20* O'Hara Glass Co., c. 1885. Extended table service.—**Key B**

2. CLIO (DAISY AND BUTTON WITH ALMOND BAND), pitcher.—*Ref. HV89* U.S. Glass Co. (Challinor), 1891. Extended table service including sauce, bowls with fan corners, celery vase, 10" plate, compote, covered bowl. Crystal, blue, vaseline, green.—**Key B**

PLATE 85 FACETS - CANE

Row 1

1. CANE AND ROSETTE (FLOWER PANELLED CANE), goblet.—*Ref. LV pl. 61* Duncan glass made in extended table service including open salt.—**Key B**

2. SCROLL WITH CANE BAND, creamer.—*Ref. K3-92* West Virginia Glass Co., 1895-1900. Extended table service including toothpick holder, salt shaker, compotes, cruet.—**Key B**

Row 2

1. FINE CUT AND PANEL, pitcher.—*Ref. L61* U.S. Glass Co. (Bryce), 1891. Extended table service including bowl, celery vase, compotes, salt shaker, tumbler, wine, tobacco jar, platter. Crystal, amber, blue, vaseline.—**Key B**

2. SUNKEN BUTTONS (MITRED DIAMOND), syrup.—*Ref. K4-129; LV31* Made in 1880's in extended table service including salt shaker, platter, compotes, wine, cordial, berry set, sauce. Crystal, vaseline, blue, canary, amber.—**Key B**

Row 3

1. HEISEY'S PANELLED CANE, pitcher.—*Ref. K7-31* A. H. Heisey #315, 1900-1904. Extended table service including wine, toothpick holder.—**Key B**

2. PANELLED CANE (BRILLIANT), creamer.—*Ref. K1-94* Fostoria Glass Co., c. 1901-04. Extended table service including wine, sauce, toothpick holder (scarce).—**Key A**

Row 4

1. UNION, carafe.—*(OMN)* New England Glass Co., 1869. —**Key D**

2. CANE COLUMN, pitcher.—*Ref. K4-11* 1880's. Extended table service including cruet, wine, sauce.—**Key A**

3. JEWEL, sugar bowl.—**Key A**

PLATE 86 FACETS - CANE

Row 1

1. ETCHED RECTANGLE, creamer.—*Ref. K1-112* —**Key B**
2. CANE MEDALLION, pitcher.—*Ref. K1-93* Westmoreland Glass Co., 1896. Made in extended table service including tumbler, berry set, pickle dish. Colors: Crystal, opaque glass.—**Key B**
3. BANDED FINECUT, goblet.—*Ref. Gob II-147*—**Key B**

Row 2

1. FLUTE AND CANE (HUCKABEE), pitcher.—*Ref. K2-72* Imperial Glass Co. #666, 1920's. Extended table service including celery vase, tumbler.—**Key A**
2. CANE, pitcher.—*Ref. L132; K3-39* Boston and Sandwich; Gillander and Sons; McKee and Brothers; 1875-85. Extended table service including berry set, jam jar, water tray, tumbler, finger bowl, wine, salt shaker, plate, pickle dish, salt dip, sauce, toothpick holder, waste bowl.—**Key B**

Row 3

1. CANE INSERT (ARCHED CANE AND FAN), Spooner.—*Ref. K6-51* Tarentum Glass Co., 1898-1906. Extended table service including compote, cake stand, rare celery vase. No known toothpick or salt shaker. Crystal, green.—**Key B**
2. STAR MEDALLION (AMELIA), pitcher.—*Ref. K4-82* Imperial Glass Co., c. 1925. *(Ref. Heacock, **Pattern Glass Preview #1**).* Made in extended table service. See Plate 235. Crystal, carnival glass. —**Key A**

Row 4

1. CANE AND CABLE, salt shaker.—*Ref. PetSal 24F* —**Key A**
2. RAINBOW, salt shaker.—*Ref. K6-89* McKee and Brothers, c. 1894. Extended table service including carafe, cigar jar, tumbler, wine. Marked "Pres-Cut". Rose-pink, gilded.—**Key B**
3. CANE AND FAN, salt shaker.—*Ref. PetSal 24G* —**Key A**

PLATE 87 FACETS - FINE CUT

Row 1

1. FINECUT, creamer.—*Ref. K8-21* Bryce Brothers, 1870's; U.S. Glass Co., 1891. Made in extended table service including tray, finger bowl, sauce, toothpick holder, plates, compote. Crystal, amber, blue, vaseline, canary.—**Key B**

2. SQUARED FINE CUT, pitcher.—*Ref. K5-32* Jones, Cavitt and Co., 1886.—**Key B**

Row 2

1. FLATTENED FINE CUT, pitcher.—*Ref. K1-86* Made in extended table service including salt shaker. Has horizontal ridges on front of pitcher.—**Key B**

2. HEAVY PANELLED FINECUT (SEQUOIA; PANELLED DIAMOND CROSS), creamer.—*Ref. K2-24* U.S. Glass Co. (Duncan #800), 1891. Extended table service including finger bowls, tray, plates, bowls, butter pat, decanter, pickle jar, straight and flared spooner, canoe-shaped bowl. Note: Only some pieces are panelled; those that are not are called "Sequoia". Crystal, blue, amber, vaseline.—**Key A**

3. HEAVY FINECUT, celery vase.—*Ref. K2-24* George Duncan and Sons, c. 1885; U.S. Glass Co., 1891. Extended table service including berry set, sauce, tumbler, individual butter, plates, covered compote, finger bowl. Crystal, amber, blue, vaseline.—**Key B**

Row 3

HEAVY PANELLED FINECUT, tumbler. See above.

Row 4

1. TINY FINECUT, goblet.—*Ref. Gob II-134* U.S. Glass Co., 1900. Made in wine set only in crystal, emerald green, ruby-stained (scarce).—**Key B**

2. CHESTNUT, tumbler.—*Ref. Gob I* Crystal, amber, blue, canary.—**Key B**

3. FINECUT, salt shaker. See Row 1 #1.

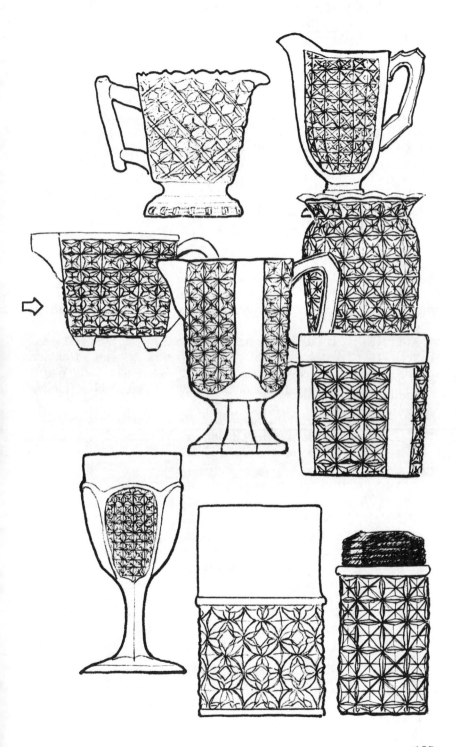

185

PLATE 88 FINE CUT

Row 1

1. PANELLED STRAWBERRY CUT (PANELLED DIAMOND), spoon holder. Made in extended table service.—**Key A**

2. VALENCIA WAFFLE (BLOCK AND STAR; HEXAGONAL BLOCK), syrup.—*Ref. K1-43; Gob I-71* Adams and Co. #85; U.S. Glass Co.; 1885-95. Extended table service including rectangular bowls, pickle jar, salt shaker. Crystal, blue, amber, apple green. —**Key C**

3. WATERFALL, pitcher.—*Ref. K5-125* O'Hara Glass Co., 1880's. Extended table service including compote, celery vase, salt shaker. Crystal, light blue, canary.—**Key B**

Row 2

1. HARTLEY (PANELLED DIAMOND CUT AND FAN), pitcher.—*Ref. K1-69* Richards and Hartley #900, 1888; U.S. Glass Co. Made in extended table service including bread plate, platter, wine, cake stand, sauce, celery vase, bowls. Crystal, amber, canary, blue.—**Key B**

2. CATHEDRAL (ORION), creamer.—*Ref. K1-19* U.S. Glass Co. (Bryce), 1891. Extended table service including wine, tumbler, rounded pitcher. Note: The "Cathedral" creamer is called "Waffle and Fine Cut" and is shown on Plate 227. Crystal, blue, amber, vaseline.—**Key B**

3. MC KEE'S COMET, pitcher.—*Ref. K4-13* McKee and Brothers, 1887. Extended table service including berry bowl, gas globe, compotes, fruit compote, sauce.—**Key B**

Row 3

1. MASCOTTE (MINOR BLOCK), goblet. See Plate 53.

2. ZEPHYR, goblet.—*Ref. Gob II-113* —**Key A**

3. FINE CUT AND BLOCK, goblet.—*Ref. K1-42; L161* U.S. Glass Co. (King), 1891. Extended table service including jelly compote, cake stands, tumbler, lamp, salt shaker. Crystal, amber-stained, sapphire blue; stained blocks.—**Key C**

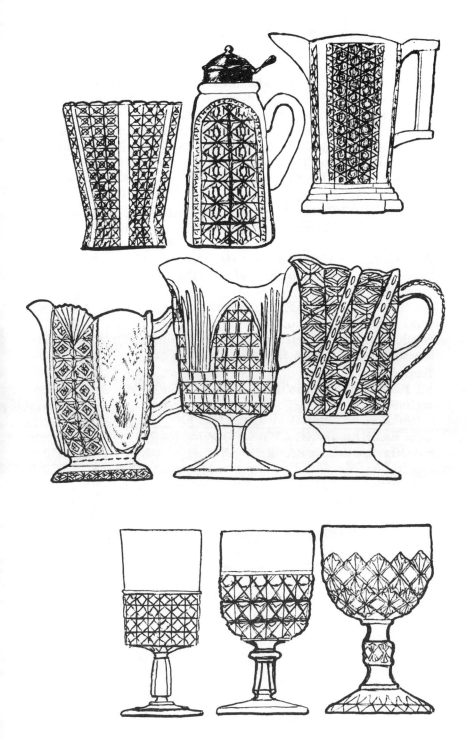

187

PLATE 89 FACETS - FINE CUT

Row 1

1. COTTAGE (DINNER BELL; FINE CUT BAND), pitcher.—*Ref. K1-38; LV64* Adams and Co., 1874; U.S. Glass, 1890's. Extended table service including tray, finger bowl, cruet, three sizes covered compotes, cake plate, salt shaker, syrup, cup and saucer, plates. Crystal, amber, dark green (rare), lt. blue, amethyst, ruby-stained.—**Key B**

2. FUNNEL ROSETTE, pitcher.—*Ref. K2-129* 1890's.—**Key A**

Row 2

1. BEADED FINE CUT, pitcher.—*Ref. K3-45* Dalzell, Gilmore and Leighton. Made in extended table service in crystal, colors. —**Key A**

2. FINE CUT AND RIB, pitcher.—*Ref. K6-60* Probably Doyle and Co.—*(Ref. Kamm).* Extended table service including tumbler, celery vase.—**Key A**

3. SANDWICH STAR, spill holder.—*Ref. L14* Extended table service including compote, dolphin-base compote, cordial, decanter, relish, all pieces are rare; the goblet is very rare. Flint glass; crystal, amethyst (rare).—**Key D**

Row 3

1. ACANTHUS SCROLL, creamer.—*Ref. K5-105* U.S. Glass #15036 (Ripley), 1895. Extended table service including cake stand, salt shaker. Crystal.—**Key B**

2. FEATHER (FINE CUT AND FEATHER; INDIANA SWIRL; SWIRL; DORIC; FEATHER SWIRL; PRINCE'S FEATHER), syrup.—*Ref. K1-73; LV 57* Made by McKee and Brothers, 1896-1905 in extended table service including wine, square sauce, jelly compote, relish, cake stand, tumbler, salt shaker, cordial, cake plate, celery vase, berry bowl, toothpick holder, bowl, 10″ plate, cruet. Crystal, green, amber, red, chocolate. See Plate 241.—**Key C**

189

PLATE 90 FACETS - BUTTONS

Row 1

1. LATE BLOCK (RED BLOCK; FOSTORIA'S VIRGINIA; FOSTER; WAFFLE BLOCK; BARRELLED BLOCK; LATTICED BLOCK), pitcher.—*Ref. K1-105; K2-83; L162* Made by Fostoria Glass Co., 1889; Specialty Glass, 1889; Doyle; Richards and Hartley, 1888; Duncan, 1887; and U.S. Glass in 1891. Extended table service including syrup, mustard and saucer, salt shaker, cruet, cup, lamp, bowls (both round and rectangular.) Crystal, ruby-stained.—**Key B**
2. OVERALL HOB, creamer.—*Ref. K6 pl. 69* Westmoreland Glass Co. #444, c. 1915. Extended table service including bowls, basket, handled olive dish.—**Key A**
3. HEXAGONAL BLOCK BAND, pitcher.—*Ref. K5-13* Made in about 1880 in extended table service.—**Key B**

Row 2

BEVELLED BUTTONS, pickle jar.—*Ref. HV99* U.S. Glass Co. (Duncan #320), 1891. Extended table service including sauce, compotes, bowls. Crystal.—**Key B**

Row 3

1. BIG LEAF AND BUTTON, bowl.—*Ref. HV97* U.S. Glass Co. (Duncan #1002), 1891. Made in bowls only. Crystal, amber-stained.—**Key C**
2. DIAMOND BLOCK WITH FAN (BLOCKADE), pitcher.—*Ref. LV65* U.S. Glass Co. (Challinor #309), 1891. Extended table service including celery vase, compotes, tumbler, finger bowl. Crystal. —**Key A**
3. TUXEDO, tumbler.—*Ref. K6 pl. 75* Fostoria Glass Co. #1578, 1907. Extended table service including cup, cruet, jelly compote, vase.—**Key A**

Row 4

1. RAINBOW VARIANT, salt shaker.—*Ref. PetSal 36L* —**Key A**
2. BUTTON PANEL WITH BARS, toothpick holder.—*Ref. HI-16* Extended table service but scarce; toothpick holder is rare. Crystal, ruby-stained.
3. BUTTON PANEL, toothpick holder.—*Ref. PetPat 58* Duncan #44, c. 1900. Extended table service including cruet, toothpick holder, toy service. Crystal, ruby-stained.—**Key B;** Toy service **Key C**

PLATE 91 FACETS - BUTTONS

Row 1

1. BUTTON AND BUTTON, creamer.—*Ref. K1-96* Bellaire Goblet Co., c. 1890. Made in extended table service.—**Key B**

2. SQUARED DAISY AND DIAMOND, pitcher.—*Ref. K2-99* Extended table service including celery vase.—**Key B**

Row 2

1. LACY DAISY, creamer. U.S. Glass Co., 1918 in extended table service including jam jar, jelly compote, cruet, rose bowl, cake plate, puff box, three-legged bowls, plates, salt shaker, individual salts, 10″ plate, fluted dish, toy pieces. Note: On some pieces the pattern runs diagonally in diamond shape. Crystal, color (scarce).—**Key A**

2. STRAWBERRY AND FAN VARIANT, pitcher.—*Ref. K5-139* —**Key C**

Row 3

1. BLOCK AND LATTICE (BIG BUTTON), pitcher.—*Ref. K4-75; K8-172* Pioneer Glass Co. #9, c. 1891. Extended table service including cruet, cracker jar, tumbler, bowls.—**Key B**

2. HENRIETTA (BIG BLOCK; DIAMOND BLOCK), creamer. —*Ref. K1-110; LV70* U.S. Glass Co. (Columbia), 1891. Extended table service including salt shaker, cake stand, individual creamer, mustard jar, sugar shaker, open salt, tumbler, cup, rose jar. Crystal, ruby-stained.—**Key A**

Row 4

1. FINDLAY'S PILLAR, creamer.—*Ref. K6-48* Findlay Glass Co., 1890. Extended table service.—**Key A**

2. NICKEL PLATE'S RICHMOND, salt shaker. See Plate 51.

3. BUTTON AND STAR (RED BLOCK AND LATTICE), salt shaker.—*Ref. PetSal 24A* Extended table service. Crystal, ruby-stained.—**Key A**

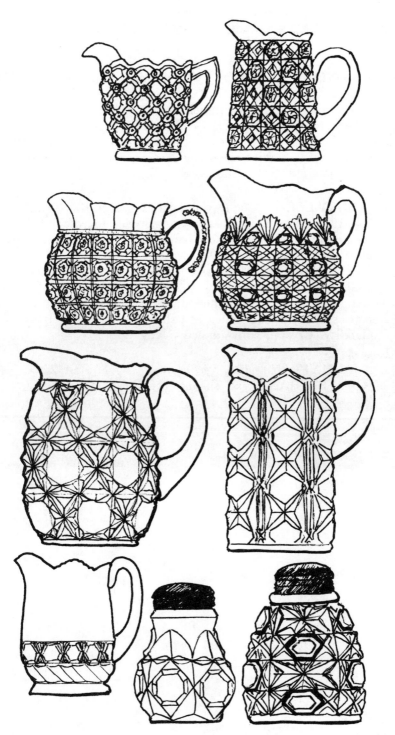

PLATE 92 FACETS - BUTTONS

Row 1

1. GLOVED HAND (COAT OF ARMS), creamer.—*Ref. K6-59; Gob II-115* U.S. Glass Co. #15100 (Gas City), 1907. Made in extended table service including toothpick holder, bowl. Crystal.—**Key B**

2. MASONIC (INVERTED PRISMS), spoon holder.—*Ref. K2-21* Indiana Tumbler and Goblet Co.; McKee and Brothers; 1894; 1917. Extended table service including bowls, cake stands, celery vase. Crystal, emerald green (rare).—**Key B**

Row 2

1. FANCY LOOP, spoon tray and details.—*Ref. K2-97* A. H. Heisey #1205, 1897. Extended table service including toothpick holder, salt shaker, jelly compote, punch bowl and cups, cracker jars, bar tumbler, claret, champagne, bowls, sherry.—**Key C**

2. NEW JERSEY (LOOPS AND DROPS), syrup.—*Ref. PetSal 34E* U.S. Glass Co. #15070 (Glassport), 1900. A State Series pattern made in extended table service including toothpick holder, individual creamer and sugar, cup, sauce, salt shaker, wine, relish, plates. Good availability. Crystal, ruby-stained.—**Key B**

Row 3

1. MANHATTAN, sauce. See Plate 17.

2. GLOVED HAND, salt shaker. See Row 1 #1.

PLATE 93 FACETS - BUTTONS AND STARS

Row 1

1. SQUARED STAR, creamer.—*Ref. K6-2* c. 1890's.—**Key B**
2. PANELLED DIAMOND CROSS (PRISM AND DAISY BAR), goblet.—*Ref. K2-24* U.S. Glass Co., 1891. Made in extended table service including wine, tumbler, cake stand. This pattern is part of the "Heavy Panelled Fine Cut" group on Plate 87.—**Key A**
3. GROGAN, goblet.—*Ref. L164#10; Gob II-98* Extended table service.—**Key A**

Row 2

1. TWO PANEL (DAISY IN PANEL; DAISY IN SQUARE), pitcher.—*Ref. L159; K3-45* Richards and Hartley; U.S. Glass Co., 1891. Extended table service including bowls, salt shaker, lamp, wine, compotes, mug, celery vase. Crystal, apple green, amber, blue, canary.—**Key A**
2. PRISM WITH DOUBLE BLOCK BAND, goblet.—*Ref. Gob II-84* —**Key A**
3. GREEK CROSS BAND, goblet.—*Ref. Gob II-53* —**Key A**

Row 3

1. NEW ERA (ERA), pitcher.—*Ref. K8-64* Bryce, Higbee and Co., mid-1880's to 1891. Made in extended table service including candelabra, toothpick holder, sauce, compotes, bread plate, jelly compote, honey dish, square olive jar, pickle tray, square plate, salt dip, salt shaker, tray, bowls.—**Key C**
2. TREMONT, spoon holder.—*(OMN)* Richards and Hartley, 1888; U.S. Glass, 1891. Made in extended table service including footed bowl, footed sauce. Crystal.—**Key A**
3. SIX PANEL FINE CUT, sugar shaker.—*Ref. SmFin-72* Dalzell, Gilmore and Leighton, 1890. Extended table service including compote.—**Key B**

Row 4

1. PANELLED FINE CUT, salt shaker.—*Ref. PetSal 161A* Extended table service.—**Key A**
2. CLOVER-DUNCAN'S, tumbler.—*Ref. K8-44* George Duncan and Sons #58; 1890. Made in extended table service including toothpick holder, wine, finger bowl. See Plate 83 for Richards and Hartley's version of "Clover."—**Key A**
3. FLAT PANELLED STAR, salt shaker.—*Ref. PetSal 173J* —**Key A**

PLATE 94 FACETS - BUTTONS AND STARS

Row 1

1. CHECKERBOARD, pitcher.—*Ref. K7-pl. 21* Westmoreland Glass Co., 1915. Extended table service including tumbler, bowls.—**Key B**
2. CURRIER AND IVES, syrup. See Plate 4.
3. STARS AND BARS (DAISY AND CUBE), pitcher.—*Ref. K1-64; LV69* Bellaire Goblet Co., 1890; U.S. Glass, 1891. Extended table service including jam jar, night lamp, celery dish, toy table set, cruet, salt shaker, tray. No goblet originally made but has been "reproduced". See Plate 195. Crystal, amber, blue.—**Key A**

Row 2

1. LOG AND STAR (MILTON; CUBE AND DIAMOND), mug.—*Ref. K5-140; Gob II-15; Gob I-67* Bellaire Goblet Co., 1890; U.S. Glass, 1891. Extended table service including two cruets, tray. No toothpick holder or syrup known. Crystal, amber, blue.—**Key B**
2. LOG AND STAR, pitcher. See above.
3. BRIDLE ROSETTES (RIBBON), tumbler.—*Ref. Gob II-15; K7-177* Cambridge Glass Co. #2653, c. 1908. Extended table service including cracker jar, trays, punch bowl, celery vase, cruet, carafe, wine.—**Key A**

Row 3

PLUTEC, pitcher.—*Ref. K3-87* McKee Glass Co., 1900. Extended table service including nut bowl, pickle dish, compote, cake stand. Pieces marked "Pres-Cut." Crystal.—**Key A**

Row 4

1. LOG AND STAR, salt shaker. See Row 2 #1.
2. BLOCK AND DENT, salt shaker.—*Ref. PetSal 155G* —**Key A**
3. MAJESTIC CROWN (FLUTED), pitcher.—*Ref. HV-88* U.S. Glass Co. (Challinor), 1891. Extended table service including sauce, trays, ice cream dish, pickle jar, waste bowl, salt shaker. See Plate 170. Crystal, purple slag.—**Key A**

PLATE 95 FACETS - BUTTONS AND STARS

Row 1

1. AETNA #300, creamer.—*Ref. K5-55* Aetna Glass and Manufacturing Co., 1886.—**Key B**

2. COARSE CUT AND BLOCK, creamer.—*Ref. K1-110* Model Flint Glass Co., c. 1890. Made in extended table service including high and low compotes, celery vase.—**Key B**

Row 2

FOSTORIA #956, creamer.—*Ref. K8-198* Fostoria Glass Co., 1901. Made in extended table service including salt shaker, berry set, sauce, plate, compote, cruet, syrup, pickle dish, tumbler. —**Key A**

Row 3

1. ENGLISH CANE, salt shaker.—*Ref. PetSal 156-i* McKee Brothers #98.—**Key B**

2. BOWLINE, salt shaker.—*Ref. PetSal 23H* —**Key A**

3. KING'S BLOCK, cruet.—*Ref. HV-132* U.S. Glass Co. (King #312), 1891. Extended table service. Crystal, vaseline—**Key B**

Row 4

HAWAIIAN LEI, bowl.—*Ref. Gob I* Bryce, Higbee and Co., after 1900. Extended table service including toothpick holder, celery dish, wine, handled basket, compote, toy set. Crystal.—**Key C**

Row 5

1. WHEELING BLOCK, creamer.—*Ref. K3-96* Cambridge Glass Co., c. 1904. Extended table service including candy tray.—**Key B**

2. DAISY-IN-SQUARE, creamer.—*Ref. PetSal 158M* U.S. Glass Co. (Duncan #330), 1891. Extended table service including bowl, sauce, tumbler, salt shaker.—**Key B**

PLATE 96 FACETS

Row 1

1. GOTHIC WINDOWS, creamer.—*Ref. K1-112* Indiana Glass Co. #166, c. 1920's. Made in extended table service.—**Key A**
2. DIAMOND BAND WITH PANELS, creamer.—*Ref. K5-61; Metz 2-142* Cooperative Flint Glass Co., 1908. Extended table service including toothpick holder, salt shaker.—**Key B**
3. PENTAGON, pitcher.—*Ref. K3-101* c. 1900's. Extended table service.—**Key B**

Row 2

1. HEART BAND, pitcher.—*Ref. K4-96* McKee and Brothers, 1897. Made in extended table service including toothpick holder, salt shaker, celery vase, tumbler. Crystal, ruby-stained.—**Key B**
2. RADIANT (DYNAST), tumbler.—*Ref. LV70* Columbia Glass Co.; U.S. Glass Co., 1891. Extended table service including salt shaker. Crystal.—**Key B**
3. JERSEY (THE KITCHEN STOVE), pitcher.—*Ref. K2-108* McKee and Brothers, 1894. Extended table service including compotes, sauce, celery vase, tumbler.—**Key C**

Row 3

1. BUTTON ARCHES (RED TOP), mug.—*Ref. K1-111; K6 pl. 9* Duncan #39, 1885; U.S. Glass, 1897; Oriental Glass, 1906; Jefferson Glass Co. Extended table service including cake stand, jelly compote, cruet, toothpick holder, tumbler, wine, salt shaker, mustard jar, toy mug, sauce. Crystal, ruby-stained.—**Key B**
2. CHANDELIER (CROWN JEWELS), salt shaker.—*Ref. K2-114* O'Hara Glass Co., 1880; U.S. Glass Co., 1891. Extended table service including tumbler, celery vase, compote. Crystal.—**Key D**
3. NEW HAMPSHIRE (BENT BUCKLE; MODISTE), mug.—*Ref. K3-97* U.S. Glass Co. #15084, 1903. A State Series pattern made in extended table service including sauce, bud vase, salt shaker, mug, toothpick holder, wine, individual sugar and creamer, square bowls, champagne, celery vase, tumbler, cruet. Very good availability. Crystal, ruby-stained.—**Key A**

Row 4

1. CUT BLOCK, syrup.—*Ref. LV40* A. H. Heisey Glass Co. #1200, c. 1900. Extended table service including individual creamer and sugar, cruet.—**Key B**
2. DIAMOND WITH PEG, toothpick holder.—*Ref. PetSal 27R* McKee Glass Co., c. 1894; Jefferson Glass Co., after 1900. Pieces found with "Krys-tol" mark were made after 1913. Extended table service in crystal, ruby-stained.—**Key B**

3. BOX-IN-BOX (FACETED ROSETTE BAND), toothpick holder.—*Ref. K6-65* c. 1900. Extended table service. Crystal, etched, ruby-stained, emerald green.—**Key B**

PLATE 97 FACETS

Row 1

1. QUINTEC, salt shaker.—*Ref. PetSal 169L* McKee Glass Co.; reproduced by Kemple. Made in extended table service including bon-bon.—**Key A**

2. POINTED JEWEL (LONG DIAMOND), creamer.—*Ref. K8-54* U.S. Glass Co. #15006 (Nickel Plate; Columbia), 1891. Made in extended table service including cup, tumbler, toy table service (called "Long Diamond"). Crystal.—**Key A**

3. FEATHERED POINTS, creamer.—*Ref. K4-120* Extended table service including salt shaker.—**Key A**

Row 2

1. SQUARED SUNBURST (STELLAR), creamer.—*Ref. K6-48* U.S. Glass Co. #15103, c. 1907. Extended table service including tumbler. Crystal.—**Key B**

2. HEAVY GOTHIC (WHITTON), goblet.—*Ref. K2-109; Gob II-13* U.S. Glass #15014 (Columbia), 1891. Extended table service including salt shaker, tumbler, wine, egg cup, compote. Crystal, ruby-stained.—**Key C**

Row 3

1. PENDANT, salt shaker.—*Ref. PetSal 168J* Probably Indiana Glass Co. (*Heacock - Pattern Glass Preview #2, pg. 10*), c. 1920. Extended table service.—**Key A**

2. STAR BASE, salt shaker.—*Ref. PetSal 173H* —**Key A**

3. POINTED GOTHIC, toothpick holder.—*Ref. K6-32* c. 1900. Extended table service.—**Key B**

Row 4

1. LOCKET, salt shaker.—*Ref. PetSal 165K* —**Key A**

2. GRAND REPUBLIC, creamer.—*Ref. HPV #2, pg. 4* Union Stopper Co. #99, 1908. Extended table service including footed punch bowl, cup, bowls, sherbet, salt shaker, celery vase.—**Key A**

205

PLATE 98 FACETS

Row 1

1. LOUISE (STARRED JEWEL), cracker jar.—*Ref. K3-80* Fostoria Glass Co. #1121, c. 1901. Made in extended table service including toothpick holder, salt shaker, compotes.—**Key B**

2. GLORIA, creamer.—*Ref. K6 pl. 41* Ohio Flint Glass Co., 1906. Extended table service.—**Key A**

Row 2

1. BORDERED ELLIPSE, pitcher.—*Ref. K4-99* McKee Glass Go.; Cambridge Glass Co. Extended table service including mug. —**Key B**

2. INVERTED FEATHER (NEARCUT #2651), creamer.—*Ref. K8-206* Cambridge Glass Co., c. 1910. Extended table service including toothpick holder, salt shaker, compotes, jelly compote, vases, cup, sherbet, plate, basket, water bottle, celery vase, pickle tray, cruets, decanter, whiskey jug, bon-bon, rectangular tray, bowls, berry set, cake stand, wine.—**Key B**

3. BRILLIANT (PETALLED MEDALLION), syrup.—*Ref. K6 pl. 65* Riverside Glass Co. #436, c. 1895. Extended table service including toothpick holder, salt shaker, cruet.—**Key A**

Row 3

1. OREGON, salt shaker. See Plate 114.

2. STYLE (MADORA), goblet.—*Ref. K6-46* Bryce, Higbee and Co. Extended table service.—**Key B**

Row 4

1. STYLE, salt shaker. See above.

2. ARROWSHEAF, pitcher.—*Ref. K3-120* c. 1900.—**Key B**

PLATE 99 FACETS

Row 1

1. NEARCUT, creamer.—*Ref. K7-169* Cambridge Glass Co. #2636, c. 1906. Made in extended table service including cruets, basket, wine, celery vase, salt shaker. See Plate 108.—**Key A**

2. FORMAL DAISY, creamer.—*Ref. K2-101* —**Key A**

Row 2

1. SHIMMERING STAR (BEADED STAR), pitcher.—*Ref. K2-55* Kokomo (Jenkins) Glass Co., c. 1905. Extended table service including salt shaker. See Plate 235.—**Key B**

2. FROSTED MEDALLION (SUNBURST ROSETTE), syrup.—*Ref. K4-120* Extended table service including covered and open compotes, bowl, tumbler.—**Key B**

Row 3

1. BEADED PANEL AND SUNBURST (CHRYSANTHEMUM), toothpick holder.—*Ref. K7-135* A. H. Heisey Glass Co. #1235, c. 1898-1903; U.S. Glass (probably), earlier. Extended table service. Crystal, color-stained.—**Key C**

2. SUNBURST ON SHIELD (DIADEM), pitcher.—*Ref. K8-52* Northwood Glass Co., c. 1905. Extended table service including water set, cruet, salt shaker. Crystal, opalescent.—**Key B**

Row 4

1. BIG STAR, salt shaker.—*Ref. PetSal 173-i* —**Key A**

2. MC KEE'S STARS AND STRIPES, salt shaker.—*Ref. K6 pl. 96* McKee and Brothers, 1898. Extended table service (scarce.) —**Key B**

3. HEISEY'S SUNBURST, salt shaker.—*Ref. K7-50* A. H. Heisey Glass Co. #343, 1904-20. There is considerable variation in this line — see two creamers and #343½ on Plate 100. Very extended table service of 107 items.—**Key C**

PLATE 100 FACETS - SUNBURSTS

Row 1

1. SUNBURST IN OVAL, creamer.—*Ref. HPV#2, pg. 3* Duncan and Miller Glass Co. #67, c. 1905, Extended table service including syrup, cruet.—**Key A**

2. ILLINOIS, pitcher.—*Ref. PetSal 163U* U.S. Glass Co. #15052, 1897 (Glassport), A State Series Pattern. Extended table service including bowls, toothpick holder, vase, candlestick, celery tray, celery vase, covered cheese dish, lamp, tumbler, ice cream tray, salt shaker, sugar shaker, 7″ round and square plates, cruet. See Plates 108, 113, 234. Crystal, emerald green (scarce).—**Key C**

Row 2

1. DAISY IN OVAL, goblet. Extended table service including tumbler.—**Key B**

2. FASHION, pitcher.—*Ref. K6-46* Imperial Glass Co. #402½, 1914. Made in extended table service of thirty-two pieces including toothpick holder, berry set, individual sugar and creamer. Made in crystal, carnival; reproduced in colors.—**Key B**

Row 3

1. DUNCAN #40, cup.—*Ref. Bones 109* George Duncan and Sons, 1898. Extended table service including toothpick holder, tumbler.—**Key A**

2. HEISEY'S #343½, creamer. See "Heisey's Sunburst", Plate 99.

Row 4

1. HEISEY'S SUNBURST, creamer. See Plate 99.

2. Another version of HEISEY'S SUNBURST, creamer. See Plate 99.

3. STARRED LOOP, cup.—*Ref. K6 pl. 57* Duncan Glass Co., c. 1900. Extended table service including tumbler, wine. See Plates 109, 234.—**Key B**

PLATE 101 FACETS - SUNBURSTS

Row 1

1. WHIRLED SUNBURST IN CIRCLE, creamer.—*Ref. K2-37* Beatty-Brady Glass Co., 1908. Basic table service.—**Key B**

2. JUBILEE (ISIS), pitcher.—*Ref. K3-41; Gob II-84* McKee and Brothers #132, 1894. Extended table service including salt shaker, celery vase, compotes, tumbler, vases, pickle dish. Crystal.—**Key A**

Row 2

FOSTORIA'S #600, individual creamer.—*Ref. K7-43* Fostoria Glass Co., 1905. Extended table service.—**Key B**

Row 3

1. AZTEC (SPINNER DAISY), spooner.—*Ref. K8 pl. 110* McKee Brothers, 1900-1910. Extended table service including water bottle, salt shaker, punch bowl, cup, jelly compote. Fair availability. —**Key A**

2. TWIN CRESCENTS, creamer.—*Ref. K2-60* —**Key A**

Row 4

NEARCUT #2697, toy creamer.—*Ref. K7-175* Cambridge Glass Co., 1909. Toy basic table service including handled spooner. —**Key B**

Row 5

1. CANNONBALL PINWHEEL (CALEDONIA; PINWHEEL), salt shaker.—*Ref. K4-140* U.S. Glass Co. #15094, 1906. Extended table service.—**Key B**

2. MEDALLION SUNBURST, salt shaker.—*Ref. Gob II-114* Bryce, Higbee and Co., c. 1905. Made in extended table service including butter pat, toothpick holder, berry set.—**Key B**

PLATE 102 FACETS - SUNBURSTS

Row 1

1. RAMBLER, creamer.—*Ref. HV 169* U.S. Glass Co. #15136 (Gas City), 1912. Extended table service including bowls, pickle dish, handled jelly dish, celery tray, sauce, bon-bon, cake stand, tumbler, salt shaker, cruet, syrup, compote. Crystal.—**Key B**

2. FERRIS WHEEL, creamer.—*Ref. K4-27; Gob I-50* Indiana Glass Co., c. 1910. Extended table service including wine.—**Key B**

Row 2

1. GEORGIA BELLE (WESTERN STAR), goblet.—*Ref. Metz 1-228; Gob I-56* U.S. Glass Co. #15097, 1906. Extended table service including salt shaker.—**Key B**

2. FEATHER SWIRL (SOLAR), salt shaker.—*Ref. Gob II-153* U.S. Glass Co. #15116, 1908 (Bryce; Gas City). Made in extended table service including cruet, tray, vase, syrup, cake stand. Crystal.—**Key B**

3. COMET IN THE STARS, pitcher.—*Ref. HPV #2 p.6* U.S. Glass Co. #15150 (Glassport), 1914. Extended table service including bowls, tumbler, sauce, handled relish. Crystal.—**Key B**

Row 3

1. RIVERSIDE'S AURORA, sugar bowl.—*Ref. Heacock* Riverside Glass Co., c. 1904. Extended table service. Crystal.—**Key B**

2. FERN BURST, cruet.—*Ref. Gob II-67* c. 1905. Extended table service.—**Key B**

PLATE 103 FACETS - SUNBURSTS

Row 1

1. ROANOKE STAR (IMPERIAL STAR), goblet.—*Ref. Gob II-38; PetSal 40L* Imperial Glass Co. #282. Made in extended table service including salt shaker, banana dish.—**Key A**

2. DIXIE BELLE, goblet.—*Ref. Gob II-38* Extended table service including salt shaker.—**Key A**

3. BUZZ-STAR (WHIRLIGIG), pitcher.—*Ref. K4-140* U.S. Glass Co. #15101 (Bryce), 1907. Extended table service including tumbler, toy table service (which is called "Whirligig"). Crystal.—**Key B**

Row 2

INDIAN SUNSET, creamer—*Ref. HTP#739* c. 1905. Extended table service including bowls, celery tray, berry set, bon-bon.—**Key B**

Row 3

1. WHIRLIGIG, toy pitcher. See "BUZZ-STAR", above.—Toy **Key C**

2. DIAMOND WHIRL, pitcher—*Ref. HV-162* U.S. Glass Co. #15109, 1915. Extended table service. Crystal.—**Key B**

Row 3

1. BISMARC STAR, goblet. c. 1900. Found in only goblets.—**Key C**

2. WHIRLWIND, salt shaker—*Ref. PetSal 43-0*—**Key A**

3. POSTSCRIPT, salt shaker.—*Ref. Gob II-58* Tarentum Glass Co., 1905. Extended table service. See Plate 107.—**Key B**

PLATE 104 FACETS - SUNBURSTS

Row 1

1. FEATHER DUSTER (ROSETTE MEDALLION; HUCKLE), pitcher.—*Ref. K2-42; LV64* U.S. Glass Co. #15043, 1895. Made in extended table service including salt shaker, compotes, plate, pickle dish, egg cup, tumbler, tray and waste bowl, berry set. Crystal, emerald green.—**Key A**

2. TWIN FEATHERS, creamer.—*Ref. K7-54* —**Key A**

Row 2

STAR AND CRESCENT, cruet.—*Ref. Gob I-50* U.S. Glass Co. (King; Ripley), 1908. Extended table service including two-handled spooner. Crystal.—**Key B**

Row 3

1. DUNCAN HOMESTEAD, water bottle.—*Ref. Bones 108* Duncan #63, c. 1900. Extended table service including punch bowl, cup, toothpick holder, celery vase, syrup, cruet, two types salt shaker, finger bowl, individual salt, individual creamer, vases, compotes, many size bowls.—**Key A**

2. FEATHER DUSTER, salt shaker. See Row 1 #1.

3. SPINNING STAR (ROYAL), syrup.—*Ref. HV-146* U.S. Glass Co. #15099. Extended table service including toothpick holder. Crystal.—**Key B**

Row 4

1. DAISY AND SCROLL (BUZZ SAW IN PARENTHESIS; U.S. VICTORIA), syrup.—*Ref. HV-146* U.S. Glass Co. #15104 (Glassport), 1907. Made in extended table service including salt shaker. Crystal.—**Key A**

2. MC KEE'S SUNBURST (AZTEC SUNBURST), salt shaker.—*Ref. PetSal 174E* McKee Brothers, c. 1910. Made in extended table service.—**Key A**

PLATE 105 FACETS - SUNBURSTS

Row 1

1. CANE PINWHEEL, pitcher (Author's name). Pieces unknown.—**Key A**

2. RAYED FLOWER, pitcher.—*Ref. K7-52* Indiana Glass Co., c. 1920. Extended table service including tumbler. See similar pattern "FLOWER WITH CANE" on Plate 132. Crystal, decorated. —**Key B**

Row 2

OXFORD, bowl.—*Ref. K6 pl. 60* McKee and Brothers, 1897. Probably made in extended table service including round and square bowls.—**Key A**

Row 3

1. HOBSTAR, creamer.—*Ref. PetSal 31F* U.S. Glass Co. #15124, (Glassport factory; Central factory), 1915. Made in extended table service including covered candy dish, pickle dish, bowls, handled spooner. See Plate 110. Crystal.—**Key B**

2. SNOWFLAKE AND SUNBURST, pitcher.—*Ref. K4-141* —**Key A**

Row 4

1. DIAMOND LACE, creamer.—*Ref. K2-69* Imperial Glass Co., 1905. Extended table service including berry set, tumbler. Crystal, carnival glass.—**Key B**

2. ROBINSON PURITAN, creamer.—*Ref. K6 pl. 39* Robinson Glass Co., 1894. Extended table service including punch bowl, tumbler, bowl, cruet.—**Key A**

3. MINNESOTA, goblet.—*Ref. K8-205* U.S. Glass Co. #15055 (Ripley; Glassport), 1898. A State Series pattern. Extended table service including toothpick holder, salt shaker, syrup, sauce, celery tray, square fruit compote, individual creamer, wine, mug, tumbler, open compote. Availability is abundant. Crystal, ruby-stained, emerald green.—**Key B**

PLATE 106 FACETS - SUNBURSTS

Row 1

1. CIRCULAR SAW (ROSETTA), creamer.—*Ref. K5-146* Beaumont Glass Co., 1904. Made in extended table service including berry set, punch bowl, berry bowl, tumbler, sauce, cracker jar, salt shaker.—**Key A**

2. PADDLEWHEEL, creamer.—*Ref. K8-41* Extended table service including salt shaker.—**Key A**

Row 2

1. WILTEC, creamer.—*Ref. K8 pl. 109* McKee Glass Co., 1894. Extended table service including vases, bowls, cigar jar, tumbler, punch bowl, spoon tray, bon-bon, sauce.—**Key A**

2. DOUBLE PINWHEEL, pitcher.—*Ref. K4-141* Indiana Glass Co., after 1915. Extended table service including salt shaker. —**Key A**

Row 3

1. BEVELLED STAR (PRIDE), pitcher.—*Ref. K2-70; LV79* Model Flint Glass Co., 1890-1897. Extended table service including compote, toothpick holder, salt shaker, — twenty-six pieces in all. Crystal, amber, emerald green, cobalt blue.—**Key A**

2. BONTEC, pitcher.—*Ref. K3-139* McKee Glass Co., c. 1900. Extended table service including bon-bon, 10″ plate, bowls, cake plate, tumbler, relish.

Row 4

1. PADDLEWHEEL SHIELD, tumbler. (Author's name). Extended table service.—**Key A**

2. SLEWED HORSESHOE (RADIANT DAISY; U.S. PEACOCK), creamer.—*Ref. K8-15* U.S. Glass Co. #15111 (Glassport), 1908. Extended table service including berry set, bowls, ice cream tray, wine. Crystal.—**Key B**

PLATE 107 FACETS - SUNBURSTS

Row 1

CARLTEC, creamer.—*Ref. K6-49* McKee and Brothers, 1894; 1917. Extended table service including oval and square creamers, berry bowl, olive tray, spoon tray, bowls, 10½" plate, rose bowl, basket.—**Key A**

Row 2

1. MEMPHIS (DOLL'S EYE), pitcher.—*Ref. Gob I* Northwood Glass Co. (*Ref. Miller*), 1908-10. Extended table service including rare toothpick holder, tumbler, berry set, fruit bowl on base, syrup, punch bowl on base, cup. Crystal, carnival glass, colors.—**Key A**
2. STAR AND LADDERS, creamer (author's name). This piece known.—**Key A**

Row 3

1. BUCKLE WITH STAR (LATE BUCKLE; ORIENT), bowl of sauce dish.—*Ref. L-166; K1-22* Bryce Walker and Company, 1875; U.S. Glass Co., 1891. Made in extended table service including compote, wine, cake stand, sauce, pickle dish. Crystal.—**Key C**
2. BUCKLE WITH STAR, pitcher. See Above.

Row 4

1. POSTSCRIPT, plate. See Plate 103.
2. ATLANTA, salt shaker.—*Ref. Gob II-63* c. 1905. Extended table service including jelly compote, wine, sauce.—**Key B**
3. ELLIPSE AND STAR, salt shaker.—*Ref. PetSal 160F*—**Key A**

PLATE 108 FACETS - SUNBURSTS

Row 1
1. GEORGIA, plate. See Plates 24, 33.
2. STAR-IN-OCTAGON, creamer.—*Ref. K7-51* —**Key A**

Row 2
1. NORTHWOOD NEARCUT (STRETCHED DIAMOND AND HOBSTAR), punch bowl.—*Ref. Hartung; HPV5 p. 20* Northwood Glass Co. #12. Made in extended table service including tumbler. Crystal, ruby-stained (rare), carnival glass.—**Key C**
2. NEARCUT, salt shaker. See Plate 99.
3. STAR AND BAR, salt shaker.—*Ref. PetSal 173C* (Do not confuse with "Stars and Bars", plate 94.)—**Key B**

Row 3
1. STAR AND RIB, salt shaker.—*Ref. PetSal 40J*—**Key B**
2. ILLINOIS, salt shaker. See Plate 100.
3. SHELTON STAR, salt shaker.—*Ref. PetSal 173-U*—**Key A**

227

PLATE 109 FACETS - SUNBURSTS

Row 1

1. OVAL STAR, pitcher (toy)—*Ref. K6-47* Indiana Glass Co. #300, c. 1910. Made in toy table service including toy water tray (scarce), spooner (used as toothpick holder by collectors).—**Key A**

2. KEYSTONE, toothpick holder.—*Ref. K6 pl. 68* McKee and Brothers, 1897. Made in extended table service including salt shaker.—**Key A**

3. BUTTRESSED SUNBURST, creamer.—*Ref. K1-114* Tarentum Glass Co., 1910. Extended table service including berry set; condiment items would be rare.—**Key A**

Row 2

1. SUNBURST AND STAR, salt shaker.—*Ref. PetSal 174D* —**Key B**

2. SNOWFLAKE (FERNLAND), spoon holder.—*Ref. K7-174* Cambridge Glass Co., c. 1910. Extended table service including tumbler, bowls, compotes, bread plate, pickle dish, celery tray, salt shaker, toothpick holder, condiment set on tray, vases, toy table service.—**Key B**

3. STARRED LOOP, tumbler. See Plates 100, 234.

Row 3

1. ARCH AND SUNBURST, salt shaker.—*Ref. PetSal 21G* —**Key A**

2. YUTEC, salt shaker.—*Ref. PetSal 177H* McKee Brothers; reproduced by Kemple Glass Co. Extended table service.—**Key A**

3. WHEEL OF FORTUNE, salt shaker.—*Ref. PetSal 43N* —**Key B**

PLATE 110 FACETS - SUNBURSTS

Row 1

1. ROTEC, pitcher.—*Ref. K6 pl. 23* McKee Glass Co., 1894 Made in extended table service including bowls, celery tray, tumbler. —**Key A**

2. BRAZILLIAN (CANE SHIELD), pitcher.—*Ref. K5-138; K7-33* Fostoria Glass Co. #600, c. 1898. Extended table service including toothpick holder, salt shaker, pickle jar, vases, sauce, handled olive, tumbler, finger bowl, compote, carafe, celery tray and vase, cracker jar, 7″, 8″ and 10″ flat berry bowls; cruet, sherbet, rose bowl. —**Key B**

Row 2

1. HOBSTAR, salt shaker, See Plate 105.

2. HORSESHOE CURVE, pitcher.—*Ref. K-149* —**Key A**

Row 3

1. U.S. REGAL, tumbler.—*Ref. K6 Pl. 35* U.S. Glass Co. (Glassport), 1906. Note: **Not** a State Series pattern for Oklahoma (*Ref. Heacock.*) Made in extended table service including flare-bottom toothpick holder, sugar shaker, butter dish with small handles, decanter, cruet, basket. Crystal.—**Key C**

2. STARDUST, salt shaker.—*Ref. PetSal-40K*—**Key A**

PLATE 111 FACETS - ORNATE

Row 1

1. NU CUT #526, creamer.—*Ref. K8-52* Imperial Glass Co., 1915.—**Key A**
2. ADA, salt shaker. See Plate 75.

Row 2

1. FRINGED DRAPE (CRESCENT), creamer.—*Ref. K6-32* McKee Glass Co., 1901; National Glass Co. Extended table service including cordial, salt shaker, cruet.—**Key B**
2. MASSACHUSETTS (ARCHED DIAMOND POINT; CANE VARIANT; GENEVA), gobler.—*Ref. K2-136; Gob II-59* A State Series pattern. U.S. Glass Co. #15054 (King), 1898. Made in extended table service including cordial, syrup, cruet, several creamers, vase, candy dish, shot glass, mug, wine, decanter, table lamp, fake rum jug. Only fair availability. See Plate 233. The "rum jug", a flask-shaped syrup with spout that does not pour, was reportedly used to transport liquor into "dry" states in the guise of syrup. For its value, see "Decanter" in Price Key D. Crystal, green, ruby-stained.—**Key B**
3. REXFORD (EUCLID; BOYLAN), goblet.—*Ref. Gob II 63,94,113* J. B. Higbee Co., c. 1910. Extended table service including toothpick holder, footed sauce, wine, cake stand, ruffle-edged bowl, flat sauce, celery vase, bowls, salt shaker.—**Key A**

Row 3

RISING SUN, cruet.—*Ref. K2-61* U.S. Glass Co. #15110 (Ripley; Glassport), 1908. Made in extended table service including three shapes sugar bowls, wine, tumbler, toothpick holder. Crystal, decorated, carnival glass.—**Key B**

Row 4

1. NEW HAMPSHIRE, salt shaker. See Plate 96.
2. MASSACHUSETTS, salt shaker. See above.
3. CANE HORSESHOE (PARAGON), cruet.—*Ref. K1-100* U.S. Glass Co. #15118 (Ripley) 1909. Extended table service including salt shaker, cake stand, tumbler, bowls, celery tray, compote, crystal.—**Key B**

PLATE 112 FACETS - ORNATE

Row 1

1. STAR OF DAVID (WETZEL), pitcher.—*Ref. K5-133* New Martinsville Glass Co. Made in extended table service including bowl, cruet, hair receiver.—**Key D**

2. COLUMNED THUMBPRINTS, creamer.—*Ref. K5-71* Westmoreland Glass Co., c. 1905. Extended table service including celery vase, syrup, salt shaker, cruet, toothpick holder, bowls, tumbler, cup, berry set.—**Key B**

Row 2

1. FANCY CUT (REX), toy pitcher.—*Ref. K2-103* Cooperative Flint Glass Co., c. 1905. Made in toy table service including punch set and water set.—**Key B**

2. ROSE WINDOWS, pitcher.—*Ref. K4-138*—**Key B**

Row 3

1. DIAMOND SWAG (FANDANGO), toothpick holder.—*Ref. K5-117; LV40* A. H. Heisey Glass Co. #1201, c. 1898-1909. Extended table service including tumbler, cruets, syrups, jelly compote, relishes, triangular jelly dish, wine, spoon tray, cracker jar, vases, banana compote, sugar shaker. Crystal.—**Key B**

2. PENNSYLVANIA (BALDER; KAMONI), syrup.—*Ref. K2-103* U.S. Glass Co. #15048 (Central; Gillander), 1898. A State Series pattern. Extended table service in every piece imaginable including toy sets, carafe, covered cheese dish, round and square sauces. Toy spooner doubles as toothpick holder and is rare in green. Good availability. See Plate 76. Crystal, ruby-stained, emerald green.—**Key B**

PLATE 113 FACETS - ORNATE

Row 1

1. STAR AND FEATHER, goblet.—**Key A**
2. DOYLE'S SHELL, pitcher.—*Ref. K8-20* Doyle and Co., 1880's; U.S. Glass Co., 1891. Made in extended table service including salt shaker. Crystal, ruby-stained.—**Key B**
3. TWIN SUNBURSTS, pitcher.—*Ref. K1-99*—**Key A**

Row 2

1. LACY CABLE, creamer.—*Ref. K1-76* c. 1866—**Key C**
2. DAISY IN DIAMOND, pitcher.—*Ref. K3-77* O'Hara Glass Co. #725, 1886; U.S. Glass Co. Extended table service including toothpick holder, salt shaker, celery vase, cruet, ice-cream tub, decanter, tumbler, waste bowl, mug. Crystal, amber, rose, blue.—**Key B**

Row 3

1. BIG X, pitcher.—*Ref. K4-130* Cambridge Glass Co., 1901. Extended table service including salt shaker.—**Key A**
2. ILLINOIS, pitcher. See Plates 100, 108, 234.

Row 4

1. BROKEN PILLAR AND REED, toothpick holder.—*Ref. Bond 30* Model Flint Glass Co. (Albany) #909, c. 1900. Extended table service. Crystal, amethyst-flashed, color-stained (scarce).—**Key B**
2. DOUBLE CROSSROADS, salt shaker.—*Ref. PetSal 26G* Extended table service including wine.—**Key B**

237

PLATE 114 FACETS - ORNATE

Row 1

1. BUCKLE WITH ENGLISH HOBNAIL, creamer.—*Ref. K2-75* Extended table service including pickle dish.—**Key B**

2. BARRED STAR (SPARTON), creamer.—*Ref. LV 49* U.S. Glass Co. (Gillander), 1891. Extended table service including compote, cake stand, salt shaker, celery vase. Crystal.—**Key B**

Row 2

1. LOUISIANA (SHARP OVAL AND DIAMOND), goblet.—*Ref. K6 Pl. 93* U.S. Glass Co. #15053 (Bryce), 1898. A State Series pattern. Made in extended table service including mug, cake stand, relish, salt shaker, bowl. Poor availability. Crystal.—**Key B**

2. OREGON (BEADED LOOP; BEADED OVALS), pitcher.—*Ref. K8-163; L76; LV 44* U.S. Glass Co. #15073, 1901. A State Series pattern. Very extended table service including compotes, cordial, mug, bread tray, toothpick, tumbler, wine, cake stand, syrup, cruet, sauce, three types sugar bowl, salt shaker. Good availability. Crystal.—**Key B**

Row 3

1. BUTTON BLOCK, salt shaker.—*Ref. PetSal 24D* —**Key A**

2. BUTTON AND STAR PANEL, salt shaker.—*Ref. PetSal 24B* Bryce, Higbee and Co., c. 1902. Extended table service including toothpick holder.—**Key B**

3. CROSSBAR AND CANE, salt shaker.—*Ref. PetSal 26F* —**Key A**

PLATE 115 FACETS - ORNATE

Row 1

1. HEART PLUME, creamer. See Plate 77.
2. V-IN-HEART, pitcher.—*Ref. K6-26*

Row 2

1. TWIN SNOWSHOES (SUNBEAM), creamer.—*Ref. K8-54* U.S. Glass Co. #15139 (Gas City), c. 1918. Extended table service including handled relish, compotes, cake stand, tumbler, wine, cruet, cup, relishes, celery vase, toothpick holder, toy table set. Crystal.—**Key A**
2. BUCKINGHAM, creamer.—*Ref. K6 pl. 33* U.S. Glass Co. #15106 (Glassport factory), 1907. Extended table service. Crystal.—**Key A**

Row 3

1. TOLTEC, toothpick holder.—*Ref. K6-pl. 10* McKee Glass, c. 1904-1910. Has trademark "Pres-Cut". Made in extended table service including tumblers, sauce, bowls, jelly compote, three cruets, cup, finger bowl, wine, 9″ and 10″ plates, celery vase, three syrups, footed sherbet, claret, spoon tray.—**Key A**
2. INTERLOCKED HEARTS (WISHBONE), goblet.—*Ref. Gob II-80; K5-69* c. 1900. Extended table service.—**Key A**
3. STARRED SCROLL (CRESCENT AND FAN), creamer.—*Ref. K8-30* c. 1900. Extended table service including tumbler, salt shaker, rose bowl, celery vase, syrup, wine. Crystal.—**Key B**

Row 4

1. IVERNA, cracker jar.—*Ref. HPV4 p. 6* Ripley and Co. #303, 1911. Extended table service including sauce, bowls, tumbler, punch bowl and pedestal, biscuit jar, vases, handled sherbet, pickle dish, celery tray, berry set, spoon tray, handled jelly. No goblet known.—**Key A**
2. ROCKET, pitcher.—*Ref. K5-148* Indiana Glass Co., 1915-25.—**Key B**

PLATE 116 FACETS - ORNATE

Row 1

1. CRYSTAL QUEEN, creamer.—*Ref. K6 pl. 25* Northwood Glass Co., 1897. Made in very extended table service including 125 items.—**Key B**

2. SQUAT PINEAPPLE (LONE STAR), creamer.—*Ref. K2-76* McKee and Brothers, 1898. Extended table service including two types salt shaker, cruet. Crystal, emerald green.—**Key C**

Row 2

1. PALM LEAF FAN, pitcher.—*Ref. K2-63* Bryce, Higbee and Co., 1904. Extended table service including tumbler, vase, jelly compote, water bottle, compote, bowls, celery vase, square cake plate, sauce, salt shaker.—**Key B**

2. GRENADE, creamer.—*Ref. K6-29*—**Key B**

Row 3

1. SWEET HEART, toy pitcher.—*Ref. K2-103* Cambridge Glass Co., c. 1910. Extended table service including sauce, berry set, toy table service, toothpick holder, lamp.—**Key A**

2. ARROWHEAD-IN-OVAL, toy creamer.—*Ref. K8-43* Higbee Glass Co., c. 1870 (bee trademark). Made in extended table service including toy table service, punch cup, wine.—**Key B**

Row 4

1. FLEUR-DE-LIS AND TASSEL (FLEUR-DE-LIS AND DRAPE), mustard jar.—*Ref. K3-50; LV59* U.S. Glass Co. (Adams; Ripley), 1891. Extended table service including tray, salt shaker, cup and saucer, cruet, bowls, compotes, finger bowl, tray, cordial, wine, tumbler, claret, flat and footed sauces. Crystal, milk glass, emerald green.—**Key B**

2. PATHFINDER, goblet.—*Ref. Gob II-135*—**Key A**

Row 5

1. ARCHED FLEUR-DE-LIS, creamer. See Plate 39.

2. BRAZEN SHIELD, goblet.—*Ref. Gob II-75; K7-13* Central Glass Co. #98; Cambridge Glass Co. (after 1904); Indiana Tumbler and Goblet Co. Extended table service.—**Key A**

PLATE 117 FACETS - ORNATE

Row 1

1. CO-OP REX, creamer.—*Ref. K6-49* Cooperative Flint Glass Co., 1907. Extended table service.—**Key B**

2. DOTTED LOOP, pitcher.—*Ref. K6-16* Made in extended table service.—**Key A**

3. BLAZING CORNUCOPIA, creamer.—*Ref. K6-29* c. 1910. Extended table service including toothpick holder with handles.—**Key A**

Row 2

1. LIBERTY, creamer.—*Ref. K4-72* McKee and Brothers, 1892. Extended table service including tumblers, tray, wine, champagne, tankard pitchers.—**Key A**

2. SHIELD, creamer.—*Ref. K8-40* c. 1900. Extended table service.—**Key A**

Row 3

1. NEAR CUT #2660, creamer.—*Ref. K7-176* Cambridge Glass Co., c. 1901. Extended table service including basket, decanter, compotes, celery vase and tray, tumbler, sherbet, cruet, punch bowl, wine, plates, cake stand, sauce, rose bowl, jelly compote, toy punch set.—**Key A**

2. LENOX, toothpick holder.—*Ref. K6-pl. 97* McKee Glass Co., 1898. Extended table service including bowls, individual salt dip, two types salt shaker, individual sugar and creamer, mug, cruet, jelly compote, tumbler.—**Key A**

Row 4

1. PLYTEC (RADIANT PETAL), salt shaker.—*Ref. PetSal 169C* McKee and Brothers. Extended table service.—**Key A**

2. ONEATA, pitcher.—*Ref. K6 pl.75* Extended table service. —**Key A**

3. CENTIPEDE, salt shaker.—*Ref. PetSal 24P* —**Key A**

245

PLATE 118 FLOWERS

HORSESHOE (GOOD LUCK; PRAYER RUG).—*Ref. L-112; K1-66* Adams and Co., 1881. Made in extended table service including jam jar, plate, covered bowl, covered compote, rare wine, platter, cake stand, celery vase, bread plate, rare master salt, relish. Covered pieces have a horseshoe finial. Good availability. Crystal.—**Key C**

Top: Footed sauce dish

Bottom: Waste jar

PLATE 119 FLOWERS

Row 1

1. TARENTUM'S VICTORIA (QUESTION MARK), salt shaker.—*Ref. K2-53* Tarentum Glass Co., 1900. Made in extended table service including tumbler, berry bowl, sauce, dresser tray. Crystal, colors, opaque, decorated.—**Key C**

2. PAMPAS FLOWER, creamer.—*Ref. K8-2* Extended table service including sauce, salt shaker, berry bowl.—**Key B**

3. PINS AND BELLS, creamer.—*Ref. K4-38* c. 1880. Scarce. —**Key B**

Row 2

1. FACETED FLOWER, pitcher.—*Ref. K3-116* Late 1800's. Extended table service including celery vase, water tray.—**Key B**

2. CURLED LEAF, pitcher.—*Ref. K3-21* Bryce, Walker and Co., 1869.—**Key B**

3. STIPPLED WOODFLOWER, creamer.—*Ref. L-136* —**Key B**

Row 3

1. DITHRIDGE #25, syrup.—*Ref. HIII-49* Dithridge and Co. Milk Glass (may be painted).—**Key C**

2. CHALLINOR TREE OF LIFE, cracker jar.—*Ref. LV80* Challinor, Taylor #313, 1885; U.S. Glass, 1893. Extended table service including syrup, salt shaker, cruet, bowl. Opaque colors, milk glass.—**Key C**

3. PANELLED 44 (ATHENIA), pitcher.—*Ref. Gob II-150* U.S. Glass Co. #15140 (Glassport factory), 1912. Made in extended table service including footed tankard, mug, bowls, cruet, tumbler, salt shaker, three-legged bon-bon, toothpick holder. May be marked with "U.S." trademark. Crystal; decorated with silver, ruby-stained. —**Key B**

Row 4

1. INTAGLIO (FLOWER SPRAY WITH SCROLLS), creamer.—*Ref. K2-110; K7-200* Northwood Glass Co., 1910. Extended table service including salt shaker, jelly compote, footed bowl, berry set, tumbler, cruet. Crystal, colors, custard.—**Key C**

2. PANELLED HEATHER, pitcher. 1890's. Extended table service including sauce, wine, vase, cake stand, covered compote.—**Key B**

PLATE 120 FLOWERS

Row 1

1. HUNDRED-LEAVED ROSE, pitcher.—*Ref. K2-128* c. 1890's. Extended table service including sauce, bowl, open and covered sugar bowls. Crystal, frosted.—**Key B**

2. AMERICAN BEAUTY (ROSE AND SUNBURSTS), creamer.—*Ref. K2-98* Northwood Glass Co., 1880's. Made in extended table service.—**Key A**

3. WILD ROSE WITH SCROLLING, butter dish.—*Ref. K8-44* McKee Glass Co., c. 1902-1910. Made in toy table service; toy spooner is collected as a toothpick holder. Crystal, opaque, decorated. —**Key B**

Row 2

1. ROSE IN SNOW, sugar bowl.—*Ref. K4-43* Bryce Brothers; U.S. Glass Co., 1870's; 1891. Made in extended table service including tumbler, plate, cake stand, sauce, relish, rare double relish. Can be easily found. Crystal, amber, canary, blue.—**Key C**

2. OPEN ROSE, goblet.—*Ref. L-122* c. 1870's. Extended table service including bowls, egg cup, tumbler, master salt, celery vase, handled berry bowl, relish, sauce. Crystal.—**Key C**

3. CABBAGE ROSE, goblet.—*Ref. L-122; K3-40* Central Glass Co. #140, 1881. Extended table service including rare wine, rare milk pitcher, cordial, nineteen sizes compotes, four sizes cake stands, egg cup, footed salt, tumbler, sauce. Fair availability. Has finial shaped like rose bud. Crystal.—**Key C**

Row 3

1. GARLAND OF ROSES, creamer.—*Ref. K4-58* c. 1900. Extended table service including footed open salt, egg cup, celery vase, toothpick holder (very rare). All pieces are rare. Crystal, vaseline.—**Key C**

2. ROSE SPRIG, pitcher.—*Ref. L-125* Campbell, Jones and Co., 1886. Extended table service including celery vase, salt shaker, footed bowl, cake plate, handled mug, plates, platter, tumbler, water tray. Fair availability. Crystal, amber, canary, blue.—**Key B**

PLATE 121 FLOWERS

Row 1

1. BEADED BOTTOM, salt shaker.—*Ref. PetSal 22* Dithridge and Co., 1898. Milk Glass.—**Key C**
2. WILD ROSE WITH BOW-KNOT, creamer.—*Ref. K2-64* McKee and Sons; National Glass Co., 1901. Made in extended table service including toothpick holder, salt shaker, tumbler, sauce, bowl, smoke set on tray. Crystal, colors, frosted.—**Key B**
3. FLORADORA (BOHEMIAN), creamer.—*Ref. K6 Pl. 59* U.S. Glass Co. #15063, 1899. Extended table service including toothpick holder, straw jar, celery vase. Crystal, rose-flashed, emerald green, frosted.—**Key B**

Row 2

1. PRIMROSE AND PEARLS, syrup.—*Ref. HIII-49* Milk Glass.—**Key C**
2. ROSE WREATH, pitcher.—*Ref. K4-142* Northwood Glass Co., c. 1909.—**Key B**
3. ROCK CRYSTAL (PURITAN), creamer.—*Ref. K5-96* McKee Glass Co., 1894. Extended table service including salt shaker, tumblers, ice cream glass, sherbet, candlestick, finger bowl, pickle tray, punch bowl, cruets.—**Key B**

Row 3

FORGETMENOT, butter dish.—*Ref. K6 Pl. 58* Fostoria Glass Co. #240, 1891. Extended table service.—**Key B**

Row 4

1. PANELLED DOGWOOD, sauce.—*Ref. HV-45* U.S. Glass Co. after 1908. Made only in various-sized bowls. Crystal, emerald green, rose-flashed, amethyst-flashed.—**Key B**
2. ROCK CRYSTAL, salt shaker. See above.
3. LOUIS XV, cruet.—*Ref. K2-199* Northwood Glass Co., 1899. Extended table service including salt shaker, tumbler, berry set (banana-boat shaped), rare toothpick holder. The pitcher has short, knobby feet. Most often found in green or custard; possibly crystal.

PLATE 122 FLOWERS

Row 1

1. ART NOVO (PANELLED DOGWOOD; DOGWOOD; WILD ROSE), miniature lamp.—*Ref. K1-69; Gob II-36* Cooperative Flint Glass Co., 1902-06. Made in extended table service including toothpick holder, salt shaker, miniatures. Crystal, rose-flashed, ruby-stained, frosted, milk glass, decorated.—**Key B**

2. ALBA BLOSSOMS, syrup.—*Ref. HIII-14* Dithridge and Co., 1895. Syrup and sugar shaker known. White opaque glass.—**Key C**

Row 2

1. LEAF AND FLOWER, celery vase.—*Ref. LV-50* Hobbs #339; U.S. Glass Co., 1891. Extended table service including salt shaker, many size bowls, rare celery basket, syrup. Crystal, color-stained.—**Key C**

2. WREATHED SUNBURST, pitcher.— *Ref. K8-23* U.S. Glass Co. #15096, 1906. Extended table service including salt shaker. Crystal.—**Key B**

3. SINGLE ROSE, salt shaker.—*Ref. K3-86* Extended table service. Known as "Wild Rose" in carnival glass. Crystal, opaque white, decorated, carnival.—**Key B**

Row 3

DELAWARE, salt shaker. See Plate 129.

Row 4

1. DANDELION, toothpick holder.—*Ref. HTP-74* Fostoria Glass Co. #1819, c. 1911.—**Key B**

2. WREATHED SUNBURST, salt shaker. See Row 2 #2.

3. FLOWERED SCROLL, syrup.—*Ref. K8-183* George Duncan and Sons #2000, 1893. Extended table service including tumbler, salt shaker, cup. Crystal, amber-stained.—**Key B**

PLATE 123 FLOWERS

Row 1

1. INTAGLIO DAISY, pitcher.—*Ref. HTP-23* U.S. Glass Co. (Glassport factory) #15133, 1911. Extended table service including cake stand, bowls, footed bowls, tumbler, toothpick holder. Crystal, decorated.—**Key B**

2. FIELD THISTLE, creamer.—*Ref. Hartung* U.S. Glass Co. (Gas City), 1912. Extended table service including celery tray, bowls, open and covered sugar bowls (open with two handles, covered with no handles), large plate, castor set, crimped olive dish, compotes, syrup, cruet, salt shaker. Crystal, carnival.—**Key B**

Row 2

1. TWO FLOWER, pitcher.—*Ref. HV-170* U.S. Glass Co. #15138, 1918. Extended table service including tall shallow compote, plate, footed bowls, handled footed nut bowl, tumbler. Crystal.—**Key B**

2. JEWEL AND FLOWER (BEADED FLOWER AND LEAF), creamer.—*Ref. K8-30* Made in extended table service including salt shaker.—**Key B**

Row 3

1. RUFFLED EYE, pitcher.—*Ref. K6-58* Indiana Tumbler and Goblet Co., 1890's. Extended table service including wine. Crystal, canary, amber, emerald green, caramel slag.—**Key C**

2. PANELLED PRIMULA, pitcher.—*Ref. K3-117* c. 1900. Extended table service including lamp, celery vase, tumbler, salt shaker, compotes, cordial, cake stand, decanter, cup and saucer, syrup, bread plate.—**Key B**

PLATE 124 FLOWERS

Row 1

1. THE SUMMIT, toothpick holder.—*Ref. K6-22* Thompson Glass Co., 1895. Extended table service including bowl, wine. Crystal, ruby-stained.—**Key B**

2. FLOWER AND HONEYCOMB, creamer.—*Ref. K7-28* U.S. Glass Co.—**Key A**

3. FLOWER AND PLEAT (MIDWESTERN POMONA), salt shaker.—*Ref. PetSal 161K* c. 1895. Extended table service including toothpick holder. Crystal, frosted, color-washed, rare ruby-stain.—**Key A**

Row 2

1. POSIES AND PODS, butter dish.—*Ref. Heacock* Northwood Glass Co., 1905. Made in extended table service including berry set. Crystal, color-stained, opalescent.—**Key B**

2. TEARDROP FLOWER, creamer.—*Ref. K7-27* Northwood Glass Co., c. 1904. Extended table service including rare cruet, sauce, berry set. Crystal, colors.—**Key B**

Row 3

1. FLOWER AND BUD, salt shaker.—*Ref. PetSal 29D* Northwood Glass Co.—**Key A**

2. THISTLE AND CLOVER, salt shaker.—*Ref. PetSal 41X* Has a clover leaf on the other side.—**Key A**

3. BEADED BLOWER, salt shaker.—*Ref. PetSal 154-M* Indiana Tumbler and Goblet Co. Made in extended table service.—**Key B**

PLATE 125 FLOWERS

Row 1

1. TULIP BAND, goblet.—*Ref. Gob II-104*—**Key B**
2. BELLFLOWER, DOUBLE VINE (RIBBED LEAF; R.L.), pitcher.—*Ref. K6-6; L30* Boston and Sandwich, 1840's; McKee Brothers, 1868, and others. Flint and non-flint. Made in very extensive table service including rare cake stand, rare castor set, rare decanter, rare handled mug, lamps, six types compotes, tumbler, rare whiskey, wine, rare 6″ plate. Crystal, cobalt blue (rare), amber (rare), opaque.—**Key D**
3. BELLFLOWER, SINGLE VINE, plate. See above.

Row 2

1. GRASSHOPPER WITHOUT INSECT, pitcher.—*Ref. K1-88* Beaumont Glass Co., 1898. Extended table service including salt shaker, cruet, syrup, celery vase on legs, jelly compote, bowls, tumbler. See "insect", Plate 5. Crystal.—**Key B**
2. FLORICUT, pitcher.—*Ref. HV-160* U.S. Glass Co. (Glassport), 1916. Extended table service including bowls with stubby feet, handled sauce, tall and medium tumbler, vases, toothpick holder. Crystal; part pressed/part cut.—**Key B**

Row 3

1. MAGNOLIA (WATERLILY; FROSTED MAGNOLIA), pitcher.—*Ref. K4-136* Dalzell, Gilmore and Leighton, 1890. Extended table service including syrup, cake stand, sauce. Crystal, frosted.—**Key C**
2. WATERLILY AND CATTAILS, pitcher.—*Ref. K4-78* Northwood; Fenton; Diamond (Dugan) Glass Co., 1889. Extended table service including tumbler, 9″ and 10″ plates, celery vase. Crystal, opalescent, carnival (rare in lavender).—**Key A**

PLATE 126 FLOWERS

Row 1

1. CRANESBILL, pitcher.—*Ref. K1-62* c. 1890. Known in basic table service; not often found.—**Key B**

2. CARNATION, pitcher.—*Ref. K2-130* Lancaster Glass Co., 1911. Made in extended table service. Crystal, decorated.—**Key C**

Row 2

1. DEWDROPS AND FLOWERS (STIPPLED VIOLET), pitcher, and detail of creamer.—*Ref. K1-49* c. 1880. Extended table service.—**Key B**

2. WILDFLOWER, pitcher.—*Ref. K1-36; LV-6* Adams and Co.; U.S. Glass Co.; others; 1874, 1898. Extended table service including sauce, goblet, footed and flat butter dishes, tumbler, various rectangular bowls, round bowl, salt shaker. Crystal, amber, blue, green, amethyst, vaseline.—**Key B**

3. PRESSED SPRAY, pitcher.—*Ref. K4-133* Pattern is impressed on **inside** of bowl.—**Key A**

Row 3

1. PANELLED SUNFLOWER, goblet.—*Ref. Gob II-15* 1880's. Extended table service including celery vase, toothpick holder. Crystal, blue.—**Key B**

2. RIBBED FORGET-ME-NOT (PERT SET), creamer.—*Ref. K1-67* U.S. Glass Co. (Bryce), 1890-91. Extended table service including handled mustard with lid, individual creamer, toy table set. Crystal, amber (scarce), blue (scarce).—**Key B;** Toy set **Key C**

3. PANELLED SAGEBRUSH, goblet.—*Ref. Gob II-13*—**Key B**

Row 4

1. WREATH AND BARS, goblet.—*Ref. Gob II-16*—**Key A**

2. NEW MARTINSVILLE CARNATION, toothpick holder.—*Ref. Mil 17* New Martinsville Glass Co., after 1901. Crystal, rare ruby-stained.—**Key B**

3. FERN GARLAND (COLONIAL WITH GARLAND), creamer.—*Ref. K4-106* McKee Glass Co. c. 1894. Extended table service including salt shaker, cup, compotes, vase, compotes, celery vase, celery tray. Pieces are marked "Pres-Cut". Also made without the impressed garland. Crystal.—**Key A**

263

PLATE 127 FLOWERS

Row 1

1. FAN BAND (SCALLOPED FLOWER BAND; BRYCE YALE), goblet.—*Ref. K8-115; Gob II-25* Bryce Higbee and Co.; U.S. Glass. Made in extended table service including compote, tray, finger bowl, wine.—**Key A**

2. FAN BAND, pitcher. See above.

3. QUATREFOIL, pitcher. c. 1880's. Extended table service including rare goblet, salt shaker, open and covered sugar bowls, covered compote. A tumbler would be very rare. Crystal, apple green.—**Key B**

Row 2

1. SPRIG IN SNOW, salt shaker.—*Ref. PetSal 40C* —**Key B**

2. STIPPLED FLOWER BAND (STARFLOWER BAND), goblet.—*Ref. L153-2* —**Key A**

3. STIPPLED STARFLOWER, goblet.—*Ref. L153-7* Late 1880's. Extended table service including celery vase, footed salt, tumbler, wine.—**Key B**

Row 3

1. SPRIG (ROYAL), pitcher.—*Ref. L78* Bryce, Higbee and Co.; McKee and Brothers, 1880's. Extended table service including celery vase, wine (scarce), compotes, cake stand, sauces, tumbler, berry bowl. See Plate 166.—**Key B**

2. JEFFERSON #271, tumbler.—*Ref. K7-152* Jefferson Glass Co., 1903. Extended table service including bowls. Crystal, blue, green.—**Key A**

3. PANELLED DAISY (BRAZIL), creamer.—*Ref. L95* U.S. Glass Co. (Bryce), 1891. Extended table service including handled mug, tumbler, sugar shaker, salt shaker, tray, finger bowl, cake stand, tall open and covered compotes, syrup, decanter. Crystal, blue, milk glass.—**Key B**

PLATE 128 FLOWERS

Row 1

1. LILY-OF-THE-VALLEY, creamer.—*Ref. L126* Boston and Sandwich, 1870's. Made in extended table service including rare master salt, celery vase. Some pieces have three fragile-looking legs. Good availability. Pieces with "legs",—**Key D;** without, **Key C**

2. THISTLE, goblet.—*Ref. L-140* Bakewell, Pears and Co., 1875. Extended table service including egg cup (scarce), cruet, compote, tumbler.—**Key C**

3. FUSCHIA, goblet.—*Ref. K8-5* Boston and Sandwich, 1865. Extended table service including celery vase, cake stand, tumbler, 8" and 10" plates, open compote.—**Key B**

4. Un-named goblet by Lee (*Handbook, Plate 153 #13*).—**Key B**

Row 2

1. *CLEMATIS, sauce.—Ref. L-75; K3-25* c. 1876. Extended table service including 12" lamp with picture of pink cat in stem, relish.—**Key B**

2. PANSY AND MOSS ROSE (PANSY, MOSS ROSE AND LILY-OF-THE VALLEY), pitcher.—*Ref. K1-61* Extended table service.—**Key B**

3. BLEEDING HEART, tumbler.—*Ref. K1-8; L-128* King, Son and Co., 1870's; U.S. Glass Co., 1898. Extended table service including waste bowl, cake stand, compotes, cordial, egg cups, handled mug, flat and footed tumblers, oval and footed salts, pickle dish. Moderately available. Crystal, opaque.—**Key C**

Row 3

1. FLOWER AND QUILL (PRETTY BAND), pitcher.—*Ref. K3-52* 1880's. Extended table service including celery vase, bowl, pickle castor, square plate.—**Key B**

2. FORGET-ME-NOT IN SCROLL, goblet.—*Ref. L-77* c. 1870's. Extended table service.—**Key B**

3. DOUBLE BAND FORGET-ME-NOT, goblet.—*Ref. Gob II-47* —**Key B**

PLATE 129 FLOWERS

Row 1

1. SCROLL WITH FLOWERS, pitcher.—*Ref. K1-65; L-140* Central Glass Co., 1870's. Made in extended table service including relish, salt shaker, plate, egg cup, mustard jar. Crystal.—**Key B**

2. DAHLIA, creamer.—*Ref. K1-73; L-126* Canton Glass Co., c. 1880's. Extended table service including relish, wines, cordial, egg cup, mug, footed sauce, rare double egg cup, platter with grape handles, cake plate, rare champagne, good availability. Crystal, amber, canary, blue, green.—**Key C**

3. PRIMROSE, pitcher.—*Ref. L-136* Canton Glass Co., 1880's. Extended table service including compote, footed sauce, bowl, card receiver in basket, wine, cake stand. Crystal, colors, slag, opaque, black.—**Key A**

Row 2

1. DELAWARE (FOUR PETAL FLOWER; NEW CENTURY), pitcher.—*Ref. K1-103* U.S. Glass Co. #15065 (Bryce), 1899. A State Series pattern. Extended table service including banana boat, sauce, rose bowl, berry set, bride's basket, tumbler, celery vase, salt shaker, covered puff jar, custard cup, vase, cruet, two types toothpick holders, bowls, pin tray, tankard pitcher. A fairly abundant pattern. Crystal, rose-flashed, emerald green, custard, milk glass (scarce).—**Key B**

2. DOUBLE DAHLIA WITH LENS, creamer.—*Ref. K8-23* U.S. Glass Co., 1900. Extended table service including toothpick holder, wine. Crystal, stained flowers and leaves, rose-flashed, emerald green.—**Key B**

Row 3

1. HANGING BASKET, pitcher.—*Ref. K6-61* 1890's. Extended table service including tumbler, compote. Crystal, colors.—**Key B**

2. FLOWER POT (POTTED PLANT), pitcher.—*Ref. L-136; K1-87* 1880's. Extended table service including two size salt shakers, cake stand, bread tray, footed sauce, open compote. Crystal. —**Key C**

3. WILLOW OAK (OAK LEAF; STIPPLED STAR; ACORN; THISTLE; WREATH), creamer.—*Ref. K1-36; L-45* Bryce Brothers, 1880's; U.S. Glass Co., 1891. Extended table service including trays, plate, mug, salt shaker, tumbler, flanged sauce, footed sauce, celery vase, waste bowl, cake stand, bowl. Crystal, amber, blue.—**Key B**

PLATE 130 FLOWERS

Row 1

1. MORNING GLORY, egg cup.—*Ref. K6-3* Boston and Sandwich, 1860's. Made in extended table service including compote, rare individual salt dip, rare footed tumbler, rare creamer, honey dish, wine. Flint glass; rare and very expensive.—**Key F+**
2. WINDFLOWER, pitcher.—*Ref. L-139; K5-5* 1870's. Extended table service including compote, tumbler, egg cup, footed salt.—Older pieces **Key 3;** others **Key B**
3. SUNFLOWER (LILY), sugar bowl.—*Ref. K1-55* Atterbury and Co., 1881. Extended table service including bowl. Crystal, amber, blue, opalescent, mosaic glass.—**Key B**

Row 2

1. STYLIZED FLOWER (FLOWER AND PANEL), spoon holder.—*Ref. K2-127* Challinor, Taylor and Co., 1885; U.S. Glass Co., 1891. Basic table service and pitchers. Crystal, brown mosaic, opalescent.—**Key B**
2. PANELLED THISTLE, pitcher.—*Ref. K1-83; L-114* J. B. Higbee Glass Co., 1905-10. Extended table service including toothpick holder, flared cup, bowls, plate, salt shaker, handled spooner. May have "bee" trademark.—**Key C**
3. CRYSTAL ROCK, pitcher.—*Ref. K6 Pl. 34* U.S. Glass Co., 1905. Extended table service including tumbler, berry set. Crystal, decorated.—**Key B**

Row 3

POINSETTIA, pitcher.—*Ref. K7-186* Imperial Glass Co. #74, 1904. Crystal, carnival.—**Key B**

Row 4

1. THISTLE AND FERN, salt shaker.—*Ref. PetSal 42A*—**Key B**
2. LATE THISTLE (INVERTED THISTLE), sugar bowl.—*Ref. K1-114* Cambridge Glass Co., c. 1903. Marked "Near Cut" on inside of base about 1906. Extended table service including cruet, covered honey dish, cake stand, compote, tumbler. Crystal.—**Key B**

PLATE 131 FLOWERS

Row 1

1. GAELIC, pitcher.—*Ref. K4-122; Gob II-64* Indiana Glass Co., c. 1910. Made in extended table service including cruet, toothpick holder, bowls, punch cup, relish, salt shaker, tumbler, pickle tray, celery vase, heart-shaped dish. Crystal, decorated.—**Key A**

2. FLOWER WINDOWS, salt shaker.—*Ref. PetSal 29M*—**Key A**

3. FLOWER AND DIAMOND, pitcher.—*Ref. HV-170* U.S. Glass Co. #15147, 1913. Extended table service including scalloped cake stand, compotes, footed and flat bowls, tall celery with two handles, tumbler. Crystal.—**Key B**

Row 2

1. HEART STEM, pitcher.—*Ref. K4-7* c. 1890. Extended table service including salt shaker, celery vase, compotes, tumbler. —**Key C**

2. STIPPLED FORGET-ME-NOT, tumbler.—*Ref. L-128; K4-126* Findlay Glass Co., 1880's. Extended table service including salt shaker, mug, cake stands, celery vase, compotes, sauces, wine, plates with baby, star, or kitten motif; tumbler, syrup. Crystal, amber (rare), opalescent (rare).—**Key C**

Row 3

1. NORTHWOOD'S SUNFLOWER, salad plate. Northwood Glass Co. Crystal decorated.—**Key B**

2. ROSE POINT BAND (WATERLILY; CLEMATIS), creamer.—*Ref. K2-116; K7-28* Indiana Glass Co., 1913. Extended table service including sauce, compote, celery vase. Crystal. —**Key B**

Row 4

1. DIAGONAL BAND, pitcher.—*Ref. 1-140* c. 1880's. Extended table service including cake stand, relish, compotes, sauce. Fairly abundant. Crystal, apple green (scarce).—**Key A**

2. ARCH AND FORGET-ME-NOT BANDS, pitcher.—*Ref. K2-82* c. 1885. Extended table service including jam jar, tumbler, berry set, sauce. Has been found with advertising for "Henderson's Wild Cherry Beverage — Free". *(Ref. Kamm).*—**Key A**

PLATE 132 FLOWERS

Row 1

1. SUNK DAISY (KIRKLAND), goblet.—*Ref. K3-89; Gob. II-138* Cooperative Flint Glass Co., 1898. Made in extended table service including toothpick holder, salt shaker. Crystal, green, decorated.—**Key A**

2. FLOWER WITH CANE (DIAMOND GOLD), sugar bowl.—*Ref. K7-29* U.S. Glass Co. #15141 (Glassport), 1895-1912. Extended table service including tumbler, toothpick holder on fancy base, custard cup. Crystal, green-stained, ruby-stained.—**Key C**

3. PANELLED SUNBURSTS AND DAISY, pitcher.—*Ref. HV-170* U.S. Glass Co. #15146, 1915. Extended table service including 6½" compote, tall compotes, bowls, twin-handled celery vase. Crystal.—**Key B**

Row 2

1. ROSETTE WITH PINWHEELS, pitcher.—*Ref. K2-39* Indiana Glass Co. #171, 1905. Extended table service including square covered honey dish.—**Key B**

2. STARRED COSMOS, pitcher.—*Ref. K4-131* Indiana Glass Co. Crystal, decorated.—**Key B**

Row 3

1. FLORAL OVAL, pitcher.—*Ref. K5-97* John F. Higbee Glass Co., c. 1910; New Martinsville Glass Co. Extended table service including plate, rectangular bowl, jelly compote, wine.—**Key B**

2. TEASEL, plate. See Plate 42.

Row 4

1. RED SUNFLOWER, sauce.—*Ref. K2-116* Cambridge Glass Co. #2760, 1910. May be marked "Near-Cut". Called "Red Sunflower" even when not stained. Extended table service including salt shaker, tumbler, berry bowls, rose bowl, lamp, cruet. Crystal, ruby-stained.—**Key B**

2. ODD FELLOW, goblet.—*Ref. L-153-9* Adams and Co., early 1880's. Extended table service including celery vase, cake stand, platter.—**Key E**

3. GARDEN PINK, goblet.—*Ref. K5-148* Indiana Glass Co. #167, 1913. Extended table service.—**Key B**

PLATE 133 FLOWERS

Row 1

1. NARCISSUS SPRAY, pitcher.—*Ref. K4-137; L153-8* Indiana Glass Co., 1915-30's. Made in extended table service including tumbler, berry set. Crystal, decorated.—**Key A**

2. MARSH PINK (SQUARE FUSCHIA), open sugar bowl.—*Ref. K2-30* 1880's. Extended table service including salt shaker, pickle dish, cake stand, jam jar, bowls, 10″ plate. Crystal, amber (rare).—**Key C**

3. DAISY AND BUTTON WITH NARCISSUS (CLEAR LILY), pitcher.—*Ref. K4-139; LV34* 1880's; Indiana Glass Co., 1920's. Extended table service including salt shaker, wine, tumbler, footed bowl, compote, decanter, tray. Crystal, gold-flashed, decorated.—**Key B**

Row 2

1. JAPANESE IRIS, creamer.—*Ref. K8-58* New Martinsville Glass Co., c. 1910. Extended table service.—**Key B**

2. PANSY, pitcher.—*Ref. K6-24* c. 1910. Carnival glass.—**Key D**

3. FLORIDA (SUNKEN PRIMROSE), pitcher.—*Ref. K4-73* Greensburg Glass Co., 1893. Extended table service including salt shaker, square berry bowl, square sauce, tumbler, relish. Crystal, decorated.—**Key B**

Row 3

NARCISSUS SPRAY, plate. See Row 1, #1.

Row 4

1. THISTLEBLOW, pitcher.—*Ref. K6-45* Jenkins Glass Co., c. 1900. Extended table service including wine, punch cup.—**Key A**

2. FLOWER MEDALLION, creamer.—*Ref. K5-147* Indiana Glass Co., 1920. Extended table service including toothpick holder, berry bowl, sauce, tumbler.—**Key C**

3. BEADED TULIP, goblet.—*Ref. L-116; K3-127* McKee Glass Co., 1894. Extended table service including cake stand, bowls, ice cream dish, bread plate, champagne, water tray, wine, sauce, plate. —**Key B**

PLATE 134 FLOWERS

Row 1

1. DIAPERED FLOWER, mustard jar.—*Ref. K6-44* The diamonds have raised borders; those of "Quilted Phlox" are sunken. Opaque blue.—**Key D**

2. QUILTED PHLOX, syrup.—*Ref. PetSal 36-H* 1898-1905. Hobbs Glass Co. Extended table service including miniature lamp, toothpick, salt shaker, cruet, rose bowl. Crystal, opaque colors; cased; milk glass; later production in emerald and apple greens, lt. blue, amethyst.—**Key C**

Row 2

1. SPOTTED BOX, creamer.—*Ref. K4-111* Opaque glass.—**Key C**

2. LITTLE DAISY, creamer.—*Ref. K5-50* Same shape as "Sunflower", Plate 130, by Atterbury and Co., 1881.—**Key B**

Row 3

BEADED ACANTHUS, pitcher.—*Ref. K3-123* Imperial Glass Co. #78, 1904. To better show the pattern, writer did not depict stippled background, which is comprised of tiny daisies.—**Key C**

PLATE 135 FLOWERS

Row 1

1. PANELLED DIAMOND AND FLOWER, goblet.—*Ref. L164-7*
—**Key B**

2. SIX PANSY (PANSY), salt shaker.—*Ref. K6-78* Consolidated Lamp and Glass Co. Made in extended table service including salt shaker, toothpick holder. Not made in crystal; opaque colors.

3. PERIWINKLE, salt shaker.—*Ref. PetSal 35i*—**Key B**

Row 2

1. BULLS-EYE AND DAISY, syrup. See Plate 26.

2. JEWELLED MOON AND STAR, salt shaker. See Plates 29, 232.

3. QUEEN'S JEWELS (QUEEN'S NECKLACE; CROWN JEWELS), creamer.—*Ref. K3-78.* Bellaire Goblet Co.; U.S. Glass Co., 1898. Extended table service including cruet, cologne bottle, pickle jar. See also Plate 232. Crystal.—**Key C**

Row 3

1. COREOPSIS, syrup.—*Ref. K5-52* c. 1902. Extended table service including stubby syrup, berry set, cracker jar. Decorated milk glass; no crystal.—**Key D**

2. HONEYCOMB WITH FLOWER RIM (VERMONT; INVERTED THUMBPRINT WITH DAISY BAND; VERMONT HONEYCOMB), pitcher.—*Ref. K2-117; K6 Pl. 19.* U.S. Glass Co. #15060, 1899; 1903. A State Series pattern for Vermont when in decorated opaque glass (custard). The honeycomb design is pressed from inside and doesn't show on opaque pieces. Made in extended table service including vase, salt shaker, toothpick, waste bowl, pickle tray, tumbler, card tray with handle on top, berry set, candlestick. Opaque pieces are moderately rare; clear pieces have been reproduced. Crystal, blue, green, custard.—**Key A**

PLATE 136 FLOWERS

Row 1

1. LATE ROSETTE, mug.—*Ref. K1-35* May have been a prize in packages of oatmeal, coffee, etc.—*(Ref. Kamm).* Known in crystal, amber and blue.—**Key B**
2. ROSETTE, salt shaker. See Row 4, #3.
3. ROMAN ROSETTE, syrup. See Plates 11, 31.

Row 2

1. FLOWERED OVAL, goblet. See Plate 26.
2. DOUBLE DAISY (ROSETTE BANDS), pitcher.—*Ref. K7-23* Probably U.S. Glass, c. 1893—*(Ref. Heacock).* Extended table service including rare compote.—**Key B**
3. ROSETTE ROW, salt shaker.—*Ref. PetSal 38E*—**Key A**

Row 3

1. SHASTA DAISY, creamer.—*Ref. K6-25* Extended table service. Crystal, opaque glass.—**Key B**
2. SEXTEC, berry creamer.—*Ref. K6 Pl. 24* McKee Glass Co., 1894. Extended table service including punch bowl syrup, cruet, salt shaker, pickle jar, orange bowl, plates, cup, handled nut bowl. —**Key B**

Row 4

1. ALABAMA, salt shaker. See Plate 20.
2. FANCY FANS, sugar shaker.—*Ref. HIII-49* Milk Glass. May be painted.—**Key D**
3. ROSETTE (MAGIC), pitcher.—*Ref. L-106; K4-46; K7-102* U.S. Glass Co. (Bryce), 1891. Extended table service including plate, tray, salt shaker, covered bowl, jelly compote, tall celery vase, fish relish, handled plate. Crystal.—**Key B**

283

PLATE 137 FLOWERS

Row 1

1. FLOWER BAND BARREL, salt shaker.—*Ref. PetSal 21U* Milk Glass.—**Key C**
2. DAHLIA AND LEAF, plate (author's name).—**Key B**
3. FISHNET AND POPPIES, syrup.—*Ref. HIII-24* c. 1895. Known in milk glass syrup.—**Key E**

Row 2

1. ASTER AND LEAF (TAPERED VINE), syrup.—*Ref. K7-pl. 63; PetSal 21J* Beaumont Glass Co. #217, 1895. Made in condiment items including salt shaker, sugar shaker. Colors only.—**Key C**
2. COSMOS (STEMLESS DAISY), syrup.—*Ref. K5-53* Consolidated Lamp and Glass Co., 1898-1905. Extended table service including berry set, condiment set, salt shaker, miniature lamp, perfume bottles, pickle castor, trays. Opaque and cased colors.—**Key D**
3. FLOWER BAND-WARMAN'S, salt shaker.—*Ref. W-140* Milk Glass.—**Key B**

Row 3

1. BEAUMONT'S FLORA, toothpick holder.—*Ref. K7-59* Beaumont Glass Co. #99, 1898. Extended table service including salt shaker, cruet, tumbler, syrup, celery vase on legs, jelly compote, bowls. Emerald green, opalescent colors.—**Key D**
2. JUMBO, creamer. See Plate 3. Without the elephant, prices are lower.

Row 4

1. FLOWER BASKET, salt shaker.—*Ref. PetSal 29H*—**Key B**
2. APPLE BLOSSOM, syrup.—*Ref. HI-50* Northwood Glass Co., c. 1896. Extended table service including sugar shaker, tumbler, cake stand, compote, cruet, miniature lamp, berry set, salt shaker. Decorated milk glass.—**Key D**

PLATE 138 FLOWERS

Row 1

1. PLEATED MEDALLION, creamer.—*Ref. K3-91* New Martinsville Glass Co., c. 1908. Made in extended table service including toothpick holder, cake stand.—**Key B**

2. FLOWER FLANGE (DEWEY), pitcher.—*Ref. K1-84* Indiana Tumbler and Goblet Co., 1898. Extended table service including cruet, plate, tray, tumbler, salt shaker. Crystal, canary, amber, blue, green, chocolate.—**Key C**

3. DAISY MEDALLION (SUNBURST MEDALLION), spoon holder.—*Ref. K5-35* 1880's. Extended table service including compote, cake stand. Crystal.—**Key A**

Row 2

1. BARRED FORGET-ME-NOT, pitcher.—*Ref. L132* Canton Glass Co., 1883. Extended table service including cake plates, compotes, cordial, wine, square handled pickle dish, relish. Fairly abundant. Crystal, canary, vaseline, amber, blue, apple green. —**Key C**

2. TRIANGULAR MEDALLION, goblet.—*Ref. K8-70* —**Key A**

3. SCROLLED SUNFLOWER, spoon holder.—*Ref. K6-53* Known in basic table service.—**Key A**

Row 3

1. STIPPLED DAISY, tumbler,—*Ref. L-101; K3-85* 1880's. Comes clear and stippled. Extended table service including sauce, wine, open compote, relish, open and covered sugar bowls. Crystal.—**Key A**

2. DAISY AND PALM, goblet.—*Ref. Gob II-86* Known in amethyst goblet.—**Key C**

3. INTAGLIO SUNFLOWER, creamer.—*Ref. K7-53* U.S. Glass Co. #15125 (Glassport), 1911. Extended table service including tall covered jar, toothpick holder. Crystal, decorated.—**Key B**

Row 1

1. MAINE (PANELLED FLOWER STIPPLED), salt shaker.—*Ref. K4-86; L77; LV 52* U.S. Glass Co. #15066, 1899. A State Series pattern. Extended table service including rare green syrup, cake stand, compote, bowls, mug, toothpick holder, salt shaker, open and covered sugar bowls, wine. No goblets were made. Limited availability. Crystal, emerald green, decorated.—**Key B**

2. PANELLED DAISIES FINECUT, goblet.—*Ref. Gob II-116* —**Key B**

3. MAINE, pitcher. See above.

Row 2

1. PANELLED FORGET-ME-NOT, goblet.—*Ref. K3-43; L130* U.S. Glass Co. (Bryce), 1891; Also Doyle and Co. Extended table service including salt shaker, bread tray, celery vase, cake stand, jam jar, footed sauce, handled sauce, wine, bowls. Crystal, amber, canary, blue, green.—**Key C**

2. LACY FLORAL, creamer.—*Ref. K5-114* Westmoreland Glass Co., c. 1905. Extended table service including syrup. Crystal, milk glass, decorated.—**Key B**

Row 3

1. THE MOSAIC (DAISY AND BLUEBELL), creamer.—*Ref. K1-93* Mosaic Glass Co. #51, 1891. Extended table service. —**Key B**

2. FLOWER FAN (SNOWFLOWER), creamer.—*Ref. PetSal 151-0* U.S. Glass Co. #35135 (Bryce), 1912. Extended table service including salt shaker, cruet, tumbler, high compote, cake stand, pickle dish, vase. Crystal.—**Key B**

3. FLOWER BAND-LEE'S, goblet.—*Ref. L107* c. 1870. Extended table service including celery vase, covered compote, footed sauce.—**Key B**

PLATE 140 FRUIT - PEARS

Row 1

1. BARTLETT PEAR, bowl.—*Ref. LV pl. 72; Gob. II* Duncan glass. Extended table service.—**Key C**

2. SWEET PEAR (SUGAR PEAR; AVOCADO), creamer.—*Ref. K4-111; Gob I-116* Indiana Glass Co. #601 (Dunkirk factory), 1922-33. Extended table service including 10″ plate. Crystal, light green, canary, pink.—**Key A**

Row 2

SWEET PEAR, plate. See above.

Row 3

BOSC PEAR, pitcher.—*Ref. K7-27* Indiana Glass Co. (Dunkirk), 1913. Extended table service including celery vase, tumbler. Crystal, flashed purple pears, gold leaves.—**Key A**

Row 4

1. BALTIMORE PEAR (GIPSY; FIG; MARYLAND; TWIN PEAR), goblet.—*Ref. L66; L154-10; K1-31* Adams and Co., 1874; U.S. Glass Co., 1891. Made in extended table service including celery vase, open and covered sugar bowls, covered compote. Crystal.—**Key C**

2. BALTIMORE PEAR, creamer. See above.

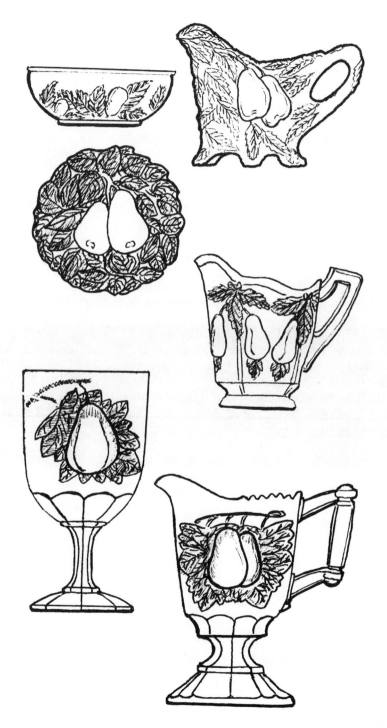

PLATE 141 FRUIT

Row 1

1. STIPPLED PEPPERS, pitcher.—*Ref. Lee* Boston and Sandwich, 1870's. Made in extended table service including footed tumbler, egg cup, footed salt, sauce. Crystal.—**Key B**

2. CORNUCOPIA, pitcher.—*Ref. K2-125* Reverse side of pitcher has a spray of cherries. c. 1885-90. Extended table service including covered compote, celery vase, cordial, wine, berry bowl.—**Key B**

Row 2

1. PINEAPPLE, pitcher.—*Ref. K8-21; LV pl. 38* Hobbs, Brockunier & Co., 1886. Extended table service including celery vase, tumbler. Crystal, opalescent colors.—**Key A**

2. CHERRY AND FIG, pitcher.—*Ref. K1-45* Extended table service.—**Key B**

Row 3

1. NORTHWOOD PEACH, creamer.—*Ref. K5-132* Northwood Glass Co., 1920. Extended table service including ruffled-edge bowl. Crystal; carnival glass.—**Key D**

2. APPLE AND GRAPE IN SCROLL, cruet.—*Ref. HIII-54* Fostoria Glass Co., 1898. Known in cruet and toothpick holder. —**Key E**

3. HEISEY'S PLANTATION (FLORIDA PINEAPPLE; PLANTATION), salt shaker.—*Ref. PetSal 169B* A. H. Heisey Co. Extended table service including 8" plate, sugar castor, sauce.—**Key B**

PLATE 142 FRUIT-CHERRIES

Row 1

1. WREATHED CHERRY, creamer.—*Ref. K7-26* Dugan Glass Co. Made in extended table service. Some pieces have cherries in relief on inside of bowl as well as outside. Crystal, opalescent, slag. —**Key B**

2. CHERRY SPRIG, creamer.—*Ref. K2-58* Blown glass, not pressed. Made in extended table service.—**Key B**

Row 2

1. STIPPLED CHERRY, pitcher.—*Ref. K4-132* 1880's. Extended table service including tumbler, bread plate, 6″ plate, berry bowl, celery vase, sauce, mug, relish.—**Key C**

2. GRAPE AND CHERRY, creamer.—*Ref. K1-94* Westmoreland Glass Co. A milk glass sugar and creamer set.—**Key C**

Row 3

1. CHERRY AND CABLE (PANELLED CHERRY; CHERRY THUMBPRINTS), sugar bowl.—*Ref. K5-63* Northwood Glass Co., 1880's. Extended table service including compotes, berry bowl, tumbler, syrup, sauce. Crystal, decorated.—**Key B**

2. CHERRY, goblet.—*Ref. L-19,66* Bakewell, Pears and Co., c. 1870. Extended table service including wine, open and covered compotes, sauce. Crystal, opalescent.—**Key C**

Row 4

1. CHERRY LATTICE, creamer. Northwood Glass Co., 1890's-1900's. Extended table service including berry set, compote.—**Key B**

2. CHERRY WITH THUMBPRINTS, pitcher.—*Ref. K4-104* Jenkins Glass Co. (Kokomo), 1920's. Extended table service including berry set, sauces, tumbler, lemonade, wine, toothpick holder, syrup, covered bowls, mug.—**Key D**

PLATE 143 FRUIT - STRAWBERRIES

Row 1

1. STRAWBERRY AND CABLE (FALMOUTH STRAWBERRY), goblet.—*Ref. Gob II-39* Extended table service.—**Key B**

2. STRAWBERRY AND CURRENT, goblet.—*Ref. L-151* c. 1880. Extended table service including syrup, celery vase, covered cheese dish, footed sauce, tumbler.—**Key C**

3. INVERTED STRAWBERRY, goblet.—*Ref. Gob II-48* Cambridge Glass Co., c. 1908. Extended table service including cruet, salt dip, tumbler, toy table service. No toothpick holder made originally.—**Key B;** Toy service **Key C**

Row 2

1. STRAWBERRY WITH CHECKERBOARD, creamer.—*Ref. K4-103* Jenkins Glass Co., c. 1920.—**Key A**

2. STIPPLED STRAWBERRY, pitcher.—*Ref. K1-117* U.S. Glass Co. (Gas City). Made in extended table service.—**Key B**

Row 3

1. STRAWBERRY (FAIRFAX STRAWBERRY), covered compote.—*Ref. L-151* Boston and Sandwich, 1860's. Made in extended table service including pickle dish, handled plate, compote, egg cup, syrup, flat and footed sauces. Crystal, milk glass.—**Key C**

2. PANELLED STRAWBERRY, pitcher.—*Ref. K4-89* Indiana Glass Co. #127, c. 1913. Extended table service including tumbler, celery vase, three size sauce dishes. Crystal, rose, decorated. —**Key B**

PLATE 144 FRUIT - BERRIES

Row 1

1. DEWBERRY, pitcher.—*Ref. K7-11* c. 1890.—**Key A**
2. BLACKBERRY, pitcher.—*Ref. K8-25; L-151* Hobbs, Brockunier and Co., 1870; Phoenix Glass Co., 1930's. Made in extended table service including rare celery vase, rare oval dish, single and double egg cups, syrup, compotes, wine, tumbler, sauce, honey dish, footed salt, lamps, champagne. Pitcher is rare but is being reproduced. Crystal, milk glass.—Milk glass **Key D**; Crystal **Key B**

Row 2

1. RASPBERRY, pitcher.—*Ref. K4-61* Late 1870's. Extended table service including tray, compotes, celery vase, tumbler.—**Key B**
2. BARBERRY, spooner.—*Ref. K1-9* McKee Glass Co.; Boston and Sandwich; 1860's; 1880's. Extended table service including wine, cordial, celery vase, cake plate, egg cup, footed salt, sauce, syrup. Good availability.—**Key B**
3. BARBERRY, goblet. See above.

Row 3

1. GOOSEBERRY, pitcher.—*Ref. L-166* Sandwich glass, 1870's. Extended table service including covered compotes, honey dish, lemonade glass, pickle dish, sauce, handled tumbler, bar tumbler, syrup, cake stand. Crystal, opaque white.—**Key C**
2. BLACKBERRY BAND, goblet.—*Ref. Gob II-62* —**Key B**
3. BERRY CLUSTER, pitcher. Extended table service including celery vase, open and covered sugar bowls, compote.—**Key C**

PLATE 145 FRUIT - GRAPES

Row 1

1. BEADED GRAPE (CALIFORNIA), creamer.—*Ref. K4-94* U.S. Glass Co. #15059 (Bryce; Ripley), 1899. A State Series pattern. Extended table service including cake stand, cordial, compotes, round and square pitchers, toothpick holder, 6" vase, wine, bowls, tray, pickle dish, sauces, salt shaker, tumblers, berry set, bread plate. Good availability. Crystal, emerald green.—**Key C**

2. PANELLED GRAPE (MAPLE), spoon holder.—*Ref. K3-61; L64* Kokomo Glass Co. after 1904. Extended table service including salt shaker, toothpick holder, cup, covered compote, bowl. Crystal, amber, other colors, milk glass.—**Key A**

Row 2

1. PALM BEACH, cruet.—*Ref. LV58* U.S. Glass Co. #15119 (Glassport), 1909. Made in extended table service including tumbler, sauce, jelly compote, wine, cruet, salt shaker, celery vase. Crystal, decorated, carnival, opalescent.—**Key B**

2. GRAPE WITH HOLLY BAND, pitcher.—*Ref. L154-16* Extended table service.—**Key B**

Row 3

1. LOGANBERRY AND GRAPE (BLACKBERRY AND GRAPE), pitcher and reverse side detail.—*Ref. K1-45* Dalzall, Gilmore and Leighton, mid-1880's. Extended table service including tumbler, celery vase, two types goblet.—**Key B**

2. GRAPE AND GOTHIC ARCHES, goblet.—*Ref. K1-101* Northwood Glass Co., c. 1890. Extended table service including plate. Crystal, milk glass, green.—**Key C**

Row 4

1. GRAPE WITH THUMBPRINT, pitcher.—*Ref. L164-4; K5-96* c. 1890's. Extended table service including salt shaker, toothpick holder, cup, covered compote, bowl. Crystal, colors, milk glass. —**Key C**

2. ARCHED GRAPE, pitcher.—*Ref. L64* Boston and Sandwich, 1870's. Extended table service including high and low compotes, cordial. Crystal.—**Key B**

3. GRAPE BUNCH, goblet. Sandwich glass, c. 1870's. Extended table service including compote, egg cup. Crystal.—**Key B**

PLATE 146 FRUIT - GRAPES

Row 1

1. RIBBED GRAPE, spoon holder.—*Ref. L-36* c. 1850. Extended table service including cordial, celery vase, compotes.—**Key D**
2. GRAPE WITHOUT VINE, creamer.—*Ref. K4-73* —**Key A**
3. GRAPE WITH VINE, creamer.—*Ref. K2-60* c. 1890's. Made in extended table service including celery vase, honey dish, salt shaker, compotes, berry bowl, sauce. Crystal, decorated.—**Key B**

Row 2

RIBBED GRAPE, plate. See Row 1 #1.

Row 3

1. BOHEMIAN GRAPE, pitcher.—*Ref. HV-40* U.S. Glass Co., 1899. Made in juice pitcher and tumbler. Crystal, emerald green, rose-flashed. Scarce.—**Key D**
2. GRAPE WITH OVERLAPPING FOLIAGE, pitcher.—*Ref. K2-48* Hobbs, Brockunier and Co., 1870's. Extended table service including celery vase. Crystal, milk glass.—**Key B**
3. BRADFORD GRAPE (BRADFORD BLACKBERRY), pitcher.—*Ref. K5-25; Gob I-15; LV pl. 22* c. 1850-60. Extended table service including champagne, cordial, wine, rare tumbler.—**Key D**

Row 4

1. LATE PANELLED GRAPE, creamer.—*Ref. K1-96* Beatty-Brady Glass Co.; Indiana Glass Co., late 1890's. Extended table service including wine, syrup, berry set.—**Key B**
2. CURRANT, pitcher.—*Ref. K8-8; L153-20* Campbell, Jones and Co., c. 1871. Extended table service including compotes, cordial, egg cup, footed tumbler, wine, cake stands.—**Key C**
3. GRAPE BAND, goblet.—*Ref. L64; K1-8* Bryce, Walker and Co., c. 1869. Extended table service including wine, compote, egg cup, pickle dish, footed salt.—**Key B**

PLATE 147 FRUIT - GRAPES

Row 1

1. BEADED GRAPE MEDALLION, spoon holder.—*Ref. L-66* Boston Silver Glass Co., 1869-1871. Variations in pattern are found — some not banded; some with extra grapes, etc. Made in extended table service including egg cup, open salt, celery vase, compote, pickle dish. Fair availability.—**Key C**

2. ASHBURTON WITH GRAPE BAND, tumbler. Tumbler known.—**Key C**

3. MAGNET AND GRAPE, tumbler.—*Ref. L-63* Boston and Sandwich, c. 1870. Has stippled or frosted leaf. Extended table service including syrups, celery vase, tumbler, bowls.—Flint **Key D**

Row 2

1. GRAPE WITH SCROLL MEDALLION, creamer.—*Ref. K2-56* c. 1880. Extended table service.—**Key B**

2. GRAPE AND FESTOON WITH SHIELD, creamer.—*Ref. K1-13* Sandwich, early; Doyle and Co., 1870's. Extended table service including egg cup, compotes, celery vase, mug, sauce. Crystal, blue.—**Key C**

Row 3

1. STIPPLED GRAPE AND FESTOON, goblet.—*Ref. L-63* Doyle and Co., 1870. Extended table service including egg cup, compote, celery vase, wine, cordial.—**Key B**

2. GRAPE AND FESTOON WITH SHIELD, goblet.—*Ref. L-65* This is a variation by Portland. See Row 2 #2.

3. GRAPE AND FESTOON, goblet.—*Ref. L-65* Portland Glass Co., 1860's. Extended table service including celery vase, plate, bowls, pickle dish, cordial, compotes, fairly abundant.—**Key B**

4. GRAPE AND FESTOON (FESTOON AND GRAPE), goblet. A variation on preceding pattern.

Row 4

1. PANELLED GRAPE BAND, pickle dish. Extended table service including covered compote.—**Key B**

2. EARLY PANELLED GRAPE BAND, open salt.—*Ref. Gob II-21* c. 1870's. Extended table service including celery vase, egg cup. —**Key B**

3. FRUIT BAND, salt shaker.—*Ref. PetSal 29-S* —**Key B**

PLATE 148 HOBNAILS AND BEADS

Row 2

1. HOBNAIL BAND (GARTER BAND), pitcher.—*Ref. K2-131; Gob II-95* c. 1890. Made in extended table service including sauce, tumbler, plates, cup and saucer, coaster, celery tray, champagne, bowls, candlesticks, wine.—**Key B**
2. HOBNAIL BAND, goblet. See above.
3. POPCORN, goblet.—*Ref. L-25* Boston and Sandwich, 1860's. Extended table service including goblet without ear of corn, sauce, wine.—**Key D**

Row 2

1. HOBNAIL, open salt dish.—*Ref. L80-83* Beatty, New Brighton, McKee, Gillander, others over many years. Very extended table service including novelties, finger lamp, mug, perfume bottles, lamp-shades, toothpick holders, trays, vases, soap dishes. Crystal, amber, canary, blue.—**Key B**
2. HOBNAIL, BALLFOOT, creamer.—*Ref. L-81* —**Key B**
3. RAINDROP, sauce dish.—*Ref. L-61* A flattened hobnail, c. 1880's. Extended table service including celery vase, miniature lamp, tumbler, compotes. Doyle's RAINDROP is called "Dot" (Plate 27). Crystal, amber, blue, light green (rare).—**Key B**

Row 3

1. BEADED TRIANGLE, salt shaker.—*Ref. PetSal 154S* Probably McKee Glass Co. c. 1902—*(Ref. Heacock).* Chocolate glass. Extended table service including toothpick holder. Scarce.
2. ACORN, syrup.—*Ref. PetSal 21A* Hobbs Glass Co.; Beaumont Glass Co. #220, 1890-1900. Made only in syrup, salt shaker, sugar shaker, mustard, and toothpick holder.—**Key C**
3. HOBB'S HOBNAIL, creamer.—*Ref. HV-125* U.S. Glass Co. (Hobbs), 1891. Made in water set — tumbler, pitchers, tray, finger bowl, butter dish, toy water set. All colors.—**Key B**

Row 4

DEW AND RAINDROP, cup.—*Ref. K4-113; L57-69* Kokomo Glass Co., 1901-05. Extended table service including tumbler, small covered compote, cordial, wine, salt shaker, sauce, sherbet, berry bowl. Crystal, ruby-flashed.—**Key B**

PLATE 149 HOBNAILS AND BEADS

Row 1

1. PANELLED DEWDROP, goblet.—*Ref. K5-31; K7-11* Campbell, Jones and Co., c. 1878. Made in extended table service including cordial, wine, celery vase, footed sauce, jam jar.—**Key B**
2. HOBNAIL WITH THUMBPRINT BASE, salt shaker.—*Ref. K1-70; K7-109* Doyle and Co.; U.S. Glass Co., 1880-1895. Extended table service including toy table set, toy tray, toothpick holder. Crystal, amber, blue, ruby-stained.—**Key B**
3. DOUBLE-EYE HOBNAIL WITH DECORATIVE BAND, cup and detail of Kamm's variation.—*Ref. L-82; K1-57* Columbia Glass Co., 1889; U.S. Glass, 1891. Extended table service including tumbler, open salt, mug, rectangular and round bowls, toothpick holder, ink stand. Crystal, blue, amber.—**Key B**

Row 2

1. FLATTENED HOBNAIL, goblet.—*Ref. L71* Extended table service including salt shaker.—**Key B**
2. DEWDROP (HOBNAIL) creamer.—*Ref. L-71* Columbia Glass Co.; U.S. Glass Co., 1891. Advertised in same set as Double-Eye Hobnail. Extended table service including sugar shaker, salt shaker, wine, castor set, syrup.—**Key B**
3. HOBNAIL WITH FAN, goblet.—*Ref. L-71* Adams and Co. #150. Extended table service including celery vase, tray, sauce, celery vase, berry bowl.—**Key B**

Row E

1. HOBNAIL "PINEAPPLE", barber bottle. Novelty item.
2. HOBNAIL WITH BARS (HOBNAIL IN BIG DIAMOND), creamer.—*Ref. LV-66* U.S. Glass Co. (Challinor #307), 1891. Extended table service including pieces with vertical bars not set into diamonds. See Plate 151.—**Key B**
3. PANELLED HOBNAIL, creamer.—*Ref. K1-67* Bryce Brothers, c. 1880. Extended table service including wine, open and covered compotes. Crystal, opaque white, canary, vaseline.—**Key B**

PLATE 150 HOBNAILS AND BEADS

Row 1

1. PANELLED BEADS, creamer.—*Ref. K8-33; Gob II-99* c. 1900. Extended table service.—**Key A**
2. DEWDROP WITH STAR, pitcher.—*Ref. K3-67* Campbell, Jones and Co., 1877. A star is on the base. Made in extended table service including cake plate, tumbler, lamp, flat and footed sauces, celery vase, pickle dish, several sizes plates, cheese dish, cake stand, compotes.—**Key B**

Row 2

GRATED RIBBON (BEADED PANELS), goblet.—*Ref. K1-54; Gob. II-96* Crystal Glass Co., 1877. Extended table service. See Plate 213.—**Key A**

Row 3

1. SEDAN (PANELLED STAR AND BUTTON), pitcher.—*Ref. K1-15; Gob. II-19* c. 1870's. Extended table service including sauce, wine, open and covered sugar bowls, salt shaker.—**Key B**
2. DOYLE'S #240, pitcher.—*Ref. K7-pl.10* Doyle and Co., 1870's; U.S. Glass Co. Made in water set — tumbler, pitchers, tray. —**Key B**

Row 4

PRINTED HOBNAIL, goblet and detail. See Plate 28.

Row 5

BUTTON BAND, goblet. See Plate 26.

Row 6 .

1. BANDED RAINDROPS, salt shaker. See Plate 29.
2. DEWDROP AND ZIG-ZAG, pitcher.—*Ref. HV-94* U.S. Glass Co. (Challinor #418), 1891. Made in limited items. Crystal, purple slag.—**Key B**

PLATE 151 HOBNAILS AND BEADS

Row 1

1. BEADED DART BAND, goblet. See Plate 81.
2. PEAS AND PODS, wine goblet.—*Ref. HV-73* U.S. Glass Co. (Bryce), 1891. Made in wine set — decanter, wine goblet, tray. Crystal, ruby-stained.—**Key C**
3. ZENITH, cruet.—*Ref. HIII-57* c. 1905. Cruet and salt shaker known. Crystal, pale blue (scarce).—**Key D**

Row 2

1. BARRED HOBNAIL (WINONA), creamer,—*Ref. K1-113; K8-162; LV56; Gob II-82* Brilliant Glass Works, 1888. Extended table service including salt shaker, sauce, bowls. Crystal, opalescent, colors.—**Key B**
2. GONTERMAN, pitcher.—*Ref. Gob I* George Duncan and Sons, 1880's. Extended table service including footed sauce, salt shaker, covered compotes, tray.—**Key B**

Row 3

1. HOBNAIL WITH BARS, cruet. See Plate 149.
2. LOOP WITH DEWDROP, creamer.—*Ref. K1-72; L-79* U.S. Glass Co. #15028, 1892. Extended table service including several size bowls, cake stands, compotes, celery vase, mug, syrup, wine, tumbler, salt shaker. Crystal.—**Key B**
3. SEEDPOD, salt shaker.—*Ref. PetSal 172-F* Extended table service including wine, tumbler, sauce, bowl. Crystal, colors. —**Key B**

PLATE 152 HOBNAILS AND BEADS

Row 1

1. BEAD COLUMN, creamer.—*Ref. K7-12* Probably Kokomo Glass Co. (*Heacock: Pattern Glass Preview #1*), c. 1905. Basic table service.—**Key A**

2. BEADED MEDALLION (BEADED MIRROR), pitcher.—*Ref. K1-39* Boston and Sandwich Glass Co., late 1860's to early 1870's. Made in extended table service including egg cup, compote, open salt, celery vase.—**Key C**

3. CORD DRAPERY (INDIANA), creamer. See Plate 63.

Row 2

1. DEWDROP IN POINTS, pitcher.—*Ref. K3-13* Greensburg Glass Co., c. 1875-85. Extended table service including cake stand, pickle dish, footed sauce, compotes, bread plate, celery vase. Fairly abundant.—**Key B**

2. BEADED PANEL, pitcher.—*Ref. K7-15* Indiana Tumbler and Goblet Co.; later Jenkins Glass Co. Extended table service including compote, egg cup, wine, salt shaker.—**Key B**

3. SCALLOPED TAPE (JEWEL BAND), pitcher.—*Ref. K2-29* Extended table service including tray, celery vase, cake stand, sauce, wine, egg cup. Crystal, amber, canary, blue, apple green.—**Key A**

Row 3

1. WELLSBURG, creamer.—*Ref. K5-63* National Glass Co. #681 (Dalzell factory), 1901. Extended table service.—**Key B**

2. POWDER AND SHOT, goblet.—*Ref. L79* Boston and Sandwich; Portland Glass; possibly others. Extended table service including master salt, sauce, egg cup, tumbler, celery vase, castor bottle. —**Key E**

Row 4

1. OVAL AND FANS, salt shaker.—*PetSal 1-D* Slag.—**Key D**

2. BEADED BULB, salt shaker.—*Ref. PetSal 22F* An opaque novelty.—**Key B**

3. BEAD AND PANEL (CHRISTMAS PEARLS), salt shaker.—*Ref. PetSal 154H* Opalescent-to-clear glass.—**Key C**

4. WISCONSIN (BEADED DEWDROP), salt shaker.—*Ref. L57; K7-46* U.S. Glass Co. #15079 (Gas City), 1903. A State Series pattern. Extended table service including many sizes bowls, cruet, syrup, compotes, mug, tumbler, wine, handled sauce, two types salt shaker, cake stand, celery tray and vase, condiment set in holder, sugar shaker, master salt, square plate, cup and saucer. Moderate availability. Crystal. See plate 153.—**Key B**

315

PLATE 153 HOBNAILS AND BEADS

Row 1
1. BEADED OVAL AND SCROLL, pitcher. See Plate 23.
2. BEADED ELLIPSE AND FAN, creamer.—*Ref. K2-94* U.S. Glass Co., c. 1905.—**Key B**
3. LACY SPIRAL (COLUSSUS), pitcher.—*Ref. K4-57* 1880's. Extended table service including open and covered compotes, jelly compote, relish dish, celery vase.—**Key A**

Row 2
1. CORD AND TASSEL, pitcher.—*Ref. L-116* Central Glass Co., 1872. Extended table service including compote, wine, mug, cordial, egg cup, sauce, bowls, cake stand, celery vase, lamp, tumbler. —**Key C**
2. JEWEL AND FESTOON (LOOP AND JEWEL), spoon holder.—*Ref. K1-66* Beatty-Brady Glass Co.; Indiana Glass Co., 1880's. Extended table service including bowls, salt shaker, sherbet, relish, master salt.—**Key B**
3. GARFIELD DRAPE (CANADIAN DRAPE), creamer. —*Ref. L-104* Adams and Co., 1880's. Extended table service including bread plate, cake stand, compotes, memorial plates, sauce, pickle dish, honey dish. Note: Campbell, Jones and Co. also made a memorial plate.—**Key C**

Row 3
1. WISCONSIN, compote. See Plate 152.
2. CHAIN AND SWAG, syrup.—*Ref. HIII-50* Milk Glass—**Key C**
3. BEADED BAND, cordial.—*Ref. L-61* c. 1884. Extended table service including syrup, compote, salt shaker, wine. Crystal; rare in color.—**Key B**

Row 4
ARCHAIC GOTHIC, creamer.—*Ref. K2-20* Basic table service.—**Key B**

Row 5
1. FESTOON, pitcher.—*Ref. L-166; K1-93* Portland Glass Co., 1880's. Extended table service including cake plate, berry set, sauce, tray, tumbler, bowls, pickle jar, 7″, 8″ and 9″ plates, wine, celery vase.—**Key B**
2. JEWEL WITH DEWDROP, salt shaker. See Plate 23.
3. TASSEL AND BEAD, salt shaker. See Plate 37.

PLATE 154 HOBNAILS AND BEADS

Row 1

1. GEORGIA GEM (LITTLE GEM), pitcher.—*Ref. K7-60* Tarentum Glass Co., c. 1900. Extended table service including toothpick holder.—**Key C**

2. RIBBED WARE (BAR AND BEAD), pitcher.—*Ref. K4-65; K8-169* U.S. Glass Co. (Gillander), 1891. Extended table service. See Plate 209. Crystal.—**Key A**

Row 2

1. FRAMED JEWEL, pitcher.—*Ref. K5-77* Canton Glass Co. #140, 1893. Extended table service.—**Key B**

2. BEADED BAND AND PANEL, wine goblet.—**Key A**

Row 3

1. COLORADO, salt shaker.—*Ref. K2-115* U.S. Glass Co. #15057 (King; Richards and Hartley), 1898. A State Series pattern. Very similar to "Lacy Medallion", Plate 39, except most Colorado pieces have "feet". Extended table service including violet bowl, vase, individual sugar and creamer, tumbler, toothpick holder, perfume bottle (rare), sauce, compotes, wine, toy table service. Crystal, green blue, ruby-stained, amethyst-flashed.—**Key B**

2. BEAD AND SCROLL, salt shaker. See Plate 26.

3. TRIPLE BEAD BAND, goblet.—*Ref. Gob II-139* —**Key A**

Row 4

1. BEADED LOBE, salt shaker.—*Ref. K3-135; K8-163* Greensburg Glass Co.'s #200, c. mid-1880's. Extended table service including compotes. See Plate 155.—**Key B**

2. BEAD AND LOOP, salt shaker.—*Ref. PetSal 154G* —**Key A**

3. IMPERIAL #81, pitcher.—*Ref. K7-67* Imperial Glass Co. after 1904.—**Key B**

4. BEADED BLOCK, salt shaker.—*Ref. W-135; PetSal 22-C* Eagle Glass and Mfg. Co. Milk Glass.—**Key C**

PLATE 155 HOBNAILS AND BEADS

Row 1

1. PLAIN BAND, pitcher.—*Ref. HTP-28* A. H. Heisey Glass Co. #1225, c. 1898-1910. Extended table service including sherbet. Crystal, ruby-stained, custard.—**Key B**

2. BEADED LOBE (WINONA), finger bowl (etched). See Plate 154.

3. BEAD AND CHAIN, creamer.—*Ref. K7-57* Central Glass Co., 1880. Extended table service.—**Key A**

Row 2

1. DOUBLE BEADED BAND, goblet.—*Ref. Gob II-138* —**Key A**

2. ALBION, butter dish. U.S. Glass Co., c. 1891. An example of U.S. Glass Co.'s special butter dishes, sometimes with no matching pieces.—**Key A**

3. TRIPLE FROSTED BAND, goblet,—*Ref. Gob II-109* —**Key A**

Row 3

1. PLAIN BAND, toothpick holder. See Row 1 #1.

2. BEAD SWAG (BEADED YOKE), salt shaker.—*Ref. K2-75* A. H. Heisey Glass Co. #1295, 1897-1905. Extended table service including toothpick holder, rose bowl, mug, wine, cup and saucer. Crystal, ruby-stained, milk glass, emerald green, some custard and vaseline.—**Key C**

3. BEAD SWAG, syrup. See above.

PLATE 156 PANELS - FLUTE

These are all goblets in the FLUTE pattern, and with many different names. Except for those noted, all can be found in Millard's *Goblets II.*—Flint - **Key B/C**; Non-Flint **Key A/B**

Row 1
1. FLUTE—*Ref. L13*
2. BANDED FLUTE
3. BILIKEN FLUTE
4. FLUTE—*Ref. L13*

Row 2
1. GIANT FLUTE
2. FRANKLIN FLUTE
3. FLARE TOP FLUTE
4. DOUBLE PETALLED FLUTE

Row 3
1. RED FLUTE
2. PITTSBURGH FLUTE
3. NEW ENGLAND FLUTE
4. LOEHR FLUTE

Row 4
1. LOOP WITH KNOB STEM
2. DUCHESS LOOP
3. SQUARE FLUTE
4. TAPERING FLUTE

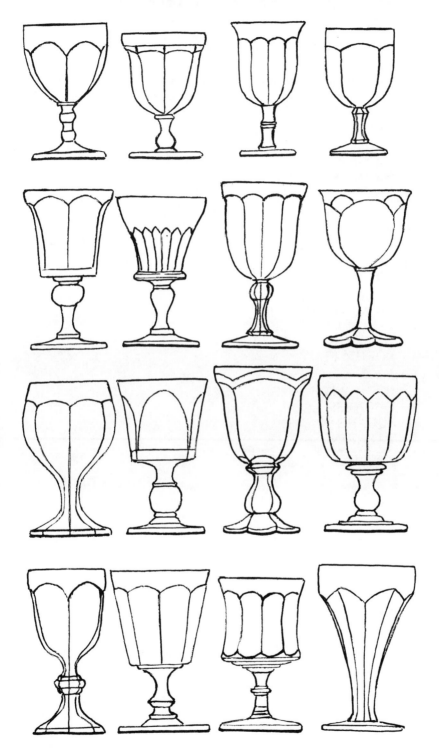

PLATE 157 PANELS

Duncan Tumblers. George Duncan and Sons, c. 1900.—**Key A**

Row 1
1. DUNCAN #69
2. DUNCAN #70

Row 2
1. DUNCAN #11
2. DUNCAN #1

Row 3
1. DUNCAN #8
2. DUNCAN #13
3. DUNCAN #212

Row 4
1. DUNCAN #37
2. DUNCAN #14
3. DUNCAN #16

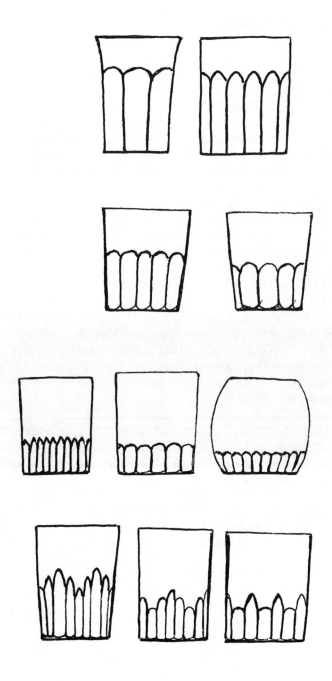

PLATE 158 PANELS

Row 1
1. DESPOT, goblet.—*Ref. Gob II-81* —**Key A**
2. DUNCAN, spoon holder.—**Key A**
3. HUBER (FALMOUTH), celery vase.—*Ref. L11* Boston and Sandwich; New England Glass; Bakewell, Pears, c. 1860's. Made in extended table service including tumblers, plates, handled egg cup, compotes, covered bowls, bitters bottle, footed salt dip, quart jug, mugs, decanters, wine, handled whiskey.—**Key A;** Flint, **Key C**

Row 2
1. CRYSTALINA, sugar bowl.—*Ref. HV-126* U.S. Glass Co. (Hobbs), 1891. Extended table service including individual creamer with half-handle, sherbet with saucer, sauce, plate, cheese plate with cover, bread plate, oval bowls. Crystal, ruby-stained, emerald green.—**Key A**
2. CRYSTALINA, pitcher. See above.

Row 3
1. U.S. PURITAN, creamer.—*Ref. HV-149* U.S. Glass Co. #15115 (King), 1909. Extended table service.—**Key A**
2. CHIPPENDALE (QUADRUPED), creamer.—*Ref. K2-107* Jefferson Glass Co.; Central Glass Co.; 1909. Extended table service including salt shaker, toothpick holder, relish. See another creamer on Plate 160.—**Key B**

Row 4
1. LATE CRYSTAL, pitcher.—*Ref. K1-21* McKee and Brothers, 1894; Richards and Hartley, 1888; U.S. Glass Co., 1898. Extended table service including high and low compotes, sauces, salt shaker, egg cup, tumbler, celery vase.—**Key A**
2. U.S. GEORGIAN, pitcher.—*Ref. HV-159* U.S. Glass Co. #15152 (Glassport; King), 1915. Extended table service including several style creamers, bowls, plate, fruit jar with cover, syrup, salt shaker, sugar shaker, footed bowl, cruet, tray. See Plate 162.—**Key B**

PLATE 159 PANELS

Row 1

1. FT. PITT, creamer.—*Ref. HV-156* U.S. Glass Co. #15123 (Glassport; Ripley), 1910. Made in extended table service including bowls, plate. Crystal.—**Key A**

2. EVANGELINE, pitcher.—*Ref. HV-168* U.S. Glass Co. #15131 (Gas City), 1918. Extended table service including compotes, bowls, wine, celery tray, handled jelly dish, jelly compote, sauce, cake stand, tumbler. Crystal.—**Key A**

Row 2

1. PLAIN TULIP, syrup.—*Ref. L-50* C. 1850's. Extended table service including wine, tumbler, celery vase, compotes.—**Key B;** Flint **Key D**

2. BOHEMIAN, goblet. Bakewell, Pears and Co.—**Key B**

3. PLAIN SCALLOPED PANEL (U.S. COLONIAL), creamer.—*Ref. K1-81* U.S. Glass Co. #15047 (Glassport), 1896. Extended table service. Crystal, emerald green, cobalt blue (scarce).—**Key A**

Row 3

1. BOUQUET, tumbler. Bakewell, Pears and Co., c. 1875. Made in water set. Cased glass.—**Key C**

2. FLAWLESS, butter tub.—*Ref. K6-15.* Duncan and Miller #72, c. 1905-10. Extended table service including basket, punch bowl and foot, individual salts, individual celery dip, cruet, syrup, celery vase, cup, vases, bowls, footed celery tray. This piece lacks the characteristic edge cutting of the pattern.—**Key A**

3. FLAWLESS, creamer. See above.

Row 4

1. CHURCH WINDOWS, creamer. See Plate 164.

2. U.S. NIAGARA, creamer.—*Ref. HV-161* U.S. Glass Co. #15162 (Glassport), 1919. Extended table service including bowls, syrup, cruet, cracker jar, plate, compote, cups, mustard jar, handled jelly. Crystal.—**Key A**

3. THUMBNAIL (FLAT-TO-ROUND PANEL), salt shaker.—*Ref. PetSal 157S* A Duncan pattern. Usually gilded.—**Key A**

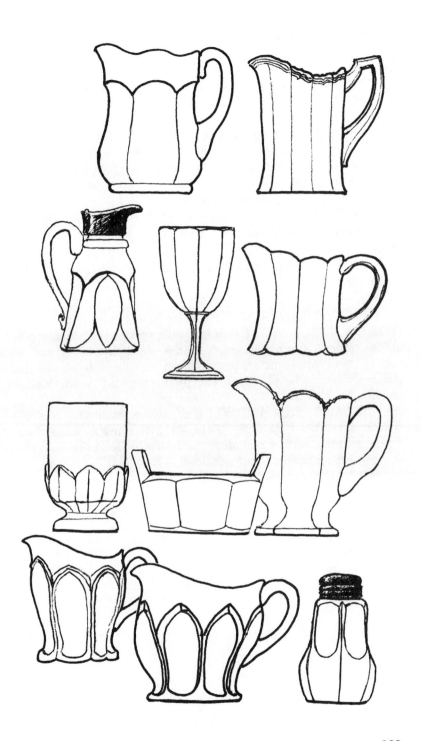

PLATE 160 PANELS

Row 1

1. COLONIAL PANEL, creamer.—*Ref. K7-10*—**Key A**
2. ARCHED PANEL, creamer.—*Ref. K1-105*—**Key A**

Row 2

1. CAMBRIDGE COLONIAL (NEARCUT COLONIAL), creamer.—*Ref. K8-189* Cambridge Glass Co. #2750, early 1900's. Made in extended table service including toothpick holder, decanter, salt shaker, syrup, tumblers, water bottle, vase, basket, plate, punch bowl, jelly compote, sauce.—**Key B**
2. LUCERNE, creamer.—*Ref. K8-37* Fostoria Glass Co. #1515, 1905. Extended table service.—**Key B**

Row 3

CHIPPENDALE (STEPPED ARCH PANEL), creamer. See Plate 158.

Row 4

1. HEISEY'S COLONIAL (PEERLESS), creamer.—*Ref. K8-189* A. H. Heisey #300, c. 1897. Extended table service including toothpick holder, cruets, syrup, decanters, wines, cordial, brandy and water bottles, candlestick, bitters bottle, claret jug, punch bowl, salt shaker. Heisey #300½ is identical except for having plain rims, not scalloped.—**Key B**
2. MILLARD (FAN AND FLUTE), syrup (etched).—*Ref. K5-60; K8-63; LV-42; LV-52* U.S. Glass #15016 (Hobbs factory), 1893. Extended table service including toothpick holder, cruet, salt shaker. Crystal, amber-stained, ruby-stained.—**Key B**
3. MILLARD, creamer. See above.

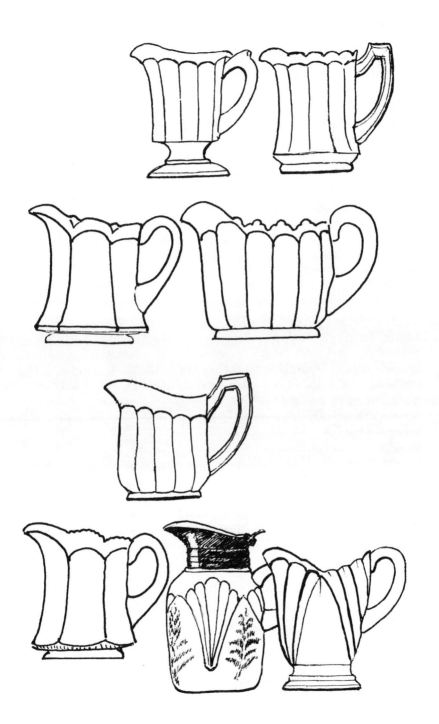

PLATE 161 PANELS

Row 1

1. CONNECTICUT FLUTE, goblet. Has eight fluted panels. —**Key A**

2. DUNCAN #71, quart tankard. Duncan Glass Co. c. 1900. Made in various sizes of tankard pitchers, some with covers; and syrup.—**Key A**

Row 2

1. LATE COLONIAL VARIANT, creamer.—*Ref. K2-87* Duncan glass #61, 1905. Extended table service including bowls, sauce, ice cream dishes, cruets, toothpick holder, open compotes, open salt, several shapes salt shakers, tumblers, water tray, water bottle, candlesticks, claret, wine, cocktail, cordial, footed whiskey, champagnes, baskets, vases, decanter, syrup, fruit jar with lid, cup, footed punch bowl.—**Key A**

2. ESSEX, creamer.—*Ref. K8-32* Fostoria Glass Co., 1905. Extended table service including claret, champagne, toothpick holder, sauce, wine, bowls, cup, syrup, sugar shaker, celery vase, sundae dish.—**Key B**

Row 3

1. DOUBLE DONUT, pitcher.—*Ref. K2-32* A Findlay, Ohio product, 1880's. Extended table service including salt shaker, celery dish, low open compote.—**Key B**

2. LATE COLONIAL, cup. Imperial Glass Co. Extended table service.—**Key A**

Row 4

1. PRETTY PANELS, syrup.—*Ref. HIII-36* Probably Hobbs, Brockunier and Co. #86, 1890 (Heacock). Syrup known. Crystal, blue, amber (scarce).—**Key B**

2. NAIL CITY, creamer.—*Ref. K3-37* Central Glass #555, 1881. Extended table service including covered compotes.—**Key A**

PLATE 162 PANELS

Row 1

ETRUSCAN, bowl.—*Ref. L20* Bakewell, Pears and Co. Extended table service including tumbler, sauce, cake stand, compotes, egg cup, bowls.—**Key B**

Row 2

1. ETRUSCAN, spoon holder. See above.
2. FOSTORIA #551, pitcher.—*Ref. K8-28* Fostoria Glass Co., 1898. Basic table service.—**Key B**

Row 3

1. JEFFERSON COLONIAL, creamer.—*Ref. K7-153* Jefferson Glass #270, 1903. Extended table service including cruet, tumbler, toothpick holder, jelly compote, salt shaker, bowls, sauce. Crystal, pale blue, green.—**Key A**
2. PRESSED OCTAGON, syrup.—*Ref. HIII-36* c. 1890. Crystal, milk glass, amber, decorated.—**Key B**

Row 4

1. DUNCAN #37, tumbler. George Duncan and Sons, c. 1900.—**Key A**
2. U.S. GEORGIAN, creamer. See Plate 158.

PLATE 163 PANELS

Row 1

1. FRONTIER, spoon holder. See Plate 30.

2. BULBOUS BASE, syrup.—*Ref. HI-16* Hobbs, Brockunier #311, c. 1887; U.S. Glass Co., 1890's. Made in extended table service including toothpick holder, cruet, salt shaker, cup, tumbler (straight sides), finger bowl, sugar shaker. Crystal, cranberry.—**Key B**

Row 2

1. DOUGLASS, toothpick holder.—*Ref. HI-27* Cooperative Flint Glass Co., c. 1903. Extended table service. Crystal, ruby-stained.—**Key A**

2. CROCUS, salt shaker.—*Ref. PetSal 26D* Milk glass.—**Key B**

Row 3

1. BELTED PANEL, salt shaker.—*Ref. PetSal 167R* A. H. Heisey Co. #333.—**Key B**

2. NORTHWOOD'S REGAL (BLOCK MIDRIFF), salt shaker.—*Ref. PetSal 155-i* Northwood Glass Co. Crystal, amber-stained, Francesware.—**Key B**

3. SPEARPOINT BAND (GOTHIC), cruet.—*Ref. K7-31* McKee and Brothers, c. 1900-1905. Extended table service including toothpick holder. Crystal, ruby-stained.—**Key C**

Row 4

1. HEISEY #339-2, salt shaker. A. H. Heisey Glass Co., c. 1895.—**Key B**

2. GOLD BAND (RANSON), cruet.—*Ref. HI-25* Riverside Glass Co., 1899. Crystal, vaseline.—**Key B**

3. LIGHTNING, salt shaker.—*Ref. K3-100* Tiffin Glass Co.; U.S. Glass Co. (Gas City), 1893. Extended table service including bowls, covered and open compotes, celery vase. Crystal.—**Key B**

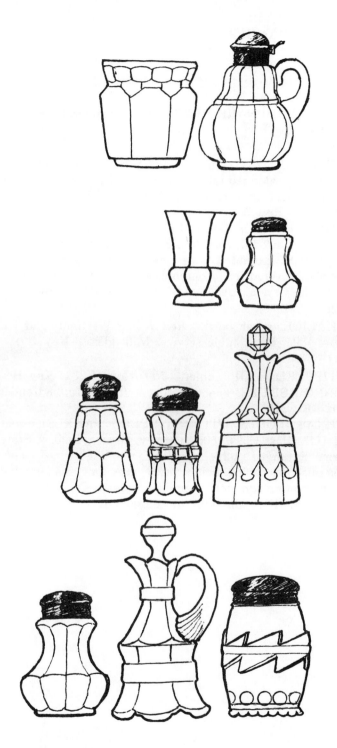

PLATE 164 PANELS

Row 1

1. U.S. #5705, cruet.—*Ref. HIII-88* U.S. Glass Co., c. 1909. Only cruet known.—**Key B**
2. WIDE AND NARROW PANEL, creamer.—*Ref. K1-108* c. 1890.—**Key A**

Row 2

1. NEARCUT #2692, creamer.—*Ref. K7-61* Cambridge Glass Co., 1909. Made in extended table service including plates, cup, tumblers, celery tray, pickle tray, cruet, salt shaker, bowls, sauce, water bottle, finger bowl.—**Key B**
2. CHURCH WINDOWS (TULIP PETALS; COLUMBIA), pitcher.—*Ref. K3-107; K4-115* U.S. Glass #15082 (King; Richard and Hartley), 1903. Extended table service including sauce, celery vase, cake stand, covered jelly compote, sardine dish, covered and open sugar bowls. Crystal, decorated. See Plate 159.—**Key A**

Row 3

CHALICE, sugar bowl.—*Ref. K1-29* Westmoreland Glass Co. #252, c. 1896. Basic table service. Milk glass.—**Key C**

Row 4

1. STIPPLED LOOP, goblet.—*Ref. Gob II-27* —**Key B**
2. MARQUISETTE, spoon holder.—*Ref. L-159* Extended table service.—**Key B**
3. TEXAS (LOOPS WITH STIPPLED PANELS), cruet.—*Ref. K2-58* U.S. Glass Co. #15067 (Ripley; Bryce), 1900. A State Series pattern. Extended table service including wine, sauce, rare ruby-stained toothpick holder, two sizes salt shakers, individual creamer, bowls, tumbler, compotes, plate. Crystal, rose-flashed, ruby-stained. (Reproductions in colors.)—**Key B**

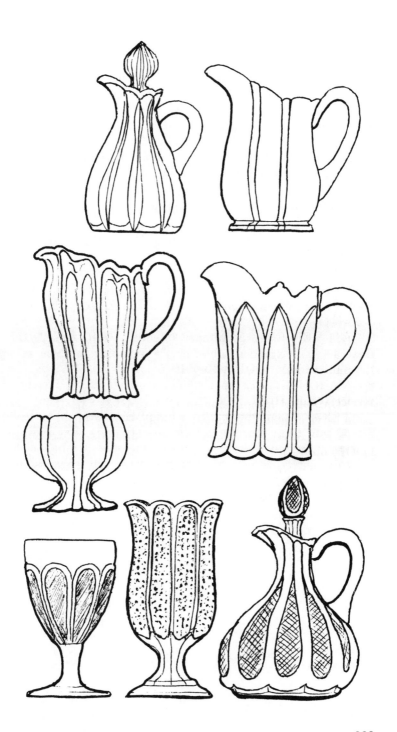

PLATE 165 PANELS

Row 1

1. LOOP (O'HARA), plate.—*Ref. L4* Boston and Sandwich; O'Hara Glass Co., 1850's-1860's. Made in extended table service including celery vase, egg cup, compotes, master salt, wine, champagne, open and covered sugar bowls.—Flint **Key C**

2. PETAL AND LOOP (O'HARA), plate.—*Ref. L4* Boston and Sandwich; O'Hara Glass Co. Extended table service including compotes, candlestick.—Flint **Key C**

Row 2

LOOP, covered bowl. See above.

Row 3

1. SANDWICH LOOP (FLUTE), goblet. A flute type — See Plate 156.

2. HAIRPIN, goblet. Sandwich glass c. 1850's. Made in extended table service including decanter, wine, tumbler, champagne, compote, egg cup, open and covered sugar bowls. Crystal, milk glass. —**Key C**

3. ETCHED GRAPE, pitcher (etched).—*Ref. K2-122* U.S. Glass Co., 1900-05. Extended table service including tumbler, celery vase. Crystal, emerald green.—**Key B**

Row 4

1. YUMA LOOP, spill holder. O'Hara Glass Co., 1860's. Extended table service including footed tumbler.—**Key B**

2. PORTLAND PETAL, goblet. Portland Glass Co. Comparable to LOOP, above.

3. U.S. #5701, cruet.—*Ref. HIII-88* U.S. Glass Co., c. 1909. —**Key A**

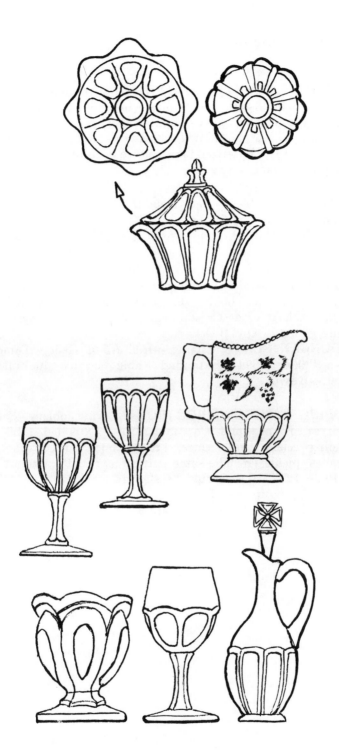

PLATE 166 PANELS

Row 1

1. EUREKA, footed tumbler.—*Ref. L6* McKee and Brothers. Made in extended table service including wine, bowls, compotes, cordial, egg cup, champagne, sauce.—Flint **Key C**

2. POGO STICK (CROWN), creamer.—*Ref. K7-23* Lancaster Glass Co., c. 1910. Extended table service including compote, handled relish, salt shaker.—**Key B**

Row 2

1. MIOTON, goblet.—*Ref. Gob II-25* Extended table service. —**Key A**

2. OVOID PANELS, goblet.—*Ref. Gob II-26* —**Key A**

Row 3

1. X-RAY, pitcher.—*Ref. K5-136* Riverside Glass Co., 1899-1902. Extended table service including rare syrup, salt shaker, cruet, jelly compote, toothpick holder, berry set, clover-leaf tray, compote, tumbler, celery vase. Crystal, emerald green, amethyst (scarce), usually gilded.—**Key B**

2. DUNCAN FLUTE, pitcher.—*Ref. K5-30* George Duncan and Sons #2004, 1894. Extended table service including salt shaker.—**Key A**

Row 4

1. SPRIG WITHOUT SPRIG (ROYAL), wine goblet.—*Ref. K8-pl. 28* Bryce, Higbee and Co., mid-1880's. Extended table service including celery vase, sauce, bread plate, bowls, cake stands, compotes, pickle jar. The same pattern as SPRIG without flowers. See Plate 127. Values would be slightly less than SPRIG.

2. X-RAY, syrup. See Row 3 #1.

3. CHICK, sugar bowl. See Plate 7.

PLATE 167 PANELS

Row 1

1. PANELLED FINETOOTH, goblet.—*Ref. Gob II-28* Made in extended table service including wine, relish dish with shield (scarce).—Flint **Key C**

2. SCALLOP SHELL, creamer.—*Ref. K2-38* The base is circular, the body square.—**Key A**

Row 2

1. SUNRAY (BALLOON; SUNBURST DESIGN), goblet.—*Ref. Metz* Fostoria Glass Co., 1935-40. Extended table service. "Depression" glass.

2. PLEATING (FLAT PANEL), pitcher.—*Ref. K8-70; LV51* U.S. Glass Co. #15003 (Ripley; Bryce), 1891. Extended table service including toothpick holder, celery vase, compotes, cake stand. See Plate 205. Crystal, ruby-stained.—**Key B**

Row 3

1. CLEAR RIBBON VARIANT, creamer.—*Ref. K1-83* c. 1890.—**Key A**

2. CLEAR RIBBON, spoon holder.—*Ref. L70* George Duncan and Sons, 1880's. Extended table service including high compote, celery vase, relish, footed sauce, bread tray.—**Key B**

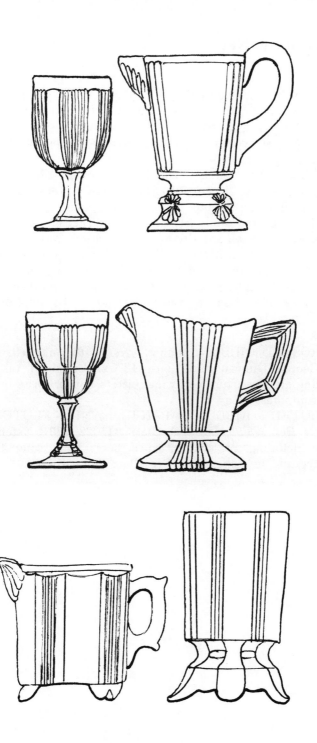

PLATE 168 PANELS

Row 1

1. FOSTORIA #952, pitcher. Fostoria Glass Co., late 1880's. Made in extended table service including tumbler.—**Key B**

2. REEDING, creamer.—*Ref. K8-32* Cambridge Glass Co. c. 1905. Extended table service including toothpick holder, cordial.—**Key B**

Row 2

1. PLEAT AND PANEL (DERBY), creamer.—*Ref. L-157; K2-24* Bryce, Walker and Co., c. 1870's; U.S. Glass Co., 1891. Extended table service including compote, covered bowl, cake stand, square plate, water tray, covered candy jar, lamp, footed sauce, relish, bread plate, salt shaker. Crystal, amethyst, canary, blue.—**Key B**

2. RIBBON, spoon holder.—*Ref. L67* Bakewell, Pears and Co., c. 1870. Extended table service including rare wine, dolphin-stamped compote, rectangular bowl, compote, covered cheese dish, water tray, celery vase, footed sauce, waste bowl.—**Key B**; dolphin compote, **Key E**

Row 3

1. FROSTED RIBBON, pitcher.—*Ref. L-69* Bakewell, Pears and Co.; George Duncan and Sons, 1870's. Extended table service including ale glass, tumbler, wine, bitters bottle, waste bowl, celery vase, compotes.—**Key C**

2. FLUTED RIBBON (PANEL AND FLUTE), spoon holder.—*Ref. K3-95; L67* U.S. Glass #15022, 1891. Extended table service including salt shaker, sauce, berry bowl, compotes, syrup, decanter, pickle dish, relish. See Plate 208.—**Key A**

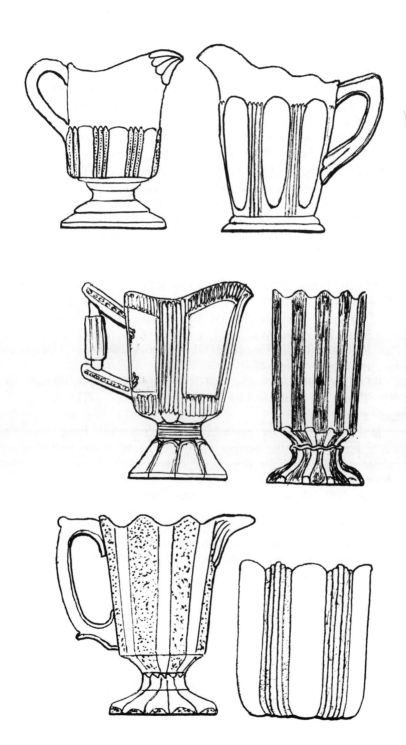

PLATE 169 PANELS

Row 1

PHILADELPHIA, compote.—*Ref. L61* New England Glass Co., 1860's. Extended table service including celery vase, egg cup, wine.—**Key B**

Row 2

1. HAND (PENNSYLVANIA; PENNSYLVANIA HAND), pitcher.—*Ref. K3-9; L107* O'Hara Glass Co., 1880. Extended table service including bread tray, celery vase, compotes, wine, bowls, jam jar, honey dish, flat sauce, platter, pickle dish, footed sauce, salt shaker. Moderate availability. See Plate 180.—**Key C**
2. STIPPLED PANEL AND BAND, creamer.—*Ref. K1-16* c. 1860's.—**Key C**

Row 3

1. STIPPLED BAND (PANELLED STIPPLED BOWL), spoon holder.—*Ref. L-107; Gob II-41* c. 1870's. Extended table service including open compote, footed salt, sauce, tumbler.—**Key B**
2. ASHLAND (SNOWDROP), goblet.—*Ref. Gob II-31* Portland Glass Co., c. 1880's. Extended table service including leaf-shaped dish, ice cream tray.—**Key B**
3. REGINA, pitcher.—*Ref. K5-103* Cooperative Flint Glass Co., 1902. Extended table service including tumbler.—**Key A**

Row 4

1. DOUBLE RIBBON, pitcher.—*Ref. K1-53; L67* King Glass Co., 1870's. Extended table service including bread plate, footed sauce, compotes, pickle dish, egg cup, salt shaker. Clear or frosted. —**Key B**
2. ROCKET BOMB, salt shaker.—*Ref. PetSal 170N* Usually gilded.—**Key B**
3. FROSTED RIBBON-DOUBLE BARS, goblet.—*Ref. Gob II-43* King Glass Co. c. 1875. Extended table service. This pattern comes in a non-frosted version called KINGS RIBBON, which includes a toy table set.—**Key B**

349

PLATE 170 PANELS

Row 1

1. DUNCAN'S #2001, salt shaker. See Plate 190.
2. GALLOWAY, pitcher. See Plate 62.

Row 2

1. JANSSEN, goblet.—*Ref. Gob II-125* —**Key B**
2. OPTIC FLUTE, creamer.—*Ref. K7-45* Imperial Glass Co. #6, c. 1902. Made in extended table service including celery vase, jelly compote, sauce, wine, lemonade set (no base pattern on tumblers), oval handled tray.—**Key B**

Row 3

1. MAJESTIC CROWN, goblet. See Plate 94.
2. DIAMOND STEM, pitcher.—*Ref. K6-58* —**Key A**

PLATE 171 PANELS

Row 1

1. WHEELING, creamer (engraved).—*Ref. LV65* Hobbs Glass Co. #115, 1880's. Made in extended table service including salt shaker.—**Key B**

2. SIDE WHEELER, creamer.—*Ref. K5-31* c. mid-1880's. Extended table service including salt shaker.—**Key A**

Row 2

1. OGLEBAY, creamer (engraved).—*Ref. Heacock* Hobbs Glass Co. #332, 1891. Extended table service including syrup, tumbler, bowls, celery vase.—**Key A**

2. NESTOR, creamer.—*Ref. K5-37* Northwood Glass Co. (National), 1903. Extended table service including jelly compote, toothpick holder, berry set, water set, cruet, salt shaker, cruet tray. **The design is painted on** — without it the pattern is hard to identify. Apple green, medium blue, amethyst.—**Key C**

Row 3

1. LATIN CROSS, creamer.—*Ref. K3-35* —**Key C**

2. THE JEFFERSON, pitcher.—*Ref. K7-149* Jefferson Glass Co. #254, c. 1907. Extended table service including toothpick holder, tumblers, salt shaker, plate, spoon tray, finger bowl, syrups, cruet, cup. Crystal, ruby-stained, opaque white.—**Key B**

3. GATHERED KNOT, pitcher.—*Ref. K7-181* Imperial Glass Co. #3, 1902. Extended table service including salt shaker, toothpick holder, compote, pickle jar, celery vase, sugar shaker, berry bowl, cracker jar, vases.—**Key A**

Row 4

1. CHAIN THUMBPRINTS, creamer (etched).—*Ref. K3-55* c. 1885-90. Extended table service.—**Key A**

2. ORINDA, creamer.—*Ref. K5-111* National Glass Co. (Lancaster #1492), 1901. Extended table service including salt shaker, toothpick holder.—**Key A**

PLATE 172 PANELS

Row 1

1. DIAMOND POINT LOOP, creamer.—*Ref. K2-111* c. 1890's. Extended table service including celery vase, plate, berry bowl. Crystal, amber, canary, apple green, blue, engraved.—**Key B**

2. CURTAIN TIE-BACK, creamer.—*Ref. K3-118; Gob I-35* c. Mid-1880's. Extended table service including tumbler, wine, celery vase, berry bowl, bread plate, salt shaker.—**Key B**

Row 2

1. TRIAD, creamer.—*Ref. K4-40* Basic table service. Crystal, etched.—**Key B**

2. SPIRAL AND MALTESE CROSS, creamer.—*Ref. K1-30* c. 1870's. Extended table service. Crystal, amber.—**Key A**

3. PANEL AND RIB, creamer.—*Ref. K4-17* c. 1885. Extended table service. Crystal, yellow, vaseline, amber.—**Key A**

Row 3

1. PANELLED LADDER, goblet.—*Ref. Gob II-3* —**Key A**

2. PRISON STRIPE, creamer.—*Ref. K7-139* A. H. Heisey #357, c. 1904-1909. Extended table service including toothpick holder, salt shaker, sauce, bowls, tumbler, cup, cruet, syrup, two creamers. —**Key B**

3. WASHBOARD (ADONIS), pitcher.—*Ref. K6 Pl. 12* McKee and Brothers, 1897. Extended table service including plate, compotes, celery vase, jelly compote, syrup, cake stand, covered bowls, salt shaker. Crystal, blue, canary, green.—**Key A**

PLATE 173 PANELS

Row 1

1. STIPPLED BAR, spoon holder.—*Ref. LV63* U.S. Glass Co. #15044. Made in extended table service. Crystal.—**Key A**

2. ZIG-ZAG (MITRED BARS; MITRED DIAMOND POINTS), pitcher.—*Ref. K2-33; Gob I-68; W-130* Bryce Brothers, 1880's; U.S. Glass Co., c. 1898. Extended table service including salt shaker, wine, celery vase, cake stand, oval bowl. Crystal, amber.—**Key B**

Row 2

1. GREEN HERRINGBONE (EMERALD GREEN HERRING-BONE; FLORIDA), pitcher.—*Ref. K1-46; L161-1* U.S. Glass Co. #15056 (Bryce), 1898. A State Series pattern. Extended table service including wide-mouthed vase, salt shaker, syrup, square berry bowls, square sauce, tumbler, wine, compote, celery vase, square plates, relish. Crystal, emerald green. Called Green Herringbone even in colorless crystal.—Crystal **Key B**; Green **Key C**

2. PANELLED PLEAT (ROBINSON'S LADDER), goblet.—*Ref. Gob II-42; K6 Pl. 37* Robinson Glass Co., 1893. Basic table service and goblet are known. See Plate 212.—**Key B**

3. CUTTLEBONE, goblet.—*Ref. Gob II-42*—**Key B**

Row 3

TREE, creamer.—*Ref. K8-31* —**Key A**

Row 4

1. FINE FEATHER, salt shaker.—*Ref. PetSal 28P* —**Key A**

2. PANELLED HERRINGBONE (PRISM AND HERRING-BONE), salt shaker.—*Ref. K7-185; Gob II-137* Imperial Glass Co., c. 1902. Extended table service including cup, bowl, pickle dish, vase, low compote, wine.—**Key A**

3. MITRED PRISMS, salt shaker.—*Ref. Gob I-68* Extended table service including celery vase.—**Key A**

PLATE 174 PANELS

Row 1
1. PRISM AND FLUTE (PRISM), footed tumbler.—*Ref. L16* Bakewell, Pears and Co., 1870's. Extended table service including cake stands, celery vase, egg cup, compotes, master salt, sauce, cordial, wine, syrup, pickle dish, champagne, covered bowls. Often engraved.—**Key A**
2. LOOP WITH PRISM BAND, pitcher.—*Ref. K2-121* Extended table service.—**Key B**

Row 2
1. ETCHED BAND, goblet. Portland Glass Co.—**Key B**
2. TRIPLE FINETOOTH BAND, goblet.—*Ref. Gob II-108* —**Key A**
3. PLEATED BANDS, goblet.—*Ref. Gob II-66* —**Key A**

Row 3
1. WELLINGTON (STAPLE), toothpick holder.—*Ref. K5-74; PetSal 40G* Westmoreland Glass Co., 1903. Extended table service including wine. See Plate 208.—**Key B**
2. CARTRIDGE BELT, goblet.—*Ref. Gob II-133* —**Key A**
3. MIOTON-PLEAT BAND, goblet.—*Ref. Gob II-131* —**Key A**

359

PLATE 175 PANELS

Row 1

1. THREADING, creamer.—*Ref. K3-15* George Duncan and Sons Glass Co., c. 1880's. Made in extended table service including compotes, open and covered sugar bowls. Crystal.—**Key A**

2. JERSEY S, creamer.—*Ref. K4-67* Jersey Glass Co., 1825. Known in open salt and creamer.—**Key E**

Row 2

1. HEISEY'S BANDED FLUTE, toothpick holder.—*Ref. Burns-3* Heisey Glass Co., 1907-1932. Extended table service. Crystal. —**Key B**

2. THREAD BAND (author's name), creamer (engraved). Duncan and Miller Glass Co., 1900-1920's. Extended table service.—**Key A**

3. COLONIS (45 COLONIS), pitcher.—*Ref. K5-146* U.S. Glass Co. #15145 (Glassport), 1913. Extended table service including tumbler, cordial, sauce, celery vase, cake stand, compotes, egg cup, oval dish, tray, pickle dish, syrup. Most pieces lack the identifying horizontal rib. Crystal.—**Key A**

Row 3

1. RIPPLE (RIPPLE BAND; HERRINGBONE BAND), open salt dish.—*Ref. K3-20* Boston and Sandwich, late 1870's. Extended table service including compotes, wine, lamp.—**Key A**

2. FLUTED SCROLLS, creamer.—*Ref. K2-119* Northwood Glass Co., late 1880's. Extended table service including tumbler, epergne, footed bowl. Crystal, amber, sapphire blue, custard.—**Key A**

3. FLUTED SCROLLS (FOGGY BOTTOM), salt shaker.—*Ref. PetSal 29-0* See above.

Row 4

1. RIPPLE, pitcher. See Row 3 #1.

2. SILVER QUEEN (ELMINO), goblet (etched).—*Ref. Gob II-109; K4-85* Ripley and Co., 1885; U.S. Glass Co., 1891. Extended table service including syrup, catsup, tumbler (very plain), spooner with two handles, handled sauce, footed sauce, wine and goblet, cake stand. Crystal, ruby-stained. See Plate 207.—plain items **Key A;** others **Key B**

3. HEISEY'S URN, salt shaker.—*Ref. Burns 63* A. H. Heisey #379, 1905-07. Extended table service including toothpick holder.—**Key B**

PLATE 176 PANELS

Row 1

1. NICKEL PLATE'S ROYAL, creamer.—*Ref. K5-35* Nickel Plate Glass Co. #77, 1890; U.S. Glass Co., 1891. Made in extended table service including barrel-shaped tumbler, footed covered bowl. Crystal.—**Key A**

2. TRIPLE BAND, pitcher.—*Ref. K4-126* The pitcher came with a pewter lid.—**Key C**

Row 2

1. TRIPLE LINE, creamer.—*Ref. K7-2*—**Key A**

2. SCALLOPED LINES (SCALLOPED BAND), goblet.—*Ref. Gob II-14* Extended table service including plate, wine.—**Key A**

3. DOT AND DASH, creamer.—*Ref. K5-11* Central Glass Co. #650, c. 1880. Extended table service.—**Key A**

Row 3

FEATHER BAND, pitcher.—*Ref. K4-134* U.S. Glass Co. #15122 (Bryce), after 1910. Extended table service including sauce, bowls, two sizes water pitcher, flat and footed sugar bowls. Crystal. —**Key A**

Row 4

1. CROCHET BAND, goblet.—*Ref. Gob II-70*—**Key A**

2. MULTIPLE CIRCLE, goblet.—*Ref. Gob II-39*—**Key A**

3. VENICE, pitcher.—*Ref. K4-105* U.S. Glass Co. (Adams factory), 1891. Extended table service.—**Key A**

PLATE 177 PANELS

Row 1

1. SCROLL BAND, pitcher.—*Ref. K5-125*—**Key A**
2. EMPRESS (DOUBLE ARCH), creamer.—*Ref. K7-59* Riverside Glass Works, 1898. Made in extended table service including cruet, jelly compote, bowl, toothpick holder, compote, cup, oil lamps, berry set, water set, mustard, rare breakfast sugar and creamer, salt shaker. Crystal, color, gilded.—**Key C**

Row 2

1. WINGED SCROLL (IVORINA VERDE), syrup.—*Ref. K7-137* A. H. Heisey Glass Co., 1888-1905. Extended table service including toothpick holder, cruet, celery vase, bowls, salt shaker, cake stand, smoker's set. Crystal, custard, milk glass (very rare).—**Key B**
2. FOSTORIA'S PRISCILLA, creamer.—*Ref. K8-200* Fostoria Glass Co. #1898, c. 1899. Extended table service including scarce toothpick holder, water set, berry set, vase, compote, two shapes salt shakers, lamps, syrup, egg cup, celery vase.—**Key B**

Row 3

1. DRAPED GARLAND, syrup.—*Ref. PetSal 159Q* Extended table service including salt shaker. Crystal, ruby-stained.—**Key B**
2. LEAF MEDALLION (THE REGENT), pitcher.—*Ref. K5-122* Northwood Glass Co., c. 1904. Extended table service including salt shaker, cruet and tray, jelly compote, water set, berry set, toothpick holder. See Plate 200. Crystal, emerald green, amethyst, cobalt blue.—**Key B**

PLATE 178 PEOPLE

Row 1

1. THREE FACE (THE SISTERS), champagne goblet.—*Ref. L89; K3-111* George Duncan and Sons, 1878; U.S. Glass Co., 1891. Made in extended table service including three size cake stands, oil lamp, claret, wine, salt shaker, sauce, compotes, celery vase, toothpick holder, cracker jar, jam jar, salt dip, tumbler. Lots of reproductions.—**Key E**

2. GIBSON GIRL, tumbler.—*Ref. K2-26* Kokomo Glass Co., 1904. Extended table service including salt shaker, 10″ plate.—**Key F**

3. GIBSON GIRL, creamer. See above.

Row 2

1. CLASSIC MEDALLION (CAMEO), pitcher.—*Ref. K1-22* c. 1880's. Extended table service including open and covered compotes, open and covered sugar bowls, celery vase.—**Key A**

2. ACTRESS (THEATRICAL; GODDESS OF LIBERTY; ANNIE; PINAFORE), creamer.—*Ref. PetSal 21E; K4-5; L164-11; Gob I 80 & 121* LaBelle Glass Co., c. 1872; Crystal Glass Co., c. 1879. Extended table service including cake stand (Annie Pixley and Maud Granger); covered cheese dish (Sanderson Moffit as "The Long Fisherman", Stuart Robson and William Crane as "Two Dromios"); water pitcher (Romeo and Juliet); milk pitcher; creamer; butter (Fanny Davenport and Lillian Nielson); goblet (Kate Claxton and Lotta Crabtree); plus sauce, relish, pickle dish, pickle jar, trays, platter, candlestick, salt shaker, bowls. Carries high prices but available. Crystal, frosted.—**Key E**

Row 3

ACTRESS, goblet. See above.

Row 4

1. ACTRESS, salt shaker. See above.

2. ACTRESS, pitcher. See above.

PLATE 179 PEOPLE

Row 1

1. LEAF ROSETTE, sugar bowl.—*Ref. K7-56* Has a woman's head on finial. Made in extended table service including salt shaker. See Plate 194.—**Key B**

2. SPANISH AMERICAN (ADMIRAL DEWEY; DEWEY), tumbler.—*Ref. K2-123* Beatty-Brady Glass Co., 1890's. Made in extended table service including rare tumbler, celery vase. See Plate 194.—**Key C**

3. WASHINGTON CENTENNIAL, platter. See Plate 34.

Row 2

1. VALENTINE (TRILBY), pitcher.—*Ref. L164-12* U.S. Glass Co. (Glassport), 1895. Extended table service including cologne bottle, match holder, tumbler, celery.—**Key E**

2. COIN — COLUMBIAN (SPANISH COIN), salt shaker.—*Ref. Metz 1,113* U.S. Glass Co., 1893. Extended table service including champagne, wine, toothpick holder, syrup.—**Key E;** Syrup **Key F**

3. ACTRESS CHAIN (THREE-FACED MEDALLION), goblet.—*Ref. L154-2; Gob II-8*—**Key C**

Row 3

MEPHISTOPHELES, ale glass.—*Ref. Gob II (Front.)* Novelty. There may be a goblet; a German mug is found but it is not like this piece. For value see "tumbler".—**Key D**

Row 4

1. BELMONT'S ROYAL, creamer. See Plate 38.

2. CERES (CAMEO; GODDESS OF LIBERTY), spoon holder.—*Ref. K2-51* Atterbury and Co., c. 1870. Extended table service including sauce, compote, mug, covered candy jar. Crystal, opaque colors, amber.—**Key C**

3. COIN — U.S., toothpick holder.—*Ref. K3-80* U.S. Glass Co. #15005 (Central; Hobbs), 1891. Extended table service including salt shaker, open compotes (Quarters, halves, dimes), bread plate, sauce (quarters), cake stand, tumbler (dollar, dime), cruet, syrup, celery vase (50¢ and quarter), berry bowls (quarter and dollar). Many reproductions. Very available at high prices.—**Key F+**

PLATE 180 PEOPLE

Row 1

1. BABY FACE, spoon holder.—*Ref. L89* George Duncan and Sons. Extended table service including knife rest. A scarce pattern. —**Key E**

2. BEARDED HEAD (VIKING; PROPHET; OLD MAN OF THE MOUNTAIN), pitcher.—*Ref. K1-81* Hobbs, Crockunier and Co., 1876. Made in extended table service including egg cup, platter, celery vase, cake plate, mug, pickle dish, master salt, bread tray, compotes, bowls. No goblet or tumbler was originally made. Fairly abundant.—**Key D**

3. WESTWARD HO! see Plate 2.

Row 2

1. JAPANESE (GRACE), pitcher.—*Ref. K2-16* George Duncan and Sons Glass Co., 1881. A variety of scenes appears on the pieces of this pattern, each with their own name from early glass researchers. See "Bird In Ring", plate 7. Made in extended table service including compote, jam jar, pickle jar in silver frame, covered compote. —**Key D**

2. MAN'S HEAD, pitcher.—*Ref. K5-12* c. 1879. Seldom found.—**Key C**

3. QUEEN ANNE (VIKING; BEARDED MAN; SANTA CLAUS; NEPTUNE; OLD MAN), creamer.—*Ref. K5 Pl. 26; K1-89* This pattern should be called QUEEN ANNE, the original company name by LaBelle Glass Co., 1880's. Extended table service including celery vase, compotes, footed sauce, master salt.—With "head", **Key D**

Row 3

1. TREE OF LIFE WITH HAND, pitcher.—*Ref. LV Pl. 11* Boston and Sandwich; Portland Glass Co.; George Duncan and Sons; 1869; 1873. Extended table service including compote, berry bowl, plate, sauce, celery vase, finger bowl.—**Key E**

2. HAND, pickle jar. See Plate 169. Note: the pattern HAND AND BAR, a very plain set, features a similar clenched fist as a finial. See Plate 185.

3. HAND AND CORN, salt shaker.—*Ref. PetSal 30K* Novelty.—**Key E**

4. HAND AND FISHSCALE, salt shaker.—*Ref. PetSal 30L* Novelty.—**Key E**

PLATE 181 PEOPLE

Row 1

1. CUPID AND VENUS (GUARDIAN ANGEL), goblet.—*Ref. L70* Richards and Hartley Flint Glass Co., 1875-1884. Made in extended table service including bowls, wine, bread platter, jam jar, champagne, celery vase, compotes, mugs, pickle castor, sauces, plates, cruet. Readily available but expensive.—**Key D**

2. CLASSIC, sugar bowl.—*Ref. L97* Gillander and Sons, 1880's. Extended table service including compotes, celery vase, bowls, footed sauce, plates for campaigns for President Cleveland, Blaine, Hendricks, and Logan; and a warrior. Pieces with log feet are especially desirable. Fair availability.—**Key F**

3. CLASSIC, goblet. See above.

Row 2

1. MINERVA, detail. See below.

2. MINERVA (ROMAN MEDALLION), spoon holder.—*Ref. K1-41* c. 1870's. Extended table service including pickle dish, footed sauce, sherbet, cake stand, compotes, jam jar, plate, platter, flat sauce, bread plate.—**Key D**

3. PSYCHE AND CUPID, pitcher.—*Ref. L75* c. 1880's. Extended table service including compotes, celery vase, sauce, wine, jam jar, open and covered sugar bowls, castor set.—**Key C**

Row 3

1. REBECCA AT THE WELL, cake stand. c. 1876. Bakewell, Pears and Co. Museum quality.

2. BICYCLE GIRL, pitcher.—*Ref. K5-126* Dalzell, Gilmore and Leighton, 1880's. Known only in pitcher.—**Key F +**

PLATE 182 PLAIN

Row 1

1. Cake Stand—*Ref. HV106* U.S. Glass Co. (Duncan), 1891. Made in several sizes.—**Key A**

2. TEXAS STAR (SNOWFLAKE BASE), pitcher.—*Ref. K5-149; PetSal 41-i* Steiner Glass Co., 1891. Has star on base. Made in extended table service including sauce, salt shaker, tumbler. See Plates 234 and 236.—**Key A**

Row 2

1. IONIC (ARABIAN), pitcher.—*Ref. K5-75* McKee Glass Co., 1894. Marked "Pres-Cut". Made in extended table service of 60 pieces including salt shaker, carafe, cake stand, cruet, celery vase.—**Key A**

2. IONIC, pitcher. See above.

Row 3

1. THE MIRROR, creamer.—*Ref. K8-26* Greensburg Glass Co., early 1880's. Extended table service of many pieces. Bowls have fine-cut pattern bases.—**Key A**

2. MONTANA, pitcher (etched).—*Ref. HV-123* U.S. Glass Co. (Ripley), 1891. **Not** part of State Series. Known in water sets — pitchers and tumblers. Crystal.—**Key B**

Row 4

1. DUNCAN #47, tumbler.—*Ref. Bones 114-115* c. 1900.

2. DUNCAN #6, tumblers.—*Ref. Bones, 114-115* c. 1900.

3. DUNCAN #313 soda.—*Ref. Bones 114-115* c. 1900.

PLATE 183 PLAIN

Row 1

1. VIGILANT, creamer (engraved).—*Ref. K5-82* Fostoria Glass Co. #403, 1894. Made in extended table service including toothpick holder, salt shaker, celery dish, tumbler, sauce, compotes, cruet, syrup.—**Key A**

2. INOMINATA, creamer.—*Ref. K4-45* c. 1875-80.—**Key A**

Row 2

1. BOSTON (PLAIN FLAT RING), creamer.—*Ref. K2-41* McKee Brothers, 1894. Extended table service. Plain or engraved.—**Key A**

2. OHIO, pitcher.—*(OMN)* U.S. Glass Co. #15050 (Ripley), 1897. A State Series pattern. Made in extended table service including cruet, salt shaker, sugar shaker, wine. Crystal, rare in ruby-stain, engraved. Hard to find.—**Key B**

Row 3

1. TRUNCATED CONE, salt shaker.—*Ref. PetSal 42P* —**Key A**

2. SUNKEN TEARDROP, salt shaker.—*Ref. K4-26* Extended table service. See Plate 187.—**Key A**

3. HOMESTEAD (CORDATE LEAF; LEAF WITH SPRAY), salt shaker.—*Ref. K8-116; K2-17* Bryce, Higbee and Co., mid-1880's. Extended table service including 12″ vase, open salts, cup, individual salts, footed sauce, wine, celery vase (that sometimes sells for footed tumbler). The butter dish is footed with flanged handles. Frequently etched with large leaf (detail). See Plate 185.—**Key B**

PLATE 184 PLAIN

Row 1

1. U.S. BLOSSOM, creamer.—*Ref. LV40* U.S. Glass Co. #15045, 1895. Extended table service. Milk glass, decorated.—**Key C**

2. NEVADA, creamer (enamel decoration on frosted background.)—*Ref. HV-28* U.S. Glass Co. #15075, 1902. A State Series pattern. Basic table service. Crystal, decorated.—**Key B**

Row 2

1. DELOS, creamer.—*Ref. K5-67* National Glass Co., 1900. Extended table service including open compote.—**Key A**

2. THE UNITED STATES, pitcher.—*Ref. K5-68* U.S. Glass Co., 1903. Extended table service including toothpick holder. Sold by Montgomery Ward enamelled with white flowers in a 34-piece set.—**Key B**

Row 3

1. DALZELL'S COLUMBIA, pitcher (engraved).—*Ref. K6 pl. 43* Dalzell, Gilmore and Leighton, 1893. Extended table service of sixty-two pieces.—**Key A**

2. IDAHO, pitcher (etched).—*Ref. HV-121* U.S. Glass Co. (Ripley), 1891. Extended table service including wine, tumbler, cup, tray.—**Key A**

3. SALOON, salt shaker.—*Ref. PetSal 171-1* c. 1888; was actually used in saloons.—**Key A**

PLATE 185 PLAIN

Row 1

1. HARMONY, creamer (etched).—*Ref. K8-1* —**Key A**
2. ANGELSEY, creamer.—*Ref. K4-13* c. 1880.—**Key A**

Row 2

1. HAND AND BAR (HAND), creamer.—*Ref. HV-84; Metz 2-82* U.S. Glass Co. (Bryce), 1891. Made in extended table service including compotes. Has clenched fist holding a bar as finial. See Plate 184. Crystal.—With bar **Key B;** without **Key A**
2. DOUBLE ZIG-ZAG, creamer.—*Ref. K3-11* McKee Glass Co., 1880. Extended table service.—**Key A**

Row 3

1. HOMESTEAD, goblet. See Plate 183.
2. CENTRAL #560, creamer.—*Ref. K3-17* Central Glass Co., 1881. Extended table service including compotes, sauce, bowls.—**Key A**

PLATE 186 PLAIN

Row 1

1. URN, creamer.—*Ref. K6-2* c. 1880, probably Central Glass Co. (Kamm).—**Key A**

2. IONA, creamer (engraved).—*Ref. K4-2* Extended table service including celery vase.—**Key A**

Row 2

1. EMPIRE, creamer (etched).—*Ref. K3-40* McKee Glass Co., 1896. Extended table service including compotes.—**Key A**

2. WHEEL AND COMMA, creamer.—*Ref. K3-5* Aetna Glass and Mfg. Co., 1881-83. Extended table service including sauce, berry bowl. Found plain or acid-etched flower or leaf designs.—**Key B**

Row 3

1. ETCHED FERN (ASHMAN), goblet (etched).—*Ref. K1-89* Portland Glass Co., c. 1880's. Extended table service including cake stand, compotes, celery vase, bread tray, footed cake basket, cake stand, footed sauce.—**Key D**

2. CROSSED DISCS, creamer.—*Ref. K4-35* c. 1890. Extended table service including egg cup.—**Key A**

Row 4

1. CASCO, goblet. Portland Glass Co.—**Key B**

2. ADAMS SAXON, cruet.—*Ref. K3-11* Adams and Co.; U.S. Glass Co., c. 1890-95. Often etched. Extended table service including water tray, finger bowl, cake stand, tumbler, mug, salt shaker, toothpick holder, syrup, celery vase, rectangular pickle dish, wine, 6″ plate. Crystal, ruby-stained.—**Key B**

3. ADAMS SAXON, creamer. See above.

PLATE 187 PLAIN

Row 1

1. CENTRAL 1879, creamer.—*Ref. K6-3* Central Glass Co., 1879. Extended table service including lamps, compote.—**Key A**
2. PANELLED RINGED STEM (PLAIN TWO-MOLD), creamer.—*Ref. K2-18* c. mid-1880's.—**Key A**
3. IVY SPRAY, creamer (engraved).—*Ref. K2-11* —**Key A**

Row 2

1. ANGULAR, creamer.—*Ref. K6-10* c. 1880's.—**Key A**
2. CENTRAL #520, creamer.—*Ref. K3-16* Central Glass Co., 1881. Extended table service including compotes.—**Key A**
3. SUNKEN TEARDROP, creamer. See Plate 183.

Row 3

1. FLAT OVAL, creamer (engraved).—*Ref. K3-113* Extended table service including covered compote.—**Key B**
2. BIG TOP, compote.—*Ref. HV-92* U.S. Glass Co. (Challinor #316-318), 1891. Made in several sizes of compotes only. Crystal.—**Key B**
3. RIBBED DROPLET BAND, pitcher.—*Ref. Heacock* George Duncan and Sons #89, c. 1887. Extended table service including bowls, sauce, compotes, celery vase, tumbler (without "feet").—**Key B**

PLATE 188 PLAIN

Row 1

1. SEASHELL (BOSWELL), creamer (engraved).—*Ref. Gob II-66; K4-1; LV pl. 20* Made in basic table service. Finials are spiral shells.—**Key B**

2. PLEAT BAND, pitcher.—*Ref. K5-139* Indiana Tumbler and Goblet Co. #137, 1898. Basic table service and milk pitcher. —**Key A**

Row 2

1. PRISM RING, creamer.—*Ref. K3-10* Duncan #415, early 1890's. Extended table service including compotes, celery vase, claret, cordial, wine.—**Key A**

2. SAWTOOTH BOTTOM, goblet.—*Ref. Gob II-33* —**Key A**

Row 3

1. FOSTORIA'S STERLING, pitcher.—*Ref. K5-33* Fostoria Glass Co. #141, 1888. Basic table service.—**Key B**

2. TAUNTON, salt shaker (etched).—*Ref. LV50* Extended table service.—**Key A**

PLATE 189 PLAIN

Row 1
1. CROSSBAR HANDLE, creamer—*Ref. K6-9* —**Key A**
2. MARY JANE, pitcher.—*Ref. K2-33* c. 1890.—**Key A**

Row 2
1. ATLAS (LITTLE BALLS), pitcher. This is the pitcher to the ATLAS pattern shown on Plate 12.—*Ref. K3-44*
2. GRECIAN, creamer—*Ref. K2-55* c. 1890's.—**Key A**
3. ADAMS # 329 (PLAIN TWO-MOLD), pitcher. (Etched)—*Ref. K4-28* U.S. Glass Co. (Adams), 1891. Extended table service including wine, cordial, claret, salt shaker, celery tray, waste bowl, compotes, cake stand, sauce, cruet.—**Key A**

Row 3
1. HEISEY #1225, pitcher—*Ref. K7 Pl. 33* A. H. Heisey Glass Co., c. 1895. Extended table service including salt shaker, cruet, syrup, celery vase, compote, covered bowl. Crystal, stained green, ruby or gold.—**Key B**
2. FROSTED EAGLE, creamer (etched). See Plate 10.
3. FROSTED EAGLE, pitcher. See Plate 10.

PLATE 190 PLAIN

Row 1

1. V-BAND, creamer—*Ref. K6-27*—**Key A**
2. LITTLE BAND, creamer—*Ref. K2-40* c. 1880.—**Key A**

Row 2

1. CONNECTICUT, creamer (etched). See Plate 61.
2. AETNA, pitcher (etched).—*Ref. K5-130* Aetna Glass and Mfg. Co. #325, 1886. Made in water set: pitcher, tumblers, waste bowl, tray.—**Key B**
3. NEWPORT, pitcher.—*Ref. HV-118* U.S. Glass Co. (Richards and Hartley factory), 1891. Made in crystal pitchers only.—**Key B**

Row 3

1. DUNCAN #2001, tumbler.—*Ref. K7-21* George Duncan's Sons and Co., 1891. Extended table service including tumbler, footed sauce, bowls, cake stand, celery vase, tray, finger bowl, salt shaker. Crystal, ruby-stained. See Plate 170.—**Key A**
2. IMPERIAL #4, pitcher.—*Ref. K7-183* Imperial Glass Co., 1902. Extended table service including jelly compote, wine, celery vase, individual creamer and sugar, compotes. Note: Imperial's #6 is identical to #4 except for vertical panels.—**Key A**

PLATE 191 PLANTS

Row 1

BULGING CORN, salt shaker.—*Ref. K5-92* Libbey and Sons, 1889. Part of a condiment set in the pattern MAIZE. See below.

Row 2

1. EAR OF CORN, vase.—*Ref. K2-62* Northwood-Dugan Glass Co., late 1890's. Made in extended table service including two types of creamer. Decorated crystal, opalescent—**Key C**

2. MAIZE, cruet.—*Ref. K5-92* Libbey and Sons Co., 1889. Extended table service including salt shaker, sugar shaker, toothpick holder, condiment set in holder, tumbler, decanters, carafe, rose bowl, celery vase, berry and finger bowls. Opaque white, ivory, carnival, decorated.—**Key C**

3. CORN, sugar shaker.—*Ref. PetSal 25N* Dithridge and Co., c. 1900. Salt and sugar shakers only. Opaque colors.—**Key C**

Row 3

1. CORN WITH HUSK, salt shaker.—*Ref. PetSal 25R; K5-92* The salt shaker to MAIZE pattern. See above.

2. MAPLE LEAF (LEAF), pitcher.—*Ref. K4-143* Gillander and Sons, late 1880's. Extended table service including large ice cream bowl, compotes, plates, sauces, tumbler, bread plate, bowls, celery vase, cake stand, jelly compote, dolphin-based compote, platter, tray. Crystal, vaseline, canary, blue, sapphire, amber.—**Key C**

Row 4

CORN SPHERE, salt shaker.—*Ref. PetSal 25P* Opaque glass.—**Key C**

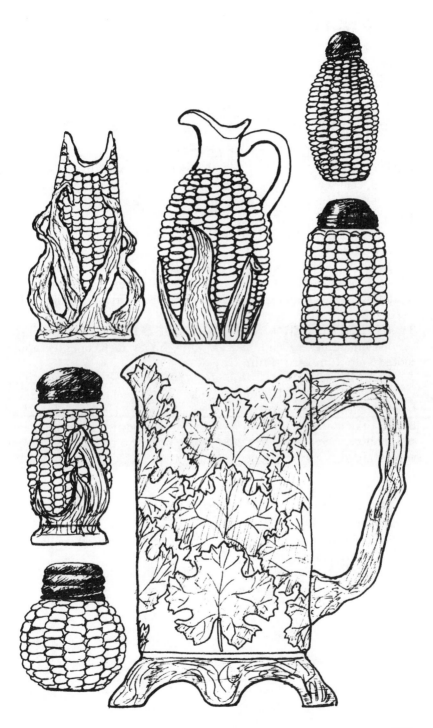

PLATE 192 PLANTS

Row 1

1. ANTHEMION, pitcher—*Ref. L58; K5-137* Model Flint Glass Co., 1890. Extended table service including cake stand, celery vase, plate, relish, sauce, tumbler, berry bowl. Crystal.—**Key B**

2. PANELLED ANTHEMION, pitcher.—*Ref. K4-59* c. 1885. Extended table service.—**Key B**

3. RIBBED PALM (SPRIG; ACANTHUS), pitcher.—*Ref. K4-55* McKee and Brothers, 1868. Extended table service including wine, egg cup, celery vase, plate, three types of lamp, sauce, tumblers, wine. Glass sometimes has a pink hue. Crystal.—**Key C**

Row 2

1. PRESSED LEAF WITH CHAIN, goblet.—*Ref. L153-16; Gob II-10* —**Key A**

2. BLOCK AND PALM (EIGHTEEN-NINETY), goblet.—*Ref. K5-58* Beaver Falls Glass Co., c. 1890's. Extended table service including coke stand, salt shaker, sauce. Crystal, milk glass. —**Key B**

3. INVERTED FERN, goblet.—*Ref. L36* c. 1860's. Extended table service including egg cup, sauces, wine, honey dish, open compote, footed salt, tumbler.—Flint **Key C**

4. PLUME, celery vase.—*Ref. K2-64* Adams and Company, 1874; U.S. Glass Co. 1891. Extended table service including cake stand, bowls, sauce, celery vase (two types), footed sauce, covered footed bowls, cake stand, open footed bowls, square bowls, lamp, vase. Fair availability. See Plate 243 for horizontal type. Crystal, ruby-stained.—**Key B**

Row 3

1. STIPPLED PALM, Pitcher.—**Key B**

2. MISSOURI (PALM AND SCROLL), goblet.—*Ref. K2-133* U.S. Glass Co. #15058, 1899. A State Series pattern. Extended table service including cruet, salt shaker, syrup, relish. Limited availability. Crystal, emerald green.—**Key B**

3. PARAGON, pitcher.—*Ref. K6-39* Dalzell, Gilmore and Leighton, 1894. Extended table service.—**Key B**

PLATE 193 PLANTS

Row 1

1. ARROWHEAD (ANDERSON), creamer.—*Ref. K3-64* c. 1900. Made in extended table service.—**Key A**

2. MEDALLION SPRIG (STYLISTIC LEAF), salt shaker.—*Ref. L-102* West Virginia Glass Co., c. 1894. Extended table service including toothpick holder, syrup, lemonade set. All pieces scarce.—**Key C**

3. CO-OP #323, creamer.—*Ref. K5 Pl. 3* Cooperative Flint Glass Co., 1905. Extended table service including toothpick holder, berry bowl.—**Key C**

Row 2

1. PANELLED FERN, pitcher.—*Ref. K5-43* c. 1878. Extended table service including covered jelly compote. Opaque white and blue.—**Key B**

2. ACANTHUS, miniature pitcher.—*Ref. K7-63* c. 1870.—**Key B**

3. HEART, goblet. Bakewell, Pears and Co. Extended table service including jelly compote.—**Key B**

Row 3

1. LEAF-IN-OVAL (PENELOPE), cup.—*Ref. K8-53* Extended table service including punch bowl. Crystal, ruby-stained.—**Key A**

2. ACANTHUS LEAF, creamer.—*Ref. K2-53* Extended table service including bowl. Milk glass or slag.—**Key D**

Row 4

1. HERRINGBONE BUTTRESS (HERRINGBONE RIB), salt shaker.—*Ref. K5-123; Gob II-18* Indiana Tumbler and Goblet Co. #140, 1899. Extended table service including cracker jar, cup, mug. Crystal, chocolate glass, green. See Plate 212.—**Key B**

2. CACTUS (PANELLED AGAVE), syrup.—*Ref. K1-78* Indiana Tumbler and Goblet Co., 1900-1903. Extended table service including celery vase, mug, cruet, cracker jar, compotes, mustard jar, berry set, flat and stemmed butter dishes, salt shaker, toothpick, tumbler, relish, plate. Crystal, chocolate; other colors rare.—Chocolate **Key D**; Crystal **Key B**

3. MURANO (LEAF AND FAN), salt shaker.—*Ref. PetSal 167B* Greensburg Glass Co., 1894. Extended table service including castor bottle.—**Key B**

PLATE 194 PLANTS

Row 1

1. MARSH FERN, salt shaker.—*Ref. K3-143* Riverside Glass Co. #327, 1889. Extended table service including bowl, compote. —**Key B**

2. SWAG WITH BRACKETS, creamer.—*Ref. K1-86* Jefferson Glass Co., c. 1903. Extended table service including toothpick holder, salt shaker, jelly compote, celery vase, tumbler. Crystal, opalescent, vaseline, other colors.—**Key B**

3. MARSH FERN, pitcher. See Row 1 #1.

Row 2

1. ARCHED LEAF, goblet. c. 1870's. Extended table service including footed salt, plate.—**Key C**

2. LEAF UMBRELLA, salt shaker.—*Ref. PetSal 32S* Northwood Glass Co. #263, c. 1889. Made in extended table service including rare butter dish, toothpick holder, berry set, syrup, sugar shaker, celery vase, finger bowl, covered powder jar. Cased cranberry and colored glass.—**Key F**

3. LONG FAN WITH ACANTHUS LEAF (FAN WITH ACANTHUS LEAF; BIJOU), pitcher.—*Ref. K2-125; K8-62* Greensburg Glass Co., mid-1880's. Extended table service including sauce, salt shaker, berry bowl.—**Key B**

Row 3

1. PANELLED SPRIG, syrup.—*Ref. HI-41* Northwood Glass Co., 1895-1905. Extended table service including cruet, sugar shaker, toothpick holder, celery vase, pickle castor set, salt shaker, jam jar. Crystal, colors, opalescent.—**Key B**

2. LEAF ROSETTE, salt shaker. See Plate 179.

3. FLORIDA PALM (TIDAL; PERFECTION), celery vase.—*Ref. K3-110* Greensburg Glass Co., 1880's; 1904. Extended table service including cake stand, berry bowl, wine, plate, compotes.—**Key C**

PLATE 195 PLANTS

Row 1

1. PRESSED LEAF (N.P.L.), spoon holder.—*Ref. L125* Central Glass Co., 1881; McKee and Brothers, 1868. Extended table service including compotes, wine, cake stand, oval dishes, cordial, egg cup, bowls, lamp, sauce.—**Key B;** Flint **Key D**

2. BIRCH LEAF, compote. c. 1870's. Extended table service including egg cup, master salt. Crystal, milk glass.—**Key B**

Row 2

1. STARS AND BARS WITH LEAF, pitcher. See STARS AND BARS, Plate 94.

2. DIAMOND CUT WITH LEAF, goblet.—*Ref. L109* Extended table service including mug, cordial, plates, open and covered sugar bowls, salt shaker, wine. Crystal, canary, blue, green.—**Key B**

3. TWIN LEAVES, creamer.—*Ref. K7-1* Basic table service. —**Key B**

Row 3

1. LEAF AND RIB, salt shaker.—*Ref. PetSal 32E* —**Key A**

2. PANELLED PALM, syrup.—*Ref. Gob II-37* U.S. Glass #15095 (Ripley factory), 1906. Extended table service including tumbler, toothpick holder, bowls, wine, cake stand, salt shaker, sauce. Crystal, rose-flashed.—**Key A**

3. LONG MAPLE LEAF, pitcher. Late 1880's. Extended table service including mug, salt shaker. Crystal.—**Key B**

PLATE 196 PLANTS

Row 1

1. RIBBED IVY, goblet—*Ref. L39* c. 1850's. Made in extended table service including champagne, wine, tumblers, whiskey, castor bottle, jelly compotes, decanters, open salts, honey dish, egg cup, hat.—**Key C**; whiskey tumbler **Key F**

2. FROSTED LEAF (STIPPLED LEAF), goblet.—*Ref. L94* Portland Glass Co., c. 1850's. Extended table service including wine, tumbler, egg cup, compote, salt, sauce, celery vase, decanter, rare flint champagne.—Flint **Key E**

3. STIPPLED IVY, footed salt dish.—*Ref. L119* Extended table service including jelly compote. Like BUDDED IVY without little buds. See Plate 197.—**Key C**

4. HAMILTON WITH LEAF, pitcher.—*Ref. L57* Boston and Sandwich Glass Co., 1870's; others later. Extended table service including tumbler, wine, cordial, egg cup, celery vase, compotes, footed salt, two size lamps, compote. Crystal, clear and frosted—**Key D**; tumbler, **Key D (double)**

Row 2

1. IVY IN SNOW (FOREST WARE), pitcher.—*Ref. L119* Cooperative Flint Glass Co., 1880's. Extended table service including cake stand, tumbler, wine, jam jar, cup and saucer, compotes, celery vase, sauce, plate, relish, bowl. Crystal, amber, ruby-stained.—**Key B**

2. SOUTHERN IVY, pitcher.—*Ref. L166* c. 1880's. Extended table service including berry bowl, cruet, egg cup, tumbler, sauce. Crystal.—**Key B**

Row 3

1. FROSTED LEAF, decanter. See Row 1, #2.

2. PANELLED IVY, pitcher.—*Ref. K3-69* U.S. Glass Co., 1880's. Extended table service including compotes, cake stand, jelly compote, sauce.—**Key B**

3. ROYAL IVY, sugar shaker.—*Ref. K5-87* Northwood Glass Co., c. 1889. Extended table service including toothpick holder, syrup, cruet, pickle castor, jam jar, lamp, berry set, tumbler, salt shaker. Frosted crystal, art glass colors, cased, opaline.—**Key C**

PLATE 197 PLANTS

Row 1

1. STIPPLED LOOP WITH VINE BAND, goblet.—*Ref. Gob II-50*—**Key B**

2. BEADED ACORN (BEADED ACORN MEDALLION), egg cup.—*Ref. L65* Boston Silver Glass Co., c. 1869. Extended table service including wine, champagne, footed and flat sauces, relish, compotes, 6″ plate.—**Key C**

3. FALLING LEAVES, pitcher.—*Ref. K4-132* Extended table service including berry bowl, oval dish. Leaves are impressed on inside of bowl. Crystal.—**Key B**

Row 2

1. SPIRALLED IVY, pitcher.—*Ref. L147* Mid-1880's. Extended table setting including tumbler, sauce. Crystal.—**Key B**

2. BUDDED IVY, goblet.—*Ref. L119* Extended table service including compote.—**Key C**

3. HOPS BAND (MAPLE; PRESSED LEAF BAND), creamer.—*Ref. K3-19* King Glass Co., c. 1871. Extended table service.—**Key A**

Row 3

1. RIBBED ACORN, bowl.—*Ref. L39* Boston and Sandwich. Extended table service including compotes, sauce, honey dish.—**Key B**

2. CROSSED FERN, creamer.—*Ref. K3-111* Made in extended table service including covered compote, berry bowls, footed sauce, family-sized butter with four feet. Crystal, opaque white, opaque turquoise.—**Key B**

Row 4

1. STIPPLED CLOVER, butter dish.—*Ref. L141* Extended table service including cordial.—**Key C**

2. OAK WREATH, pitcher—*Ref. K6-5* Central Glass Co., 1880's. Extended table service including sauce.—**Key B**

PLATE 198 PLANTS - OAKS

Row 1

1. PANELLED ACORN BAND, pitcher.—*Ref. L125* Boston and Sandwich, early; other companies later. Made in extended table service including compotes, celery vase, egg cup, sauce.—**Key C**

2. ACORN BAND-TYPE I (ACORN VARIANT), goblet.—*Ref. L125* Portland Glass Co. Extended table service including rare wine, celery vase, egg cup, compotes, flat and footed sauces.—**Key C**

3. ACORN BAND-TYPE 2 (ACORN VARIANT), goblet.—*Ref. L125* Portland Glass Co. See above - Type 1.

Row 2

1. OAK LEAF BAND, goblet. Portland Glass Co.—**Key C**

2. OAK LEAF BAND WITH MEDALLION, goblet. Portland Glass Co.—**Key C**

3. OAK LEAVES, goblet.—*Ref. L153-4* —**Key B**

4. ACORN, goblet—*Ref. L125* c. 1870's. Extended table service including celery vase, egg cup, compotes.—**Key C**

Row 3

1. PANELLED OAK, creamer—*Ref. K7-41* Lancaster Glass Co., 1911. Extended table service including celery vase, tumbler. Crystal.—**Key C**

2. CHESTNUT OAK (OLD ACORN), pitcher.—*Ref. K2-86; L125* Early 1870's. Extended table service.—**Key B**

3. WHITE OAK, creamer.—*Ref. K2-65* —**Key C**

Row 4

1. NETTED OAK (ACORN; NETTED ROYAL OAK), sugar shaker.—*Ref. HIII-33* Northwood Glass Co., c. 1895-1905. Extended table service including syrup, water set, cruet, berry set. Crystal, milk glass, apple green, amethyst, blue.—**Key B**

2. ROYAL OAK, sugar shaker.—*Ref. K5-86* Northwood Glass Co., 1889-90. Extended table service including water set, cruet, salt shaker, pickle castor, berry set. Frosted Crystal, rubina.—**Key D;** Syrup **Key E**

3. ROYAL OAK, syrup. See above.

PLATE 199 PLANTS

Row 1

1. POND LILY, goblet—*Ref. Gob II-117* —**Key C**
2. HANGING LEAF, salt shaker.—*Ref. W123; PetSal 32M* Milk glass.—**Key C**
3. CABBAGE LEAF, pitcher.—*Ref. L65* c. 1870's and '80's. Extended table service including rabbit plate, compote, leaf-shaped pickle dish, celery vase, cake stand, cup, egg cup, covered cheese dish. Crystal, amber, frosted, opalescent.—**Key D**
4. HOLLY goblet.—*Ref. L116* Boston and Sandwich Glass Co., 1860's-'70's. Made in extended table service including tumbler, wine, egg cup, covered and open compotes, celery vase, cake stand, sauce, pickle dish.—Flint **Key E**

Row 2

1. GARDEN OF EDEN, goblet. See Plate 6.
2. HOLLY BAND, pitcher.—*Ref. K6-64* c. 1870's. Extended table service including compote, celery vase, tumbler.—**Key D**
3. ARTICHOKE (VALENCIA), salt shaker. See Plate 51.

Row 3

1. PANELLED HOLLY AND DIAMOND, creamer.—*Ref. K2-59* Opaque glass.—**Key C**
2. HOLLY CLEAR, creamer.—*Ref. K5-81* Indiana Tumbler and Goblet Co. (National Glass Co.), 1903. Extended table service including tumbler, toothpick holder on pedestal, vase, covered compotes, rare mug. Crystal, amber opalescent. Called HOLLY AMBER in amber opalescent. HOLLY AMBER pieces are priced so high that professional evaluation would be warranted.—**Key E**
3. HOLLY AMBER, syrup. See above.

PLATE 200 PLANTS

Row 1

1. BASKETWEAVE WITH FROSTED LEAF, pitcher. c. 1890-1900. Extended table service including cake plate, compote, cordial, egg cup, syrup, water tray. Crystal, canary, blue, green. —**Key B**

2. BARRED FISHSCALE, creamer.—*Ref. K5-59* c. 1875-85. Opaque colors.—**Key C**

Row 2

1. LEAF MEDALLION (REGENT), cruet. See Plate 177.

2. CIRCLED SCROLL, creamer.—*Ref. K4-70* Dugan Glass Co., c. 1903. Extended table service including salt shaker, sauce, berry bowl, tumbler. Crystal, colors, opalescent.—**Key B**

Row 3

1. CLOVER, pitcher. Extended table service including tumbler, toothpick holder.—**Key B**

2. THREE LEAF CLOVER, spill holder.—**Key B**

3. LEAF AND STAR (TOBIN), creamer.—*Ref. K6-17; Gob II-136* New Martinsville Glass Co. #711. Extended table service including toothpick holder, water set. Crystal, ruby-stained, marigold-flashed.—**Key B**

Row 4

1. LEAFY SCROLL, creamer.—*Ref. K4-91* U.S. Glass Co. #15034 (Gillander factory), 1896. Extended table service. Crystal.—**Key B**

2. RIPLEY'S WYOMING, pitcher.—*Ref. HV 121* U.S. Glass Co. (Ripley factory), 1891. Extended table service including tumblers. Crystal.—**Key B**

3. SCROLL WITH ACANTHUS, salt shaker. See Plate 37.

411

PLATE 201 PLANTS

Row 1

1. ORIENTAL, pickle jar.—*Ref. K7-77* Made in extended table service including tumbler, celery vase, covered compote.—**Key C**

2. BAMBOO, pitcher.—*Ref. K5-Pl. 2* LaBelle Glass Co., 1883. Extended table service including compotes, salt shaker, tumbler. Crystal, engraved.—**Key B**

3. SCROLLED SPRAY, creamer.—*Ref. K2-91* Made in extended table service including salt shaker. Opaque glass.—**Key C**

Row 2

1. BARLEY (SPRIG; INDIAN TREE), pitcher.—*Ref. K1-34; L116* Late 1870's. Extended table service including cake stands, compote, cordial, jam jar, plate, wine. Fairly abundant.—**Key B**

2. TREE OF LIFE WITH SPRIG, creamer.—*Ref. K2-27* Portland Glass Co., 1870's. Made in extended table service including celery vase, syrup. Not all pieces have the little wheels.—**Key B**

3. HOLLAND (OAT SPRAY), pitcher.—*Ref. K4-37* McKee Glass Co., 1894. Extended table service including compote.—**Key A**

Row 3

1. WHEAT AND BARLEY (DUQUESNE; HOPS AND BARLEY; OATS AND BARLEY), pitcher.—*Ref. K1-41; L50* Bryce Brothers, late 1870's; U.S. Glass, 1891. Extended table service including jelly compote, syrup, open and covered high compotes, footed tumbler, cake stand, mug, 7″ and 9″ plates, flat and footed sauces, toothpick holder. Crystal, amber, blue.—**Key B**

2. FERN, goblet.—*Ref. K8-66* Union Glass Co., c. 1880. Known in goblets.—**Key A**

3. PANELLED WHEAT (WHEAT), pitcher.—*Ref. K1-40* Hobbs, Brockunier and Co., 1871. Extended table service including open and covered compotes. Crystal, milk glass.—**Key C**

413

PLATE 202 RIBS AND COLUMNS

Row 1

1. LONG BUTTRESS, sugar bowl.—*Ref. K7-46* Fostoria Glass Co. #1229, c. 1904. Extended table service including toothpick holder, salt shaker, tumblers, salt dip, individual creamer and sugar, celery vase, pickle dish, syrups, pickle jar, vases. Crystal.—**Key B**

2. THE BEDFORD (LONG PUNTY), creamer.—*Ref. K3-81* Fostoria Glass Co., 1901-05. Made in extended table service including toothpick, celery vase, tumbler. Crystal.—**Key B**

Row 2

1. ELEPHANT TOES, creamer.—*Ref. HV-28* U.S. Glass Co. (Richards and Hartley factory), 1905. Extended table service. Crystal, staining.—**Key A**

2. PITTSBURGH, creamer.—*Ref. K4-63; LV63* U.S. Glass Co. (Bryce), 1891. Extended table service including handled relishes, celery vases, syrup, sauces, handled jelly, cake baskets, covered bowls, salt shaker, individual salt, tumbler, wine, champagne, decanters, pickle castor sets, bowls, cruet. Crystal.—**Key B**

3. VIRGINIA (BANDED PORTLAND; MAIDEN'S BLUSH; PORTLAND WITH DIAMOND POINT BAND), tumbler.—*Ref. K2-89* U. S. Glass Co. #15071 (Gillander; Gas City; Richards and Hartley), 1901. A State Series pattern. Extended table service including toothpick holder, salt shaker, cruet, vase, wine, compotes, water bottle, jam jar, tumbler, relish boat, puff box, candlesticks, tray, cologne bottles, bowls, sardine dish. Good availability. Crystal, green- and rose-flashed; ruby-stained.—**Key C**

Row 3

BARRED OVAL (OVAL AND CROSSBAR), pitcher.—*Ref. K6-25; LV41* U. S. Glass Co. #15004 (Duncan), 1891. Extended table service including water bottle, compote, small plate, salt shaker. Crystal, ruby-stained.—**Key A**

Row 4

1. PORTLAND, cruet.—*Ref. K1-107* U.S. Glass Co. (Glassport; Ripley; Central), #15121, after 1900. Extended table service including toothpick holder, salt shaker, pomade jar, puff box, cake stand, several size compotes, decanter, vases. Crystal.—**Key C**

2. PORTLAND, goblet. See above.

3. VIRGINIA, syrup. See Row 2 #3.

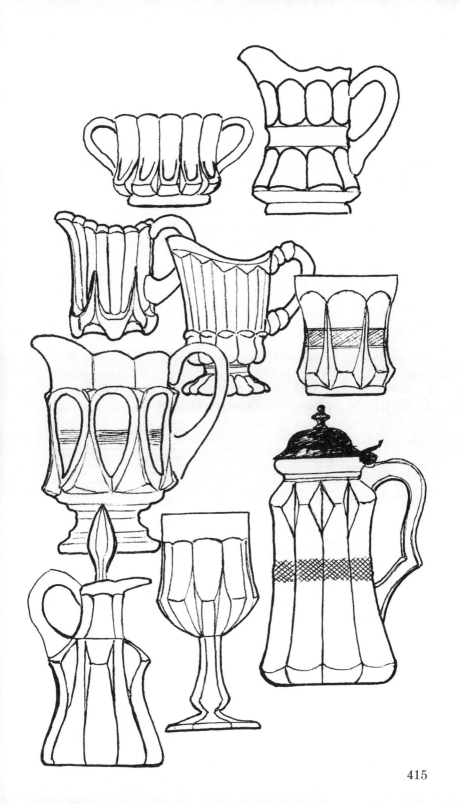

PLATE 203 RIBS AND COLUMNS

Row 1

1. ADAMS #52, creamer.—*Ref. HV72* U.S. Glass Co. #329 (Adams), 1891. Crystal.—**Key A**
2. BELLE, creamer.—*Ref. K5-64* Ohio Flint Glass Co., 1897. Made in extended table service including sixty items. Crystal, etched, engraved.—**Key A**

Row 2

1. DOUBLE BEETLE BAND, pitcher.—*Ref. K3-47* Columbia Glass Co., 1880's. Extended table service including flat and footed sauce, open and covered sugar bowls. Crystal, yellow, amber, blue.—**Key B**
2. SUNK HONEYCOMB (CORONA), syrup.—*Ref. K2-57* Greensburg Glass Co.; McKee and Brothers, c. 1903. Extended table service including cruet, decanter, toothpick holder, wine, salt shaker, rare jelly compote, berry set, individual creamer and sugar. Crystal, ruby-stained.—**Key B**
3. SEMI-OVAL, salt shaker.—*Ref. PetSal 39-B* —**Key A**

Row 3

1. OPPOSING PYRAMIDS, creamer. See Plate 49.
2. FULTON, pitcher. See Plate 13.

PLATE 204 RIBS AND COLUMNS

Row 1

1. CHELSEA, tumbler.—*Ref. K8-65* Cambridge Glass Co., c. 1906. Extended table service including cup, soda glasses, ten sizes goblets, several size tumblers, punch bowl, celery tray, bowls, nut cup, plates, vases, baskets, syrup jug with plate. Marked "Near Cut" after 1906. Crystal.—**Key A**

2. PIONEER #15, creamer.—*Ref. K3-94* Pioneer Glass Co., c. 1885-1890. Extended table service including celery vase, tumbler, berry bowl, sauces. Crystal, ruby-stained.—**Key A**

2. CUT LOG, creamer—*Ref. K1-118; K8-61; LV53* Greensburg Glass Co., 1885. Made in extended table service including mug, wine, salt shaker, cruet, compotes, syrup, "canoe" bowl, relish, vase, handled relish, individual creamer and sugar, celery vase, finger bowl. Good availability.—**Key C**

Row 2

1. CLIMAX (SMOCKING BANDS; BULLET BAND; LITTLE BULLET), pitcher (etched).—*Ref. K7-44* U.S. Glass Co. (Columbia factory), 1891. Extended table service including covered compote. Crystal, blue.—**Key A**

2. TORPEDO (FISH-EYE; PIGMY), pitcher.—*Ref. K2-107* Thompson Glass Co. c. 1889. Made in extended table service including berry bowl, rose bowl, waste bowl, open flared bowl, cake stand, jelly compote, sauce, master salt, salt shaker, decanter, syrup, tumbler, celery vase, cup and saucer, lamp.—**Key D**

3. TEARDROP, pitcher.—*Ref. K7-18* Dalzell, Gilmore and Leighton Glass Co., late 1890's. Made in extended table service including candlestick, wine, compote.—**Key A**

Row 3

1. BROKEN COLUMN (IRISH COLUMN; NOTCHED RIB; RATTAN AND BAMBOO), pitcher.—*Ref. K4-116; LV71* Columbia Glass Co., 1887; U.S. Glass Co. #15021, 1891. Very extended table service including banana dish, handled basket, pickle castor, cruet, syrup, cracker jar, water bottle, rare 7″ plate, rare sugar shaker, rare covered compote, salt shaker, celery vase. Being reproduced. Crystal, ruby-stained, cobalt blue.—**Key D**

2. BALL (NOTCHED BAR), cruet.—*Ref. K7-17; Gob II-160* McKee Glass Co. #492, 1894. Extended table service.—**Key B**

Row 4

1. TRUNCATED CUBE (THOMPSON #77), salt shaker.—*Ref. K5-82; Gob II-39* Thompson Glass Co., 1892. Extended table service including wine, toothpick holder, tumbler, cruet, celery vase. See Plate 220. Crystal, ruby-stained.—**Key B**

2. BALL, salt shaker. See Row 3 #2.
3. BROKEN COLUMN, syrup. See Row 3 #1.

PLATE 205 RIBS AND COLUMNS

Row 1

1. PLEATING, spoon holder. See Plate 167.
2. CELTIC CROSS, creamer (engraved).—*Ref. K2-111* Geo. Duncan and Sons #771, 1883. Made in extended table service including bowls, compotes.—**Key A**
3. OLD COLUMBIA, creamer.—*Ref. HPV#1, 16* U.S. Glass Co. (Columbia), 1891. Extended table service including cup, toothpick holder. Crystal.—**Key A**

Row 2

U.S. RIB, creamer.—*Ref. K7-42* U.S. Glass Co. #15061 (Glassport), 1899. Extended table service of many pieces. Crystal, emerald green.—**Key B**

Row 3

1. MARIO, pitcher. See Plate 16.
2. VULCAN, creamer.—*Ref. K5-101* National Glass Co. (McKee factory), 1900; Ohio Flint Glass Works, 1902. Extended table service including toothpick holder, salt shaker, 8″ compote, sauce, celery vase, syrup, cruet, olive dish, vases, wine.—**Key B**
3. FOOTED PANELLED RIB, creamer.—*Ref. LV 59* U.S. Glass Co. (Challinor #308), 1891. Basic table service. Crystal.—**Key B**

Row 4

1. CORDOVA (PRISM BUTTRESS; POINTED THUMBPRINT AND PANEL), goblet.—*Ref. K1-105; LV66* O'Hara Glass Co., 1890; U.S. Glass Co., 1891. Made in extended table service including salt shaker, toothpick holder, inkwell, handled lamp, compotes, cake stand, syrup, egg cup, tumbler, wine. Crystal, ruby-stained, green.—**Key A**
2. CONTINENTAL, pitcher.—*Ref. K8-187* A.H. Heisey #339, 1903-1910. Extended table service including toothpick holder, two kinds of butter dishes, two kinds of creamers, two kinds of spooners, two kinds of sugar bowls (flat, footed). Crystal.—**Key C**
3. DELTA, syrup.—*Ref. HIII-23* c. 1895. Syrup known. Amber, crystal.—**Key C**

421

PLATE 206 RIBS AND COLUMNS

Row 1

1. YOKED LOOP (SCALLOPED LOOP), goblet.—*Ref. Gob II-54* Extended table service including open and covered sugar bowls, tumbler.—**Key C**

2. SNAKESKIN (OVERSHOT), goblet—*Ref. L135* Extended table service including plate. See Plate 245.—**Key B**

3. PRISM, egg cup.—*Ref. L13* c. 1860's. Made in extended table service including decanter, wine, champagne.—**Key C**

Row 2

1. SUNKEN ARCHES,. creamer.—*Ref. K5-58* Riverside Glass Works #370, 1891. Extended table service.—**Key B**

2. LOOP AND PETAL, goblet.—*Ref. Gob II-1* —**Key B**

3. PALMER PRISM, goblet.—**Key B**

Row 3

1. HEISEY'S COARSE RIBBING, creamer.—*Ref. K8-51* A.H. Heisey Glass Co., 1902.—**Key B**

2. LOOPS AND OVALS, goblet.—*Ref. Gob II-26* —**Key B**

3. PRISM BARS, creamer.—*Ref. Gob II-54; K4-42* c. early 1890's. Extended table service.—**Key A**

Row 4

1. TRIANGULAR PRISM, goblet.—*Ref. Gob II-29* Made in extended table service including whiskey tumbler, wine, master salt, cup, low and high compotes, bowls.—Flint **Key D;** Non-flint **Key B**

2. FLUTE AND CROWN, pitcher.—*Ref. K2-118* Westmoreland Glass Co., 1896. Extended table service including salt shaker, toothpick holder. Milk glass.—**Key C**

3. RIBBING, creamer.—*Ref. K7-1* c. 1875.—**Key A**

PLATE 207 RIBS AND COLUMNS

Row 1

1. ICICLE, sugar bowl.—*Ref. L19-20-22* Bakewell, Pears and Co., c. 1870's. Extended table service including compotes, pickle dish, relish, individual butter dish, sauce, flat and footed butter dishes, master salt, 5″ lamp.—**Key B**

2. BLAZE, sugar bowl.—*Ref. 213* New England Glass Co., c. 1869. Extended table service including compote, plates, sauces, salt shaker, tumbler, wine, egg cup. Crystal.—Flint **Key D**

3. BANDED ICICLE, pitcher.—*Ref. Gob II-137* Bakewell, Pears and Co., 1870's. Extended table service including compotes, sauce, celery vase. Crystal.—**Key B**

Row 2

1. BANDED ICICLE — LATE, goblet.—**Key A**

2. BELTED ICICLE (LATE ICICLE), pitcher.—*Ref. K8-63* Fostoria Glass Co. #162. Made in extended table service including salt shaker, tumbler.—**Key B**

3. WAVE, creamer.—*Ref. K7-14* c. 1880's—**Key A**

Row 3

1. SILVER QUEEN, creamer. See Plate 175.

2. RIB AND BEAD (NAOMI), creamer.—*Ref. K8-60* National Glass Co. (McKee), c. 1901. Extended table service including toothpick holder. Crystal, ruby-stained.—**Key B**

3. DUNCAN #10, tumbler. George Duncan and Sons, c. 1900.—**Key A**

Row 4

1. FINE RIB, footed salt dish.—*Ref. L36* Extended table service including cordial, covered compote, claret, celery vase, wine.—Flint **Key D**

2. STEDMAN, syrup.—*Ref. L13* McKee and Brothers. Extended table service including champagne, decanter, cordial, egg cup.—Flint **Key C**

3. RIBBED DRAPE, toothpick holder.—*Ref. K7-150* Jefferson Glass Co. #250, 1907. Extended table service including tumbler, sauce, bowl. Crystal, blue, custard, decorated with flowers.—**Key B**

PLATE 208 RIBS AND COLUMNS

Row 1

1. BRYCE #160, salt shaker.—*Ref. HV82* Bryce Brothers; U.S. Glass Co., c. 1891. Made in extended table service including sugar shaker, tray.—**Key A**
2. RIBBED BANDS, creamer.—*Ref. K7-7* c. 1880's.—**Key A**
3. PUFFED BANDS (SNOW BAND), creamer.—*Ref. K2-45* c. 1880's. Extended table service including wine, compotes, relish, sauce. Crystal, blue.—**Key A**

Row 2

1. TRIPLE BAR (SCALLOPED PRISM), creamer.—*Ref. K8-103* Doyle and Co. #84, 1880's; U.S. Glass Co., 1895. Extended table service including tumbler. Crystal.—**Key A**
2. TRIPLE BAR AND LOOP, creamer.—*Ref. K2-80* c. 1880's. Milk Glass.—**Key C**

Row 3

1. FLUTED RIBBON, tumbler. See Plate 168.
2. DUNCAN #16, tumbler. George Duncan and Sons, c. 1900.—**Key A**
3. DUNCAN #14, tumbler. George Duncan and Sons, c. 1900.—**Key A**

Row 4

1. WELLINGTON, salt shaker. See Plate 174.
2. DUNCAN #904, cup.—*Ref. Bones* George Duncan and Sons, c. 1900.—**Key A**
3. DUNCAN #37, tumbler. See Plate 162.—**Key A**

PLATE 209 RIBS AND COLUMNS

Row 1

1. RIB BAND, creamer.—*Ref. K8-38* Opaque white glass.—**Key C**
2. REX, creamer.—*Ref. K5 pl. 23* McKee Glass Co. #136, 1894. Extended table service including tumbler, cup, plate, pickle tray, finger bowl, syrup, cruet, straw jar, soda glasses, sundae, fruit bowl with lid, wine, footed sherbet.—**Key A**

Row 2

1. INSIDE RIBBING (PRESSED OPTIC), creamer.—*Ref. K8-37* Beaumont Glass Co. #101, 1900. Extended table service including celery vase, toothpick holder.—**Key A**
2. BAR AND FLUTE, creamer. See Plate 15.

Row 3

1. RIBBED WARE, spoon holder. See Plate 154.
2. BEATTY RIB (RIBBED OPAL), pitcher.—*Ref. L147; K6-54* A. J. Beatty Glass Co., 1888; U.S. Glass Co. Extended table service including two sizes toothpick holder, banana boat, berry bowl, sauce, cup, tumbler, cracker jar, salt shaker, sugar shaker. Opalescent white, blue and canary (scarce).—**Key C**

Row 4

1. HEAVY RIB, creamer.—*Ref. K7-62* —**Key A**
2. INSIDE FLUTE, pitcher.—*Ref. K5-140* —**Key A**

PLATE 210 RIBS AND COLUMNS

Row 1

1. FISHSCALE (CORAL), pitcher.—*Ref. K1-58; L156* Bryce Brothers, 1880's; U.S. Glass Co., 1891. Made in extended table service including berry bowl, salt shaker, tray, finger bowl, covered bowl, celery vase, compote, sauce, jelly compote. Crystal. Good availability.—**Key A**

2. FILE (RIBBED SAWTOOTH), pitcher.—*Ref. K2-30* Columbia Glass Co.; Imperial Glass Co.; U.S. Glass Co.; 1890-1907. Extended table service including cake plate, vases, salt shaker. Crystal. —**Key B**

3. DUNCAN #76, tumbler.—*Ref. Bones 115* George Duncan and Sons, c. 1900.—**Key A**

Row 2

1. HEART-SANDWICH, pitcher.—*Ref. K7-16* A very early Boston and Sandwich pattern, made in other pieces but not common. Museum quality.

2. PALING (BANDED PALING), pitcher.—*Ref. K3-24; Gob II-14* c. 1880's. Extended table service.—**Key A**

3. STRIGIL, pitcher.—*Ref. K2-83* c. late 1880's. Extended table service including egg cup, celery vase, compote, tumbler, sauce, wine.—**Key A**

Row 3

1. PICKET BAND (STAVES WITH SCALLOPED BAND; PEN), goblet.—*Ref. K3-33; Gob II-49* Doyle and Company, c. 1870's. Extended table service including wine. Crystal, blue.—**Key A**

2. TRIPLE PRISM GRID, salt shaker.—*Ref. K7-208* Imperial Glass Co. #256½, c. 1915. Extended table service.—**Key A**

3. TRANSVERSE RIBS, salt shaker.—*Ref. Gob II-42* Extended table service.—**Key B**

PLATE 211 RIBS AND COLUMNS

Row 1

1. ZIPPER SLASH, pitcher.—*Ref. K3-83* George Duncan's Sons and Co. #2005, after 1900. Extended table service including toothpick holder, wine, bowls, celery vase, tumbler, open and covered compotes, sherbet, cup, footed sauce, banana dish. Crystal, frosted, ruby-stained, amber-stained.—**Key B**

2. LACY VALANCE (PERSIAN SHAWL), creamer.—*Ref. K2-34* c. 1890's. Made in extended table service including salt shaker, flat-sided honey dish, celery vase, bread tray, compotes with handles, syrup. Has a triangular medallion with scrolls in end panels.—**Key A**

Row 2

1. LADDERS, creamer.—*Ref. K5-79* Tarentum Glass Co. #292 1901. Extended table service including vase, cup, celery vase. Crystal.—**Key A**

2. BEADED COARSE BARS, goblet.—*Ref. Gob II-15* Extended table service including water bottle.—**Key A**

Row 3

1. ZIPPERED BLOCK (CRYPTIC), goblet.—*Ref. K3-131* Duncan, 1890; U.S. Glass, 1891. Extended table service including bowls, water bottle, tumbler, salt shaker. Crystal, ruby-stained (scarce).—**Key A**

2. SERRATED RIB, salt shaker.—*Ref. PetSal 37G* Surfaces of panels are higher than "zippers".—**Key A**

Row 4

1. ZIPPER BORDERS, syrup (etched).—*Ref. HIII-47* c. 1898. Syrup known. Crystal, ruby-stained.—**Key B**

2. IOWA (PANELLED ZIPPER), cruet.—*Ref. PetSal 164D* U.S. Glass Co. #15069 (Glassport), 1900. A State Series pattern. Extended table service including wine, toothpick holder, salt shaker, tumbler, cup. Crystal, rose-flashed.—**Key B**

PLATE 212 RIBS AND COLUMNS

Row 1
1. PANELLED PLEAT, creamer. See Plate 173.
2. IMPERIAL'S #77, pitcher.—*Ref. K7-66* Imperial Glass Co., c. 1902.—**Key A**

Row 2
1. HERRINGBONE BUTTRESS, pitcher. See Plate 193.
2. PARIS (ROUGHNECK), creamer.—*Ref. K5-40; PetSal 171B* Bryce, Higbee and Co., c. 1900. Extended table service including cake stand, salt shaker, footed sauce, jelly compote, vase, wine, cruet, compote, cake basket, cake stand, berry bowl, tumbler, cake plates.—**Key B**

Row 3
1. FISHBONE BOW, salt shaker.—*Ref. PetSal 161B* —**Key A**
2. FISHBONE, salt shaker.—*Ref. PetSal 28U* Extended table service.—**Key A**
3. WINDOW AND DRAPE, salt shaker.—*Ref. PetSal 177E* Originally contained snuff.—**Key B**
4. PANELLED FISHBONE, salt shaker.—*Ref. PetSal 28V* —**Key A**

Row 4
1. GREEN HERRINGBONE, salt shaker. See Plate 173.
2. HERRINGBONE BUTTRESS, goblet. See Row 2 #1.
3. BANDED SERRATED PRISM, goblet.—*Ref. Gob II-17* Extended table service including salt shaker.—**Key A**
4. BEADED RIB, salt shaker.—*Ref. PetSal 36S* —**Key A**

PLATE 213 RIBS AND COLUMNS

Row 1

1. NELLY (SYLVAN; FLORENCE), creamer.—*Ref. K5-39* McKee Glass Co., 1894. Extended table service including salt shaker, celery vase, compote, berry bowl, sauce, tumbler, cake stand. Crystal. —**Key A**

2. EDGEWOOD, creamer—*Ref. K5-103* Fostoria Glass Co. #675, 1899. Made in extended table service including salt shaker, toothpick holder, carafe, syrup, cup, sherbet.—**Key A**

Row 2

1. NOTCHED PANEL, creamer.—*Ref. PetSal 34H* Tarentum Glass Co., 1902. Extended table service including toothpick holder, salt shaker. Crystal, ruby-stained.—**Key B**

2. PRISM COLUMN, creamer.—*Ref. K6-15* U.S. Glass #15023, 1892. Extended table service including syrup, celery vase, compote, 6″ plate, cake stand, mustard can, ice tub. Crystal, light green. —**Key A**

Row 3

1. ZIPPER (COBB; LATE SAWTOOTH), pitcher.—*Ref. K2-19* Richards and Hartley Flint Glass Co., 1888. Made in extended table service including covered jam jar, celery vase, open and covered compotes, footed sauce, toy banana stand, sugar shaker, syrup. Crystal, blue—**Key B**

2. SERRATED PANELS, bowl.—*Ref. HV-164* U.S. Glass Co. #15089 (Gas City), 1904. Extended table service. Crystal.—**Key B**

Row 4

1. GRATED RIBBON, creamer. See Plate 150.

2. THE PRIZE, creamer.—*Ref. K5-67* National Glass Co. (McKee), c. 1901. Extended table service including tumbler, toothpick holder, salt shaker, syrup. Crystal, emerald green, ruby-stained.—**Key B**

PLATE 214 RIBS AND COLUMNS

Row 1

1. FOSTORIA'S #1231, creamer.—*Ref. K8-40* Fostoria Glass Co., c. 1903. Extended table service including vases, finger bowl, cup, rose bowl, pickle jar, punch bowl, sherbet, sauce, bowls.—**Key B**

2. SERRATED SPEAR POINT, goblet.—*Ref. Gob II-74* —**Key A**

Row 2

1. MARDI GRAS, creamer. See Plate 78.

2. HEISEY'S #1250, pitcher.—*Ref. K7-136* A. H. Heisey and Co., c. 1897. Extended table service including tumbler, salt shaker, bonbon, spoon tray, cruet, celery vase, compotes, cracker jar, 5" and 6" plates, bowls, pickle jar, sauce, berry set.—**Key B**

Row 3

1. MICHIGAN (LOOP AND PILLAR; PANELLED JEWEL; DESPLAINES), goblet.—*Ref. K1-106* U. S. Glass Co. #15077 (Glassport), 1902. A State Series pattern. Extended table service including plate, vases, tumbler, cruet, rare ruby-stained toothpick holder, salt shaker, toy table set, individual sugar and creamer, sauce, mug, handled lemonade. Crystal, rose-flashed (maiden's blush), green-flashed, decorated, vaseline-stained, green-stained. Reproduced in other colors. Moderate availability. See Plate 17. —**Key B**

2. STAR AND NOTCHED RIB, salt shaker.—*Ref. PetSal 173G* —**Key A**

3. IRIS WITH MEANDER (IRIS), pitcher.—*Ref. K6-63* Jefferson Glass Co., 1904. Made in extended table service including toothpick holder, tumbler, sauce, salt shaker. Crystal, blue, green, amethyst; opalescent colors.—**Key B**

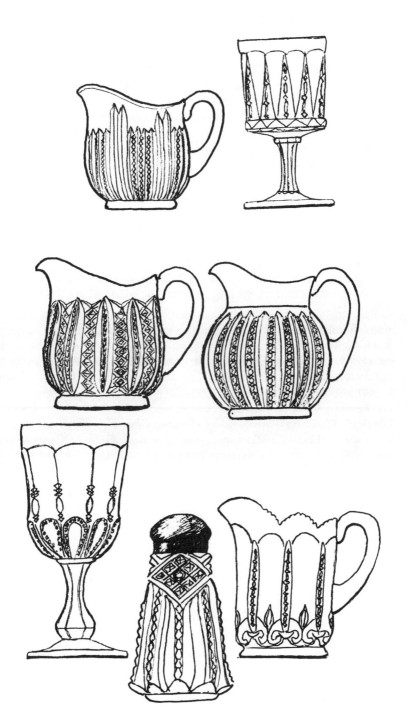

PLATE 215 ROPES

Row 1

1. BUTTRESSED ARCH, creamer.—*Ref. K3-109* —**Key A**
2. CABLE VARIANT, goblet.—*Ref. L164-2* —**Key B**
3. ROPE BANDS (ARGENT; CLEAR PANELS WITH CORD BAND), pitcher.—*Ref. K5-14* U.S. Glass Co. (Bryce), 1891. Extended table service including wine, tumbler, celery vase, platter, cake stand, covered compote, open and covered sugar bowls, sauce. Crystal.—**Key A**

Row 2

1. BEADED ROPE PANEL, salt shaker.—*Ref. PetSal 37S* —**Key A**
2. ROPE PANEL, salt shaker.—*Ref. W. 136* Milk glass.—**Key B**
3. CABLE, goblet.—*Ref. L36* c. 1850's. Extended table service including rare creamer, cake stand, rare water pitcher, compote, egg cup, lamps, rare footed tumbler, bowls, wine, champagne, decanters, syrup, master salt. Crystal; rare in opaque white, blue, green. —**Key C**

Row 3

1. CABLE WITH RING, creamer.—*Ref. K1-5* Boston and Sandwich Glass Co., 1860's. Made in extended table service including open compote, honey dish, lamp, sauce. No goblet or tumbler known. Crystal.—**Key E**
2. PANELLED CABLE, creamer.—*Ref. K6-14* U.S. Glass Co. (Bryce), 1891. Extended table service. Crystal.—**Key A**
3. ROPE AND RIBS, sugar shaker.—*Ref. HIII-59* Central Glass Co., c. 1890. Made in extended table service. Crystal, amber, blue, canary.—**Key A**

PLATE 216 ROPES

Row 1

1. ROPED DIAMOND, goblet.—*Ref. Gob II-109* —**Key B**
2. RETICULATED CORD (DRUM), goblet.—*Ref. Gob I-130; Gob II-139* U.S. Glass Co. (O'Hara), 1891. Made in extended table service including open-handled plate. Crystal, color (scarce).—**Key B**
3. RETICULATED CORD, pitcher. See above.

Row 2

1. CORD AND BARS, goblet.—*Ref. Gob II-87* —**Key A**
2. LOOP HERRINGBONE, syrup.—*Ref. HV-173* U.S. Glass Co., 1901. Crystal syrup known.—**Key B**
3. CABLE, plate. See Plate 215.

Row 3

1. LOOPED ROPE, syrup.—*Ref. K7-19* Extended table service. Opaque white.—**Key C**
2. TRIPLE BAR WITH CABLE (PENTAGON), creamer.—*Ref. K2-115; LV43* George Duncan and Sons, c. 1880-1885. Extended table service.—**Key B**

PLATE 217 SHELLS

Row 1

1. CRYSTALINA, plate. See Plate 158.
2. SHELL ON RIBS (SHELL), creamer.—*Ref. HV 129* U. S. Glass Co. (Columbia), 1891. Basic table service. Crystal.—**Key B**
3. LEAF BRACKET, cruet.—*Ref. K5-106* Indiana Tumbler and Goblet Co., 1900. Extended table service including berry bowl, tumbler, celery tray, salt shaker, triangular bowl, toothpick holder. Crystal, opalescent, chocolate, green.—**Key B**

Row 2

1. CRYSTALINA, bread plate. See Plate 158.
2. ARGONAUT SHELL (NAUTILUS), pitcher.—*Ref. K4-32* Northwood Glass Co., 1900. Extended table service including berry set, toothpick holder, salt shaker, compotes, tumbler. Custard, opalescent, carnival. A very choice pattern.
3. SHELL (JEFFERSON SHELL), creamer.—*Ref. K7-58* Dugan Glass Co., 1903. Extended table service including toothpick holder. Note: This was called "Jefferson Shell" until William Heacock recently discovered its true manufacturer, Dugan. Crystal, plain and opalescent blue, green, canary.—**Key B**

Row 3

BANDED SHELLS, sauce.—*Ref. HIII 64* U.S. Glass Co. (Challinor), 1891. Extended table service including salt shaker, sugar shaker, syrup. Opaque glass.—**Key C**

Row 4

1. SHELL AND JEWEL (VICTOR), tumbler.—*Ref. K1-68* Westmoreland Glass Co.; Fostoria Glass Co.; 1893. Extended table service including salt shaker, sauce, tumbler, compote, cake stand. No goblet made. Crystal, blue, green.—**Key B**
2. SHELL AND SCALE, salt shaker.—*Ref. PetSal 172H* Made in extended table service including cake stand.—**Key B**
3. SHELL AND TASSEL ROUND, vase. See Plate 5.

Row 5

1. GENEVA (SHELL AND SCROLL), tumbler.—*Ref. K2-117* National Glass Co. (McKee), 1900. Extended table service including footed bowls, syrup, toothpick holder, salt shaker. Crystal, custard, decorated.—**Key C**
2. TRIPLE SHELL, salt shaker.—*Ref. PetSal 172J* Eagle Glass and Mfg. Co., 1898. Milk glass.—**Key C**

PLATE 218 SQUARES AND RECTANGLES

Row 1

1. STAR-IN-SQUARE, creamer.—*Ref. K8-48* Duncan and Miller Glass Co. #75, c. 1904. Extended table service including salt shaker, toothpick holder.—**Key B**

2. HANOVER (BLOCK WITH STARS), creamer.—*Ref. K1-113* Richards and Hartley, 1888; U.S. Glass Co., 1891. Made in extended table service including cheese plate and cover, cake stand, compotes, bowls, puff box without stars, tumbler, wine, sauce. Crystal, amber, blue.—**Key B**

Row 2

1. INDIANA (FEATHER; PRISON WINDOW), pitcher.—*Ref. LV 39; PetSal 169J* U.S. Glass Co. #15029 (Gas City), 1896-97. A State Series Pattern. Extended table service. Not easily found. See Plates 54 and 221. Crystal.—**Key B**

2. WAFFLE AND STAR BAND (BLOCK AND STAR SPEAR POINT; VERONA), creamer.—*Ref. K1-113; Gob II-110* Tarentum Glass Co., c. 1910. Extended table service including punch bowl, toothpick holder. Crystal, ruby-stained.—**Key C**

Row 3

1. SKILTON (OREGON), goblet—*Ref. Gob II 59; LV 44* Richards and Hartley Flint Glass Co., 1888; U.S. Glass Co., 1891. Extended table service including rectangular and round bowls, footed sauce, handled relish, salt shaker, wine, tumbler, compotes. Crystal, ruby-stained.—**Key B**

2. COLUMN BLOCK (PANEL AND STAR), creamer.—*Ref. K3-75* O'Hara Glass Co. #500, c. 1890. Made in extended table service including salt shaker, rare toothpick holder. Crystal, vaseline.—**Key B**

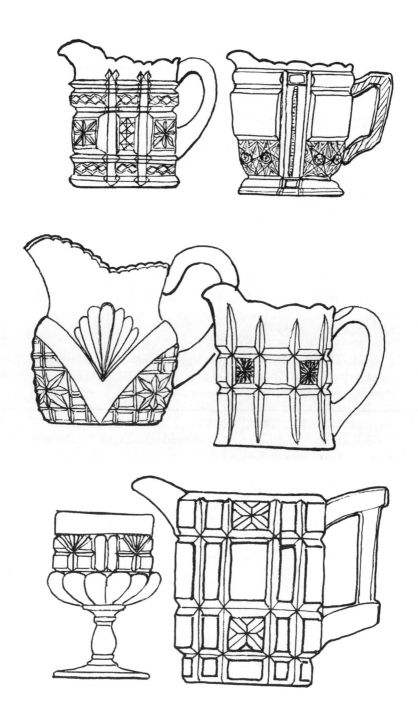

PLATE 219 SQUARES AND RECTANGLES

Row 1

1. BLOCK AND FAN (ROMEO), tumbler.—*Ref. K3-75; LV85* Richards and Hartley #544, 1888; U.S. Glass Co., 1891. Made in extended table service including cake stand, compote, cruets, plates, lamp, salt shaker, relish, sauces, celery tray and vase, castor set, syrup, footed and flat berry bowls, cracker jar, ice tub. Crystal, ruby-stained, milk glass.—**Key C**

2. PICTURE WINDOW, pitcher (etched).—*Ref. K4-139* Central Glass Co. #870. Made in extended table service including salt shaker.—**Key B**

3. CUBE AND BLOCK, pitcher—*Ref. HV 180* U.S. Glass Co. (Richards and Hartley #40), 1891. Extended table service. Crystal, ruby-stained.—**Key B**

Row 2

1. PLUME AND BLOCK (FEATHER AND BLOCK), spoon holder.—*Ref. K3-74* U.S. Glass Co. (Hartley #189), 1891. Extended table service including celery vase, compotes. Crystal, ruby-stained.—**Key B**

2. HOBBS' BLOCK (DIVIDED SQUARES), pitcher.—*Ref. K3-95* U.S. Glass Co. (Hobbs), 1891. Extended table service including tumbler, syrup, water bottle, finger bowl, celery boat, salt shaker. Crystal, frosted, amber, decorated.—**Key B**

3. BLOCK AND PLEAT (PERSIAN), mug.—*Ref. K5-36* Bryce, Higbee and Co., 1885; U.S. Glass Co. Extended table service including candy jar, open and covered compotes, bowls, celery vase, footed sauce, tray.—**Key C**

Row 3

1. MALTESE CROSS, pitcher.—*Ref. Gob I-35; K5-31* U.S. Glass Co. (Duncan #1003), 1891. Extended table service including water tray, cup, finger bowl, tumblers, salt shaker, pickle jar, celery vase. Crystal.—**Key B**

2. CROSSED BLOCK, creamer. See Plate 55.

3. TWIN PANELS, goblet.—*Ref. K8-71* Extended table service including salt shaker.—**Key A**

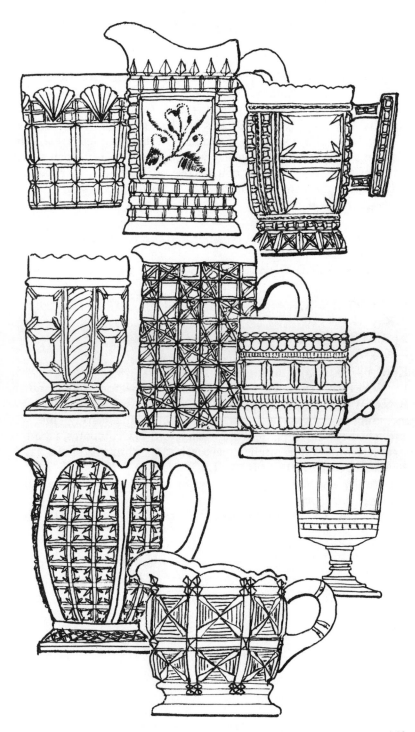

449

PLATE 220 SQUARES AND RECTANGLES

Row 1

1. WAFFLE WITH POINTS, creamer—*Ref. K4-27* Probably Duncan, c. 1890 (Kamm). Extended table service.—**Key B**
2. BLOCK ON STILTS, goblet.—*Ref. Gob II-32* —**Key B**
3. HIDALGO (FROSTED WAFFLE), creamer (etched).—*Ref. K3-56; LV49* U.S. Glass Co. (Adams), 1891. Extended table service including compotes, cruet, celery vase, cup and saucer, open salt and salt shaker, tray, finger bowl, covered compote, syrup, many odd-shaped relish dishes and bowls. Crystal, frosted, ruby-stained.—**Key B**

Row 2

1. BLOCK AND RIB, creamer.—*Ref. K3-48* Opaque white. —**Key C**
2. TRUNCATED CUBE, cruet. See Plate 204.

Row 3

1. CURTAIN AND BLOCK, salt shaker.—*Ref. PetSal 26L* —**Key B**
2. CAPSTAN, salt shaker.—*Ref. PetSal 156J* —**Key A**

Row 4

1. WAFFLE, tumbler.—*Ref. L46: K6-7* Boston and Sandwich; Bryce, Walker & Co., early 1860's. Made in extended table service including celery vase, egg cup, plate, champagne, claret, wine, water and whiskey tumblers, decanters, high and low compotes, rare quart creamer, rare water pitcher, castor bottle. Flint.—**Key D**
2. HERCULES PILLAR — LATE, syrup.—*Ref. Gob I* Hobbs, Brockunier and Co. Goblet and syrup known. Crystal, blue, amber, apple green, canary (scarce).—**Key C**
3. BLOCK AND PILLAR, salt shaker.—*Ref. PetSal 23D* —**Key A**

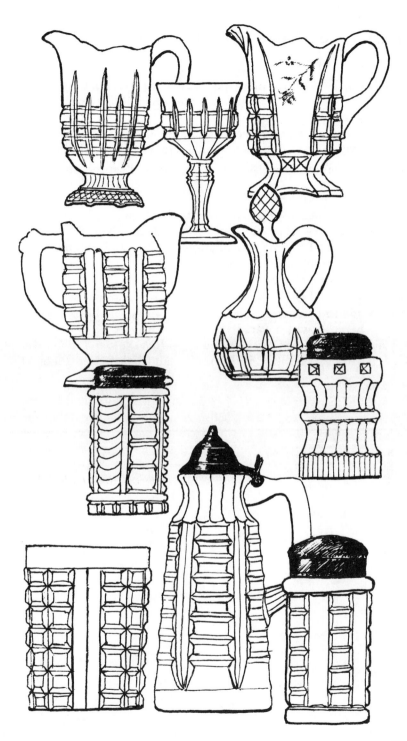

451

PLATE 221 SQUARES AND RECTANGLES

Row 1

1. DOYLE'S #80, creamer.—*Ref. K8-48* Doyle and Co., c. 1880; U.S. Glass Co., 1891. Made in extended table service. Crystal, colors.—**Key A**

2. SWAG BLOCK, creamer.—*Ref. K3-130* U.S. Glass Co. (Duncan #326), 1891. Made in extended table service including sauce. Crystal.—**Key A**

Row 2

1. BLOCK AND SUNBURST, creamer.—*Ref. K1-102* George Duncan and Sons, 1880's. Extended table service including tumbler, wine, mug, sauce, compote, tankard creamer.—**Key A**

2. CRADLED PRISMS, creamer.—*Ref. K4-112* Challinor, Taylor, 1880's. Basic table service.—**Key B**

Row 3

1. ELSON'S BLOCK, creamer.—*Ref. K5-12* Elson Glass Co. #150, 1891. Made in extended table service including tumbler, celery vase, sauces, berry bowls, covered compotes.—**Key A**

2. WAFFLE WINDOW, salt shaker.—*Ref. PetSal 176S* —**Key A**

3. INDIANA (PRISON WINDOW), salt shaker. See Plate 218.

PLATE 222 SQUARES AND RECTANGLES

Row 1

1. POINTED CUBE, wine goblet. c. 1880's. Made in water set: decanter, tray, wine.—**Key B**

2. TACKLE BLOCK, goblet.—*Ref. Gob II-49* Known in two types flint goblet, c. 1840's.—**Key C**

3. WAFFLE AND BAR, miniature creamer.—*Ref. K1-115* Duncan glass.—**Key A**

Row 2

1. PRESSED BLOCK, compote.—*Ref. Gob II-97* Made in extended table service.—**Key D**

2. DUNCAN BLOCK, creamer.—*Ref. LV41* U.S. Glass Co. (Duncan; Doyle), 1891. Made in extended table service including plate, cup, basket, water bottle, salt shaker, bowls, tumbler, cruet, sugar shaker, celery vase, individual salt, mustard jar, syrup. Crystal, ruby-stained.—**Key A**

3. BLOCK, spoon holder. Extended table service including cup, cruet, wine, covered cracker jar. Crystal, color-stained.—**Key A**

Row 3

1. WAFFLE VARIANT, individual creamer.—*Ref. K1-118* George Duncan and Sons #308, 1890; U.S. Glass, 1891. Made in extended table service including 7″ and 8″ trays, footed and flat celery vases, sugar shaker, cruets, covered cheese dish, carafe, ice cream tray, bowls.—**Key B**

2. WAFFLE OCTAGON, salt shaker. —*Ref. PetSal 43D* Has rotary agitator and top patented Christmas, 1877.—**Key B**

3. DUNCAN'S LATE BLOCK (WAFFLE BLOCK), syrup.—*Ref. K1-118* U.S. Glass Co. (Duncan#331), 1891. Extended table service including parlour lamp, celery boat, square and triangular bowls, cup, square sauce, mustard jar, cruet, punch bowl, ice tub, handled relish, jelly compote, sugar shaker, salt shaker, two size sugar bowls, rose bowls. Crystal, ruby-stained.—**Key A**

PLATE 223 SQUARES AND RECTANGLES

Row 1

1. BERLIN (REEDED WAFFLE), pitcher.—*Ref. K1-98* Adams and Company, 1874; U.S. Glass Co., 1891. Extended table service including tumbler, cup, cruet, wine, covered cracker jar. Crystal, color-stained—**Key B**

2. THUMBPRINT BLOCK (BANQUET), creamer.—*Ref. K5-57* Columbia Glass Co.; U.S. Glass Co., 1891. Extended table service including cup, rose bowl. Also has a rounded form — See Row 3 #2. Crystal.—**Key B**

Row 2

1. BLOCK AND BAR, creamer.—*Ref. K5-45* —**Key C**

2. OPEN BASKETWEAVE (OPEN PLAID), creamer.—*Ref. K1-30* Extended table service including bowls, cordial, plate, salt shaker, tumbler, wine, syrup. Crystal.—**Key B**

Row 3

1. KALONYAL, pitcher.—*Ref. K7-142* A. H. Heisey Co.'s #1776, 1905, Marked with H-in-diamond trademark. Made in extended table service including celery tray, pickle tray, spoon tray, bowls, tumbler, claret, cup, egg cup, footed sherbets, salt shaker, cordial, compotes, cake stand, punch bowl, wines, champagne, scalloped-top sherbet, mug, wager bottle (81 items in all).—**Key B**

2. THUMBPRINT BLOCK (ROUND), creamer (etched). See Row 1 #2.

3. APOLLO, goblet (etched). See Plate 16.

Row 4

1. SQUARE BLOCK, salt shaker.—*Ref. PetSal 173B* —**Key A**

2. BANDED BARREL, syrup.—*Ref. HIII-15* c. 1895. Known in syrup. Crystal, amber, green.—**Key C**

3. BLOCK WITH THUMBPRINT, salt shaker.—*Ref. L101* c. 1876. Made in extended table service including footed tumbler, celery vase, covered compote.—**Key C**

457

PLATE 224 SQUARES AND RECTANGLES

Row 1

1. PLAID, pitcher—*Ref. L76* c. 1880's. Extended table service including syrup, tumbler, wine, celery vase, compotes. Crystal. —**Key B**

2. OVERALL LATTICE, creamer—*Ref. K2-43* Indiana Tumbler and Goblet Co. Extended table service including wine, plate, ruffled bowl. Crystal, vaseline.—**Key A**

Row 2

1. GRILLE, creamer—*Ref. K7-16* A square piece with handle and spout on corners.—**Key B**

2. CUBE, goblet—*Ref. L26* Boston and Sandwich Glass Co. Extended table service including cake stand, cruet.—Flint **Key C**

3. MOESSER, goblet—*Ref. Gob II-107* —**Key B**

4. ZENITH BLOCK, goblet—*Ref. Gob II-71* —**Key A**

Row 3

1. PANELLED ENGLISH HOBNAIL, goblet—*Ref. L86* —**Key B**

2. SCREEN, salt shaker.—*Ref. PetSal 171-0* —**Key A**

3. BEATTY HONEYCOMB, sugar shaker.—*Ref. LV69* Beatty and Sons Glass Co.; U.S. Glass Co.; c. 1888-1895. Made in condiments pieces: cruet, toothpick holder, salt shaker. White and blue opalescent.—**Key E**

PLATE 225 SQUARES AND RECTANGLES

Row 1

1. BAMBOO BEAUTY, creamer.—*Ref. HV-128* U.S. Glass Co. (Columbia), 1891. Basic table service. Crystal.—**Key A**

2. TILE (OPTICAL CUBE), pitcher.—*Ref. K6-22; Gob II-70* Thompson Glass Co. #19, 1890. Extended table service including compotes — 75 items in all.—**Key A**

3. PILLOW BANDS, pitcher.—*Ref. K2-77* Extended table service including cruet, compotes, celery vase, berry bowl.—**Key B**

Row 2

1. TILE, goblet. See Row 1 #2.

2. SECTIONAL BLOCK, goblet.—*Ref. Gob II-109* —**Key A**

3. DUNCAN #46, cruet.—*Ref. Bones 110* George Duncan and Sons, c. 1900. Two sizes cruet known.—**Key A**

Row 3

1. GREENSBURG'S #130 (BLOCK BARREL), creamer.—*Ref. K5-pl. 7* Greensburg Glass Co., 1889. Extended table service including basket, covered compote, berry bowl, square handled jelly dish.—**Key B**

2. PRISM CUBE, goblet.—*Ref. Gob II-58* —**Key B**

3. MC KEE'S PILLOW, toy creamer.—*Ref. K7-48* McKee Glass Co., c. 1890's.—**Key A**

Row 4

1. HOOPED BARREL, salt shaker.—*Ref. PetSal 21-V* —**Key A**

2. WAFFLE KEG, salt shaker.—*Ref. PetSal 43-C* A.H. Heisey Co. #1425.—**Key B**

3. BASKETWEAVE (PLAID), syrup.—*Ref. L104; K5-51; Gob I-127* c. 1885. Extended table service including egg cups, lamp, mug, plate, 12″ tray, tumbler, cup and saucer, salt shaker. Crystal, amber, blue, vaseline, canary, apple green, opaque white.—**Key B**

461

PLATE 226 SQUARES AND RECTANGLES

Row 1

1. CRAZY PATCH, goblet.—*Ref. Gob II-71* —**Key B**
2. NICKLE PLATE'S RICHMOND, pitcher. A vertical variation of the pattern shown on Plates 51 and 91.

Row 2

KLONDIKE (ENGLISH HOBNAIL CROSS; AMBERETTE; ALASKA), creamer.—*Ref. K2-100; K6 pl. 15* A.J. Beatty Co., 1885; Hobbs, Brockunier, 1888; and others. Extended table service including relish, tumbler, bowls, salt shaker, pickle boat, covered compote, sauces, syrup, toothpick holder, square tray, bud vase, cake stand, cruet, champagne, cup. Abundantly available but expensive in color. Crystal, frosted, amber or lilac stained. Crystal.—**Key D**

Row 3

1. TAPPAN, toy creamer.—*Ref. K3-127* McKee Glass Co., 1894. Toy basic table service. Crystal, amber.—**Key B**
2. CHECKERBOARD BAND, creamer.—*Ref. K7-60* U.S. Glass Co. (Challinor #82), 1891. Basic table service. Crystal.—**Key B**
3. WAFFLE AND THUMBPRINT, goblet. See Plate 33.

Row 4

BEADED BLOCK, IMPERIAL'S, jelly compote. Imperial Glass Co., 1927-1930's. Depression glass in large table service. Many colors.

Row 5

1. DIAGONAL BAND WITH FAN, sauce.—*Ref. L156* U.S. Glass Co. (Ripley), 1891. Extended table service including compotes, salt shaker, celery vase, wine, plates, cordial, champagne. Crystal. —**Key B**
2. FROSTED BLOCK, creamer.—*Ref. K1-98; K3-26* Imperial Glass Co., 1913 to the 1930's. Later ware was colored pink, chartreuse, and apple green. Made in large table service. Crystal, many colors, vaseline opalescent.—**Key A**

463

PLATE 227 SQUARES AND RECTANGLES

Row 1

1. BAR AND BLOCK, tankard pitcher.—*Ref. K4-128* This is part of "Nickle Plate's Richmond" pattern on Plate 51.
2. BLOCK BAND SQUARES (BLOCK BAND), tankard pitcher.—*Ref. K7-20* —**Key A**
3. CLARK, creamer.—*Ref. LV 68* Extended table service including salt shaker.—**Key B**

Row 2

1. RING AND BLOCK, tankard pitcher (etched).—*Ref. K4-128* U.S. Glass Co. (King), 1891. Extended table service. Crystal. —**Key B**
2. SAXON, creamer.—*Ref. L20; Gob II-12* Bakewell, Pears and Co., c. 1870's. Extended table service including toothpick holder, wine, bowl, sauce, tumbler, egg cup, salt dish, celery vase, 6″ plate, covered jar, relish, pickle dish.—**Key B**
3. STARRED BLOCK, creamer.—*Ref. K4-114* c. 1896. A tankard-type pitcher is also known in this pattern, sold by Montgomery Ward in 1896.—**Key A**

Row 3

1. WAFFLE AND FINE CUT, individual creamer.—*Ref. K2-98* U.S. Glass Co., (Bryce), 1891. This is a creamer in the "Cathedral" pattern. The butter dish looks more like this variation than the creamer shown on Plate 88.
2. CO-OP BLOCK, creamer (etched).—*Ref. K5-93* Cooperative Flint Glass Co., 1899. Extended table service including sáuces, handled jelly dish, bowls.—**Key A**
3. QUARTERED BLOCK, creamer.—*Ref. K2-90* Duncan and Miller Glass Co. #55, 1903. Extended table service including toothpick holder, cup, orange bowl, berry bowl, tumbler.—**Key A**

465

PLATE 228 SQUARES AND RECTANGLES

Row 1

1. PLAIN ROMAN KEY, creamer.—*Ref. K3-18* Boston and Sandwich Glass Co. Extended table service including cordial, wine, champagne, tumbler, master salt, sauce, compote, celery vase, pickle dish.—**Key D**

2. DOUBLE GREEK KEY, pitcher. See Plate 35.

Row 2

1. ROMAN KEY-FROSTED BAND, goblet.—*Ref. Gob II-150* Extended table service including champagne, celery vase, tumbler.—**Key C**

2. HEISEY'S GREEK KEY (GRECIAN BORDER), creamer.—*Ref. K8-51* A. H. Heisey Glass Co., 1911. Extended table service including rare toothpick holder, sundae dish, bowl, sherbet, banana split, relish.—**Key C**

3. RIB AND BLOCK, goblet.—*Ref. Gob II-128* —**Key A**

Row 3

1. GREEK KEY, master salt. Portland Glass Co. Extended table service including salt shaker, ice tub, lamp, berry bowl, sauce, sherbet.—**Key C**

2. U.S. SHERATON, creamer.—*Ref. K5-100* U.S. Glass Co. #15144, 1912. Very large table service including miniature lamp, mustard jar, jam jar, several sugar bowls, dresser set and tray, cruet, syrup, ring stand, salt shakers, footed bowls, square plates, toothpick tray, pin tray. Crystal, light green—**Key A**

Row 4

1. ROMAN KEY, celery vase.—*Ref. L94* Union Glass Co. Extended table service including compote, sauce, champagne, wine.—Flint **Key D**

2. PANELLED ROMAN KEY, salt shaker.—*Ref. PetSal 37-0; K3-18* Extended table service.—**Key C**

3. ROMAN KEY COLLAR, salt shaker.—*Ref. PetSal 37N* Extended table service. Milk Glass.—**Key C**

4. ROMAN KEY BASE, salt shaker.—*Ref. PetSal 37M* Milk glass.—**Key C**

467

PLATE 229 STARS

Row 1

1. EFFULGENT STAR (STAR GALAXY), pitcher.—*Ref. K8-78; Gob II-122* Central Glass Co., 1880. Extended table service including cake stand, tumbler, celery vase. Crystal, colors.—**Key C**

2. STAR ROSETTED, goblet.—*Ref. K5-10* McKee and Brothers, 1880. Extended table service including covered compote, 10″ plate: "A Good Mother", pickle dish, 7″ plate, flat and footed sauces, open compote, bread plate. Crystal.—**Key C**

Row 2

1. STAR AND FEATHER-LEE'S, plate—*Ref. L135* —**Key C**

2. STIPPLED STAR, pitcher.—*Ref. L147* Gillander and Sons, 1870's. Extended table service including celery vase, bread plate, egg cup, pickle dish, compotes, tumbler. Crystal (reproductions in color).—**Key B**

3. STAR PATTERN, pitcher.

Row 3

1. STIPPLED SANDBUR (STIPPLED STAR VARIANT), goblet.—*Ref. Gob II, 47; K1-103* Beatty-Brady Glass Co., 1903. Extended table service including jelly compote, salt shaker, bowl, wine, sauce, compotes, tumbler. Crystal.—**Key A**

2. TWINKLE STAR (UTAH; STARLIGHT; FROST FLOWER), pitcher.—*Ref. K4-122* U.S. Glass Co. #15080 (Gas City), 1903. A State Series pattern. Stars are impressed **inside** each piece. Extended table service including salt shaker, compotes, syrup, cake stands, 9″ and 11″ plates, cake plates, tumbler, celery vase, jelly compote. A scarce pattern. Frosted Crystal.—**Key B**

469

PLATE 230 STARS

Row 1

1. STARLYTE, pitcher.—*Ref. K5-36* Lancaster Glass Co., 1910. Extended table service including celery vase, compote, salt shaker, syrup, plate, bowls, sauce, tumbler. Crystal.—**Key B**

2. PENTAGON, creamer—*Ref. K3-101* Extended table service including individual creamer.—**Key B**

Row 2

1. BETHLEHEM STAR (STARBURST), pitcher.—*Ref. K5-97* Indiana Glass Co., 1910-20. Extended table service including cruet, sauce, toothpick holder, jelly compote. Crystal.—**Key A**

2. GEM STAR, creamer. See Plate 67.

Row 3

1. STAR-OF-BETHLEHEM, pitcher.—*Ref. K7-178* Cambridge Glass Co. #2656, 1909. Extended table service including toilet bottle, water bottle, bowls, tumbler, champagne, claret, soda glass, handled celery vase, compote.—**Key A**

2. STARGLOW, pitcher.—*Ref. HV 155* U.S. Glass Co.#15120 (Gas City), 1910. Extended table service including compotes, bowls, cruet, wine, tumbler, plate, pickle dish, cake stand, castor set, celery vase, syrup, vase.—**Key B**

3. HOBBLESKIRT (RADIANT), pitcher.—*Ref. K5 pl. 5* National Glass Co., 1901.—**Key A**

Row 4

1. FEATHERED STAR, pitcher.—*Ref. HPV#2 pg. 4* Union Stopper Co., c. 1908. Extended table service including tumbler, bowl, sauce, open compote.

2. HEXAGON STAR, salt shaker.—*Ref. PetSal 173K* c. 1900. Known also in toothpick holder.—**Key A**

3. STAR AND CIRCLE, goblet.—*Ref. Gob II-8* Extended table service including 5½" compote, rare flint goblet.—Flint **Key D**

4. DAGGER, salt shaker.—*Ref. PetSal 26Q* Extended table service.—**Key B**

PLATE 231 STARS

Row 1

1.` CENTENNIAL SHIELD (FLAG), pitcher.—*Ref. K3-58* Has 38 stars. Extended table service.—**Key D**

2. STAR AND PILLAR, creamer.—*Ref. L154 #17* McKee Glass Co., 1880. Extended table service including salt shaker, celery vase, tumbler, wine. Crystal.—**Key C**

Row 2

STAR WITH ZIPPERS (STAR), salt shaker.—*Ref. PetSal 40H* —**Key B**

Row 3

1. DOYLE'S #400 (BANDED PRISM BAR), spoon holder.—*Ref. Gob II, 53; K7-73* Doyle and Co.; U.S. Glass Co., 1891. Extended table service. Crystal, amber.—**Key B**

2. SHIELD, goblet.—*Ref. K7-72* c. 1876.—**Key C**

Row 4

1. SHRINE (JEWEL WITH MOON AND STAR: JEWELLED MOON AND STAR), creamer.—*Ref. K1-101; LV 35* Beatty-Brady; Indiana Glass Co.; 1880's. Extended table service including berry set, pickle tray, jelly compote, tumbler, sauce, two sizes salt shaker. Crystal, frosted.—**Key C**

2. DIAMOND, vase.—*Ref. K6 pl 67* Ohio Flint Glass Co., 1896. Extended table service including compote.—**Key B**

Note: This has been wrongly identified as U.S. Glass Co.'s "Buckingham" (See Plate 115) and the 1st edition **Primer** repeated that error. "Diamond" is the correct attribution; Kamm shows an Ohio Flint Glass Co. ad with the "Diamond" water pitcher pictured.

3. PRISCILLA (ALEXIS; SUN AND STAR), creamer.—*Ref. K4-92; LV 72* Dalzell, Gilmore and Leighton Co., c. 1888. Extended table service including tumbler, salt shaker, toothpick, individual creamer, plate, rose bowl, compotes, wine, cracker jar, square bowl, mug, celery vase.—**Key B**

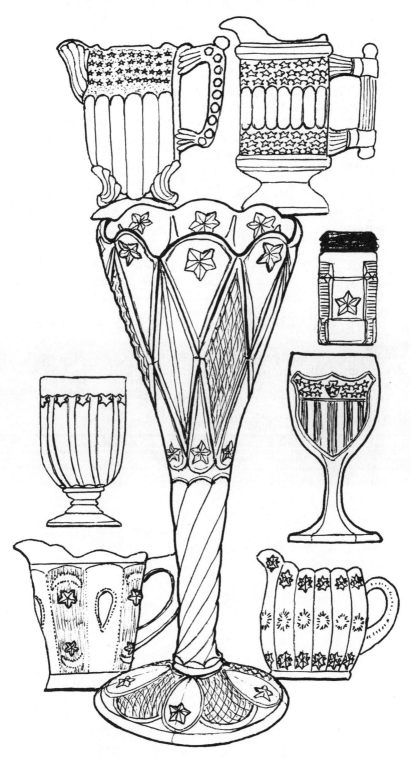

PLATE 232 STARS

Row 1

1. SANDWICH STAR AND BUCKLE, pitcher.—*Ref. K2-9* Boston and Sandwich Glass Co., early. Pieces known include spill holder, syrup, cologne bottles.—**Key D**

2. SUNK JEWEL, pitcher.—*Ref. K5-147* Fostoria Glass Co., 1903.—**Key B**

Row 2

1. DEWDROP AND STAR, goblet.—*Ref. L154-4* Extended table service included footed sauce.—**Key A**

2. STAR AND SWAG, bowl.—*Ref. L190* —**Key B**

Row 3

1. STAR AND PUNTY, pitcher.—*Ref. K5-86* Boston and Sandwich Glass Co., early. Known pieces include lamp, cologne bottle, creamer, pitcher, sugar bowl. Scarce.—**Key E**

2. MOON AND STAR, goblet. See Plate 40.

3. JEWELLED MOON AND STAR, goblet. See Plates 29 and 135.

Row 4

1. STAR AND THUMBPRINT (OLD MOON AND STAR), sugar bowl.—*Ref. K8-72* New England Glass Co., c. 1840's. Extended table service including tumblers, spill holder, lamp. All pieces rare. Crystal, canary.—**Key F**

2. SHUTTLE, salt shaker. See Plate 29.

3. QUEEN'S JEWELS (QUEEN'S NECKLACE; CROWN JEWELS), salt shaker. See Plate 135.

475

PLATE 233 STARS

Row 1

1. BANDED STAR, creamer.—*Ref. K4-110* King, Son and Co., c. 1880. Extended table service including celery vase, sauces, high and low open covered compotes, individual sugar and creamer.—**Key B**

2. FESTOONED STARS, goblet.—*Ref. Gob II 112* —**Key A**

3. MASSACHUSETTS, pitcher. See Plate 111.

Row 2

1. STAR AND PALM, goblet.—*Ref. Gob II 26* See similar pattern, "Inverted Feather", Plate 98.—**Key B**

2. DOYLE, goblet.—*Ref. K7-Pl 14* Doyle and Company, c. 1870's; U. S. Glass Co.—**Key B**

3. STAR IN HONEYCOMB (LA VERNE), pitcher.—*Ref. K2-122* Bryce Brothers, late 1880's. Extended table service including tumbler, compotes, cake stand, sauce. Crystal.—**Key B**

Row 3

1. STAR AND DART, butter dish. c. 1850's. Basic table service.—Flint **Key C**

2. STARTEC, pitcher.—*Ref. K3-137* McKee Glass Co., c. 1900. Extended table service including cruet, syrup, sauce, tumbler, bowls.—**Key A**

PLATE 234 STARS

Row 1

1. TEXAS STAR (SWIRL AND STAR; TEXAS SWIRL; SNOWFLAKE BASE), plate. See Plates 182 and 236.
2. BRITTANIC, creamer.—*Ref. K4-71* McKee Glass Co., 1894. Extended table service including banana boat, cake stand, cruet, tumbler, salt shaker, wine, compotes, toothpick holder, rose bowl, fruit basket, square bowls, round bowls, handled olive dishes, pickle dish, celery tray, celery vase, sauces, ice-cream tray, cologne bottles, carafe, syrup, cracker jar, lamps, castor set. Crystal, amber and ruby-stained.—**Key A**

Row 2

1. SUNBURST, salt shaker.—*Ref. K3-63* Jenkins Glass Co., 1910. Extended table service including cake stand, tumbler, cordial, egg cup, wine, compotes, plates, celery vase.—**Key A**
2. TEN-POINTED STAR, pitcher.—*Ref. K2-62* J.B. Higbee and Co., c. 1910. Extended table service including tumbler, sauce. —**Key B**

Row 3

1. STARRED LOOP, salt shaker. See Plate 100.
2. STAR OCTAD, salt shaker.—*Ref. PetSal 173-P* —**Key A**
3. ILLINOIS, salt shaker. See Plates 100, 108, 113.

PLATE 235 STARS

Row 1
1. ICICLE WITH STAR, pitcher.—*Ref. K4-121* —**Key A**
2. STAR-WITH-HANDLE, individual creamer.—*Ref. K8-53* —**Key B**

Row 2
1. BOXED STAR, pitcher.—*Ref. K7-12* Extended table service including tumbler.—**Key B**
2. ORNATE STAR, creamer.—*Ref. K6-21* Tarentum Glass Co., 1907. Extended table service including cordial.—**Key B**

Row 3
1. STAR AND FAN, salt shaker.—*Ref. PetSal 173F* —**Key A**
2. X-BULL'S EYE (SUMMIT), salt shaker.—*Ref. PetSal 177F* Thompson Glass Co., 1890's. Extended table service including bowls, tumblers, wine, tankard pitcher, compote.—**Key A**

Row 4
1. STAR MEDALLION (AMELIA), pitcher. See Plate 86.
2. SHIMMERING STAR, salt shaker. See Plate 99.

PLATE 236 SWIRLS

Row 1

1. BANDED SWIRL, goblet.—*Ref. Gob II 105* —**Key B**
2. NARROW SWIRL, creamer.—*Ref. K1-109* George Duncan and Sons. Was a container for mustard, horseradish, honey, etc. and had a metal lid.—**Key A**
3. NICKLE PLATE #26, pitcher.—*Ref. K5-102* Nickle Plate Glass Co., 1890; U. S. Glass Co., 1891. Extended table service including salt shaker, covered cheese dish, square and round berry bowls, mustard pot, tumbler.—**Key B**

Row 1

1. PINWHEEL, plate.—*Ref. L44* Extended table service including child's punch set.—**Key A**
2. FOSTORIA'S SWIRL, creamer.—*Ref. K5-90* Fostoria Glass Co. #175, 1890. Extended table service including bowl, vase, castor set, water bottle, salt shaker.—**Key B**

Row 3

1. CYCLONE (GRECIAN SWIRL), butter dish.—*Ref. Lee* Extended table service including champagne, wine.—**Key B**
2. TEXAS STAR (SWIRL-STAR BASE), salt shaker. See Plates 182 and 234.
3. LEANING PILLARS, syrup.—*Ref. HIII 31* Syrup and sugar shaker known, c. 1895. Crystal, amber, pale blue, amethyst.—**Key B**

Row 4

1. PARIAN SWIRL (PARIAN RUBY), syrup.—*Ref. K5-89* Northwood Glass Co., 1894. Extended table service including berry set, salt shaker, sugar shaker, toothpick holder, cruet, night lamp. Has artichoke-shaped finial on covered pieces. Satin camphor, cranberry, blue satin, light green opaque. Not made in crystal.
2. BLOWN SWIRL (FRANCESWARE SWIRL), sugar shaker.—*Ref. K6-68* Hobbs, Brockunier and Co. #326, 1885-1892. Extended table service including toothpick holder, syrup, celery vase, mustard jar, pickle tray, salt shaker. Crystal, amber-stained, frosted—**Key B**
3. RIDGE SWIRL, sugar shaker.—*Ref. Taylor Pl 1* c. 1900. This piece known. Crystal, cobalt, amber, emerald green.—**Key B**

PLATE 237 SWIRLS

Row 1

1. EAST LIVERPOOL, creamer (etched).—*Ref. K4-69* East Liverpool Glass Co., 1882-83. Extended table service including cordial, wine, cake stand, compote, 10″ plate, bowl. Limited production.—**Key B**

2. SWIRL WITH BEADED BAND, goblet.—*Ref. Gob II 147* —**Key A**

3. SWIRL AND BALL (RAY), creamer.—*Ref. K1-110* McKee Brothers, 1894. Extended table service including salt shaker, celery vase, sauce, 6″ plate, cordial set, syrup, footed jelly, candlestick, cake stand.—**Key A**

Row 2

1. RIGHT SWIRL, goblet.—*Ref. Gob II 154.* —**Key B**

2. BALL AND SWIRL, goblet.—*Ref. Gob II 32* c. 1890. Extended table service including cake stand, mugs, syrup, tumbler, wine, decanter, celery vase, cordial, compote.—**Key B**

3. SWIRL AND BALL, tankard creamer. See Row 1 #3.

Row 3

1. LUTZ (SWIRL AND BALL VARIANT), pitcher.—*Ref. K2-106* McKee and Brothers, 1894. Extended table service including mustard jar, pickle jar. Crystal.—**Key A**

2. RIB AND SWIRL, salt shaker.—*Ref PetSal 170B* Milk glass.—**Key B**

3. SWIRL BAND, creamer.—*Ref K2-12* c. mid-1880's.—**Key A**

PLATE 238 SWIRLS

Row 1

1. VESTA, open compote (etched).—*Ref. K5 pl. 24* Aetna Glass and Mfg. Co., c. 1880's.—**Key A**

2. SLASHED SWIRL, pitcher.—*Ref. K1-112* Riverside Glass Co. #0348, 1891. Extended table service including celery vase, salt shaker, compote, wine, tumbler. Crystal.—**Key A**

3. SWIRL AND CABLE, pitcher.—*Ref. K2-85* Model Flint Glass Co. Known in pitcher and creamer. Crystal.—**Key B**

Row 2

1. DOUBLE LINE SWIRL, goblet.—*Ref. Gob II-20* —**Key A**

2. TWO-PLY SWIRL, syrup.—*Ref. PetSal 41-J* Geo. Duncan and Sons #51, 1902. Extended table service including salt shaker, toothpick holder, cake stand. An early ad stated there were 75 to 100 pieces in this line in crystal and color-stained.—**Key B**

3. PRESSED SWIRL, cruet.—*Ref. HIII-56* U.S. Glass Co. (Central), 1891. Only cruet known. Crystal, amber, blue.—**Key B**

Row 3

1. WIDE SWIRL, salt shaker.—*Ref. PetSal 41M* —**Key A**

2. ORINOCO, creamer.—*Ref. K5-111* A.J. Beatty and Co., 1888. Extended table service.—**Key B**

PLATE 239 SWIRLS

Row 1
1. PECAN SWIRL, tankard pitcher.—*Ref. K4-102* —**Key B**
2. SWIRL WITH FAN, tankard pitcher.—*Ref. K7-20* —**Key B**

Row 2
1. BEADED SWIRL AND LENS, creamer.—*Ref K3-95* Crystal, colored "lens".—**Key B**
2. FERN SPRAYS, vase.—**Key B**

Row 3
1. RING AND SWIRL, goblet.—*Ref Gob II 139* —**Key A**
2. SWIRLED COLUMN (BEADED SWIRL), creamer.—*Ref. LV 41; K3-113* Geo. A. Duncan and Sons, 1890; U.S. Glass Co., 1891. Extended table service including tumbler, cup, sauces, bowls, celery vase, plate, salt shaker, sugar shaker, syrup, cruet, covered footed bowls. Crystal, emeral green.—**Key A**

Row 4
1. BAR AND SWIRL, goblet.—*Ref Gob II 79* —**Key A**
2. CHALLINOR #27, pitcher.—*Ref HV55* U. S. Glass Co. (Challinor), 1891. Opaque glass with painted flowers.—**Key C**

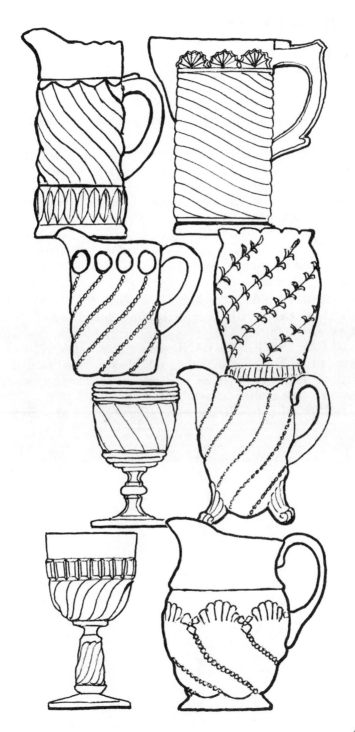

PLATE 240 SWIRLS

Row 1

1. DIAGONAL BAR BAND, creamer.—*Ref. K2-12* c. 1880's. Extended table service.—**Key A**
2. WAVEY (WAVE), tankard creamer.—*Ref K7-44* Probably a container for mustard, jelly, honey, pickles, etc.—**Key B**

Row 2

1. BEADED SWIRL AND DISC, pitcher.—*Ref. K8-36* East Liverpool Glass Co., c. 1890's; U.S. Glass Co. #15085 (Bryce), 1904. Extended table service including cake stand, celery vase, compotes, cruet, toothpick holder, bowls, salt shaker. Crystal, blue, green, yellow-stained.—**Key B**
2. FLICKERING FLAME, creamer.—*Ref. K2-92* Westmoreland Glass Co., 1896. Basic table service, plus rare syrup. Sometimes painted red in grooves. Milk Glass.—**Key A**

Row 3

1. PEBBLED SWIRL, goblet.—*Ref. Gob II 20* —**Key A**
2. DIAGONAL FROSTED RIBBON, goblet.—*Ref. Gob II 23* —**Key A**
3. CLEAR DIAGONAL BAND, celery vase.—*Ref. K1-44* c. 1880's. Extended table service including salt shaker, wine, cordial, jam jar, compotes, celery vase, sauces, open and covered sugar bowls, 7" plate, "Eureka" bread plate. Crystal.—**Key B**
4. FISHSCALE SWIRL, goblet.—*Ref. Gob II 51* —**Key B**

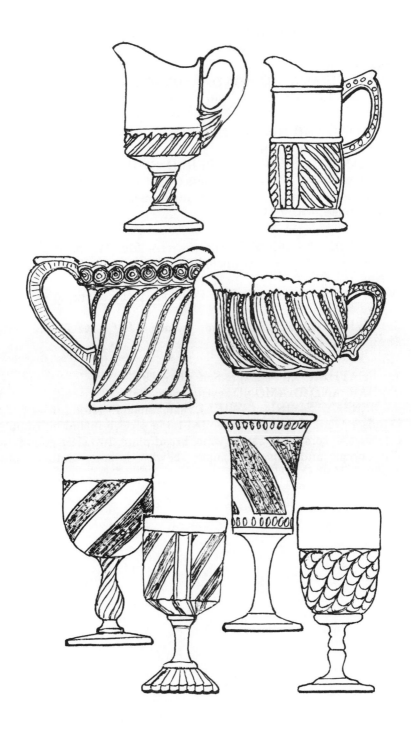

PLATE 241 SWIRLS

Row 1

1. SWIRL AND DIAMOND (AMERICA), pitcher. See Plate 43.
2. SLEWED DIAMOND, pitcher. See Plate 77.

Row 2

1. SWIRL AND DIAMOND, tumbler. See Row 1 #1. Some pieces are plain on top, or etched.
2. DIAMOND SWIRL (ZIPPERED SWIRL AND DIAMOND), sugar bowl.—*Ref. K4-93* U. S. Glass Co., 1895. Extended table service including salt shaker, syrup, individual creamer and sugar. Crystal, ruby-stained.—**Key B**

Row 3

1. SWIRL AND PANEL, salt shaker.—*Ref. PetSal 40X* c. 1900. Extended table service including toothpick holder, egg cup. —**Key C**
2. SPIRALLED DIAMOND-POINT, pickle jar.—*Ref. K8-75* —**Key B**
3. SWIRLED STAR, spoon holder.—*Ref. K7-75* c. 1885-1895.—**Key B**

Row 4

1. FEATHER, salt shaker. See Plate 89.
2. BAR AND DIAMOND, syrup. See Plate 47.
3. JERSEY SWIRL (SWIRL), salt shaker.—*Ref. K3-49; L69* Windsor Glass Co. 1887. Extended table service including tumbler, celery vase, compotes, sauce, wine, bread plate, two sizes goblet, salt dip, open and covered sugar bowl. Crystal, amber, blue, canary.—**Key C**

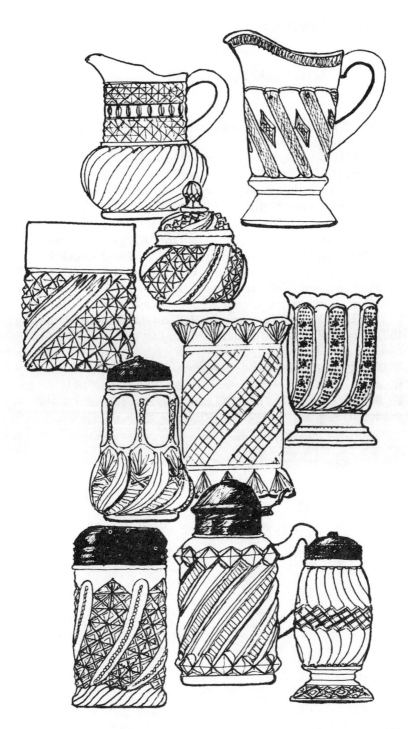

PLATE 242 SWIRLS

Row 1

1. SNAIL, butter dish. See Plate 40.
2. DOUBLE SCROLL, pitcher. See Plate 39.

Row 2

1. DOUBLE SNAIL, pitcher.—*Ref. K5 pl. 30* George Duncan and Sons, 1890-91. Known is four size pitchers.—**Key C**
2. SNAIL, creamer (etched). See Plate 40.
3. FOSTORIA'S VICTORIA, creamer.—*Ref. K5-73* Fostoria Glass Co. #183, 1890. Extended table service including syrup, tumbler, sauce, cruet, berry bowl, salt shaker.—**Key B**

Row 3

1. S-REPEAT, syrup.—*Ref. K4-115* Northwood Glass Co., c. 1900-1910; Dugan-Diamond Glass Co.; National Glass Co., 1903. Extended table service including salt shaker, cruet, toothpick holder, celery vase, tumbler, compotes, decanter, wine, tray. Crystal, amethyst, light green, sapphire blue.—**Key B**
2. WEDDING BELLS, cruet.—*Ref. K4-113* Fostoria Glass Co., c. 1901. Extended table service including salt shaker, tumbler, toothpick holder, egg cup, celery vase, compotes, punch bowl, berry bowl. Crystal, rose-flashed (maiden's blush).—**Key B**

Row 4

1. FOSTORIA'S VICTORIA, tumbler. See Row 2 #3.
2. KING'S #500, syrup. See Plate 58.

PLATE 243 SWIRLS, DRAPED

Row 1

1. COOLIDGE DRAPE, oil lamp. A lamp like this was in the room where Calvin Coolidge took the oath of office after President Harding's death. 1880. Lamp only. Crystal, cobalt blue.—See **Key E** for decanter

2. SWIRL AND DOT, celery vase.—*Ref. LV63* Extended table service including salt shaker.—**Key B**

Row 2

1. CURTAIN (SULTAN), mug.—*Ref. K3-118; L85* Bryce Brothers, 1875-85. Extended table service including tumbler, celery boat, salt shaker, compotes, cake plate, waste bowl, square plate, footed sauce. Crystal.—**Key B**

2. HEAVY DRAPE, pitcher.—*Ref. K7-39; K8-91* Fostoria Glass Co. #1300, 1904. Extended table service including toothpick holder, egg cup, salt shaker, tumbler, wine, berry set, celery vase, compotes. Crystal.—**Key D**

Row 3

1. SCALLOPED SWIRL (YORK HERRINGBONE), salt shaker.—*Ref. K6 pl. 32* Ripley and Company U.S. Glass Co. #15026, 1892. Extended table service including toothpick holder, wine, compotes, tumbler, individual creamer. Crystal, ruby-stained, green (scarce).—**Key C**

2. PILGRIM BOTTLE, salt shaker.—*Ref. K6-21* Belmont Glass Co., c. 1882; Central Glass Co. Extended table service including cruet, salt shaker, syrup. Crystal, amber, blue, vaseline.—**Key C**

Row 4

1. PLUME, pitcher. See Plate 192.

2. RUFFLES, salt shaker.—*Ref. K6 pl. 36* U. S. Glass Co. #15008 (Gillander), 1891. Extended table service. Crystal.—**Key B**

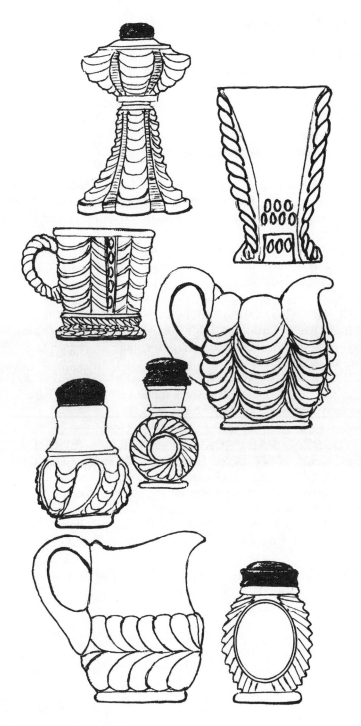

PLATE 244 MISCELLANEOUS

Row 1

1. LOG HOUSE, creamer.—*Ref. K5-41* —**Key C**
2. LOG CABIN, creamer.—*Ref. K8-59* Central Glass Co., 1875. Extended table service including rare pitcher, covered compote, covered vegetable bowl, sauce. Fair availability and expensive. Crystal.—**Key F**
3. LOG CABIN, covered compote. See above.

Row 2

1. BRICKWORK, creamer. —*Ref. K4-58* Indiana Tumbler and Goblet Co., c. 1900. Extended table service including jelly compote, salt shaker, celery vase, individual creamer. Crystal, caramel slag.—**Key A**
2. FINDLAY #19, creamer.—*Ref. K5-72* Findlay Glass Co., 1890. Extended table service including berry bowl, wine, syrup, toothpick holder, mug.—**Key B**

Row 3

1. PICKET (LONDON), pitcher.—*Ref. K1-88; L107* King Glass Co., late 1880's. Extended table service including toothpick holder, celery vase, open salt, sauce, compotes, jam jar, water tray. Crystal, plain, stippled.—**Key C**
2. BELLAIRE BASKET WEAVE, cruet.—*Ref. SmFin 50* Bellaire Goblet Co., c. 1890. Novelty items made including toothpick holder, cruet tray. Crystal, amber, blue.—**Key C**

Row 4

1. WOODEN PAIL (OAKEN BUCKET; BUCKET SET), pitcher.—*Ref. K1-55* Bryce Brothers, 1880's; U.S. Glass Co., 1891. Extended table service including jelly buckets, toothpick holder, ice bucket, open and covered sugar bowls, toy set. Crystal, amber, blue, canary, amethyst (rare).—**Key B**
2. BASKETWEAVE WITH CABLE, pitcher.—*Ref. K7-24* Atterbury and Co., c. 1874. Opaque glass.—**Key C**

Row 5

LEGGED TROUGH, creamer.—*Ref. K7-56* Has spray of berries under base.—**Key B**

PLATE 245 MISCELLANEOUS

Row 1

1. TREEBARK, pitcher.—*Ref. K1-48* Extended table service including tumblers. Crystal, amber.—**Key B**
2. SHELL AND TASSEL (SQUARE), pitcher. See Plate 5.

Row 2

1. ORANGE PEEL, goblet.—**Key A**
2. ORANGE PEEL BAND, goblet.—*Ref. Gob II 94* —**Key A**
3. TREE OF LIFE, goblet.—*Ref. LV11,12; K3-120* Boston and Sandwich; Portland Glass; Duncan Glass; U. S. Glass (1891); 1868; 1873. Extended table service including relish, egg cup, toothpick holder, bowls, wine, celery vase, compotes, tumbler, 7" plate, ice cream tray, salt shaker, cup, cake stand, footed sauce, berry bowl. Good availability. Crystal, amber, blue.—**Key C**; Flint **Key D**

Row 3

1. SNAKESKIN (OVERSHOT), plate. See Plate 206.
2. BRANCHED TREE, pitcher.—*Ref. K4-124* Dalzell, Gilmore and Leighton, 1890's. Extended table service including celery vase, compotes. Crystal, amber, blue.—**Key C**
3. THE TOWN PUMP, creamer.—*Ref. K2-108* Northwood Glass Co., 1900. Came in a set of sugar and creamer. The shaded portion on top is always a different color.—**Key D**

PLATE 246 MISCELLANEOUS

Row 1

CANADIAN, pitcher and detail.—*Ref. L112; K1-40* Burlington Glass Works (Ontario, Canada), 1870's. Extended table service including jam jar, bowl, bread tray, compotes, plates, sauce, celery vase, wine. Moderate availability. Crystal.—**Key D**

Row 2

1. BASKETWEAVE WITH FROSTED LEAF, pitcher. See Plate 200.

2. CANTON HOUSE, creamer.—*Ref. K5-16* The creamer is known without the house.—**Key C**

Row 3

1. LITTLE RIVER, pickle jar and details.—*Ref. K8-74* Jar known.—See spoon holder **Key C**

2. CAPE COD, goblet.—*Ref. L115; K8-68* Boston and Sandwich, 1870's. Pattern is like Canadian except for scenes, which show shorelines with trees, sailboat, lighthouse, etc. Extended table service including flat and footed sauce, jam jar, four size plates, cordial, celery vase, bowls with handles, open and covered compotes, wine, cup and saucer. Crystal.—**Key C**

Row 4

RING-HANDLED BASKET, salt shaker.—*Ref. PetSal 37K; W26* Milk glass.—**Key B**

PLATE 247 MISCELLANEOUS

Row 1

1. FINE RIBBED ANCHOR AND SHIELD (RHODE ISLAND), goblet. Flint goblet only is known; very scarce.—**Key E**
2. LIBERTY BELL, mug. A Centennial Exposition souvenir (1876). Milk glass.—**Key C**
3. BALLOON, creamer—*Ref. K3-76* c. 1850's. Made in Ohio. Other pieces known including plate. All pieces rare.—**Key F**

Row 2

1. ICONOCLAST, goblet.—**Key C**
2. DRAPED WINDOW, goblet.—*Ref. Gob II 152* —**Key D**
3. HARP (LYRE), spill holder.—*Ref. L14* Bryce Brothers, 1840's or 1850's. Extended table service including compote, two sizes butter dishes, two types goblet, two types whale oil lamps, sauce, honey dish, footed salt. A very choice pattern. Crystal, green. Goblet rare.—**Key F**

Row 3

1. LIBERTY BELL (CENTENNIAL), goblet.—*Ref. L58* Gillander and Sons, 1876. Extended table service including signers platter, celery vase, salt shaker, salt dip, compotes, toy table set, John Hancock bread platter, flat and footed sauces, snake-handled mug, footed bowls, pickle dish. Lots of this for sale at high prices. Crystal, milk glass (rare).—Goblet **Key D**; other **Key F**
2. CENTENNIAL 1876, goblet.—*Ref. L117, 118* c. 1876. Extended table service including bread plate.—**Key C**
3. ALASKA (LION'S LEG), pitcher.—*Ref. K1-83* Northwood Glass Co., 1897-1910. Extended table service including berry set, jewel tray, rose bowl. Crystal, emerald green, opalescent.—**Key D**

Row 4

1. LIBERTY BELL, salt shaker.—*Ref. PetSal 165H* c. 1876. Extended table service including sauce, toy table set.—**Key D**
2. DRUM, toothpick holder (toy spooner).—*Ref. K7-47* Bryce, Higbee and Co., c. 1880. Has tiny cannons for finials. Toy Table service made including mustard jar. Crystal, blue.—**Key D**
3. BEADS AND BARK, flower vase. Northwood Glass Co., 1902. Novelty in purple slag, and reportedly in green; also known in opalescent glass.—Slag **Key C**

GLASS COMPANIES

Adams and Company, Pittsburgh, Pa., c. 1851 to 1891. Joined U.S. Glass Co. in 1891 as Factory A.

Aetna Glass and Manufacturing Co., Bellaire, Ohio, 1880 to 1891.

American Flint Glass Works, Wheeling, Va. 1840's

Anchor-Hocking Glass Co., c. 1904 to present. Began as Hocking Glass Co., and in 1906 Ohio Flint Glass Co. merged with it.

Atterbury and Company, Pittsburgh, Pa., 1850's.

Bakewell, Pears and Company, Pittsburgh, Pa. Began as Bakewell, Payn and Page Co. (Pittsburgh), 1808. Still operating in the 1870's.

Beatty, Alexander J. and Sons, Steubenville, Ohio, 1879. Moved to Tiffin, Ohio and joined U.S. Glass in 1892 as Factory R.

Beatty-Brady Glass Co., Steubenville, Ohio, 1850; Dunkirk, Indiana, 1898. Joined National Glass in 1899.

Beaumont Glass Co., Martin's Ferry, Ohio, 1895. In 1905 joined Hocking Glass Co., which became Anchor-Hocking Glass Co.

Beaver Falls Cooperative Glass Co., Beaver Falls, Pa. 1879. Became Beaver Falls Glass Co., 1887.

Bellaire Goblet Co., Bellaire, Ohio, 1879; Findlay, Ohio, 1888. Joined U.S. Glass in 1891 as Factory M.

Belmont Glass Co., Bellaire, Ohio, 1866; still operating in 1888.

Boston and Sandwich Glass Co., Sandwich, Mass.; 1825-1889.

Boston Silver Glass Co., East Cambridge, Mass., 1857-1870's.

Brilliant Glass Works, Brilliant, Ohio; 1880. Moved to La-Grange in 1880 and merged with Novelty Glass Works, 1889.

Bryce, McKee and Co., Pittsburgh, Pa., 1850. Became Bryce, Walker and Co. in 1854.

Bryce, Walker and Co., Pittsburgh, Pa., 1855; became Bryce Brothers in 1882.

Bryce Brothers, Pittsburgh, Pa., 1882. Moved to Hammondsville, Pa., 1889; joined U.S. Glass in 1891 as Factory B. Moved to Mt. Pleasant, Pa. in 1896 and was still operating in 1952.

Bryce, Higbee and Co. (Homestead Glass Works), Pittsburgh, Pa., 1879. Became J. B. Higbee Glass Co. c. 1900 at Bridgeville, Pa., and was still operating in 1911.

Buckeye Glass Co., Wheeling, W. Va., 1849; moved to

506

Bowling Green, Ohio in 1888. Closed c. 1903. See Excelsior Glass Works for their other factory.

Cambridge Glass Co. (National Glass Co.), Cambridge, Ohio, 1901; still operating in 1953.

Campbell, Jones and Co., Pittsburgh, Pa., 1865. Became Jones, Cavitt and Co., 1883.

Canton Glass Co., Canton, Ohio, c. 1883; Marion Indiana, 1883; joined National Glass in 1899.

Central Glass Co., Wheeling, W. Va., 1863; joined U.S. Glass in 1891 as Factory O; became Central Glass Works later.

Central Glass Co., Summitsville, Ind. Joined National Glass in 1899; survived and was still operating in 1924.

Cumberland Glass Co., Cumberland, Maryland. Joined National Glass Co. in 1899.

Challinor, Taylor and Co. (Challinor, Hogan Glass Co.), Pittsburgh, Pa., 1866; Tarentum, Pa., 1884. Joined U. S. Glass as Factory C in 1891.

Columbia Glass Co., Findlay, Ohio 1886; joined U. S. Glass in 1891 as Factory J.

Cooperative Flint Glass Co., Beaver Falls, Pa., 1879-1937.

Crystal Glass Co., Pittsburgh, Pa., 1879; Bridgeport, Ohio, 1882. Burned in 1884. Moved to Bowling Green, Ohio, 1888. Joined National Glass Co. in 1899; reorganized by 1906; closed in 1908.

Curling, R. B. and Sons (Curling, Price and Co.), Pittsburgh, Pa, 1827; became Dithridge and Sons, 1860.

Dalzell, Gilmore and Leighton Glass Co. (Dalzell Brothers and Gilmore), Brilliant, Ohio, 1883; went to Wellsburg, W. Va. in 1884; to Findlay, Ohio in 1888; joined National Glass, 1899.

Dithridge and Co. (Ft. Pitt Glassworks), Pittsburgh, Pa., 1860. To Martins Ferry, Ohio in 1881; New Brighton, Pa., in 1887 and became Dithridge and Sons.

Doyle and Company, Pittsburgh, Pa., 1866. Joined U. S. Glass, 1891 as Factory P.

Dugan Glass Co. (Indiana Glass Co.), Indiana, Pa., 1892.

Duncan, George and Sons, Pittsburgh, Pa., 1874. Became George A. Duncan and Sons and George Duncan's Sons; joined U. S. Glass in 1891 as Factory D. Became Duncan and Miller Glass Co. in 1903.

Eagle Glass and Mfg. Co., Wellsburgh, W. Va.

East Liverpool Glass Co., East Liverpool, Ohio, 1882-1883. In 1889 Specialty Glass Co. started there.

Elson Glass Works Pittsburgh, Pa., c. 1870's.

Excelsior Glass Works (Buckeye Glass Co.), Wheeling, W. Va., 1849; moved to Martins Ferry, Ohio, 1879. Burned in 1894.

Fairmont Glass Co. joined

National Glass in 1899.

Fenton Art Glass Co., Martins Ferry, Ohio and Williamston, W. Va., 1906 to present.

Findlay Flint Glass Co., Findlay, Ohio, 1889; failed shortly thereafter.

Fostoria Glass Co., Fostoria, Ohio, 1887; Roundsville, W. Va., 1891. Added factory at Miles, Ohio in 1910. Still producing.

Franklin Flint Glass Co., Philadelphia, Pa., 1861. Operated by Gillander and Sons.

Gillander and Sons, Philadelphia, Pa., 1861. Moved to Greensburg, Pa., in 1888. Joined U. S. Glass as Factory G in 1891.

Greensburg Glass Co., Greensburg, Pa., 1889; joined National Glass in 1899.

Heisey, A. H. Glass Co., Newark, Ohio, 1895; still operating in 1953.

Higbee, J. B. Glass Co., Bridgeville, Pa., 1900; still operating in 1911.

Hobbs, Brockunierand Co. (Hobbs, J. H. Glass Co.), Wheeling, W. Va., 1863. Joined U. S. Glass as Factory H in 1891; dismantled shortly thereafter.

Imperial Glass Co., Dunkirk, Ind., 1901 to present.

Indiana Glass Co., Dunkirk, Ind., 1897-1899.

Indiana Tumbler and Goblet Co., Greentown, Ind., 1853. Joined National Glass in

1899; burned in 1903.

Jefferson Glass Co., Steubenville, Ohio, 1901; to Follansbee, W. Va. in 1907; still operating in 1920's.

Jenkins Glass Co., Greentown, Ind., 1894.

Jones, Cavitt and Co., Pittsburgh, Pa., 1884.

Kemple, John E. Glass Co., Kenova, W. Va.; East Palestine, Ohio, 1945-1970. Reproduced McKee patterns from old molds.

Keystone Tumbler Works, Rochester, Pa., 1897; joined National Glass in 1899.

King, Son and Co., Pittsburgh, Pa., 1864 as Johann, King and Co.; became King Glass Co., c. 1879.

King Glass Co., Pittsburgh, Pa., c. 1879; became U. S. Glass Factory K in 1891.

Kokomo Glass Co., Kokomo, Ind., 1899.

LaBelle Glass Co., Bridgeport, Ohio, 1872; burned in 1887; sold in 1888 to Muhleman Glass Works, LaBelle, Ohio.

Lancaster Glass Co., Lancaster, Ohio c. 1915.

Libbey, Wh. H. and Sons, Co., Toledo, Ohio, c. 1899.

McKee and Brothers, Pittsburgh, Pa., c. 1853; moved to Jeannette, Pa., 1889; joined National Glass in 1899. Was McKee Glass Co. by 1904.

Model Flint Glass Co., Findlay, Ohio, 1888; to Albany, Ind. between 1891 and 1894.

508

Joined National Glass in 1899; failed c. 1903.

National Glass Co., Pittsburgh, Ohio, 1898-1905.

New England Glass Co. (New England Glass Works), Cambridge, Mass., 1817. Became W. L. Libbey and Sons in 1880.

Nickel Plate Glass Co., Fostoria, Ohio 1888. Joined U. S. Glass as Factory N in 1891.

Northwood Glass Co., Indiana, Pa., (Became part of Dugan Glass Co., c. 1896). Joined National Glass in 1899. Became Harry Northwood Glass Co. in 1910 at Wheeling, W. Va. Failed c. 1923.

Novelty Glass Co., LaGrange, Ohio, 1880. Moved to Brilliant, Ohio, 1882. Joined U. S. Glass in 1891 as Factory T. Moved to Fostoria, Ohio in 1892 and burned in 1893.

Ohio Flint Glass Co., Lancaster, Ohio; joined National Glass in 1899.

Pittsburgh Glass Works, Pittsburgh, Pa., 1798-1852. Became James B. Lyon Glass Co. Associated with O'Hara Glass Co., Pittsburgh. Joined U. S. Glass in 1891.

Portland Glass Co., Portland, Maine, 1864.

Richards and Hartley Flint Glass Co., Pittsburgh, Pa., 1866; Tarentum, Pa., 1884. Joined U. S. Glass in 1891.

Ripley and Co., Pittsburgh, Pa., 1866; became U. S. Glass Factory F in 1891.

Riverside Glass Co., Wellsburgh, W. Va., 1879; joined National Glass in 1899.

Robinson Glass Co., Zanesville, Ohio, 1893; joined National Glass in 1899; burned in 1906.

Rochester Tumbler Co., Rochester, Pa., 1872; joined National Glass in 1899.

Royal Glass Co., Marietta, Ohio joined National Glass in 1899.

Specialty Glass Co., East Liverpool, Ohio, 1889 to c. 1898.

Steiner Glass Co., Buckhannon, W. Va., 1870's.

Tarentum Glass Co., Tarentum, Pa. was operating in 1894; still operating in 1915.

Thompson Glass Co., Uniontown, Pa., 1889 to 1898.

Union Flint Glass Works, Pittsburgh, Pa., 1854. Moved to Bellaire, Ohio in 1880; Martin's Ferry, Ohio in 1880; sold to Dithridge Flint Glass Works in 1882. New plant at Martin's Ferry; to Ellwood, Pa., in 1895. Became Northwood Co. in 1896.

Westmoreland Glass Co. (Westmoreland Specialty Co.), Grapeville, Pa., to present.

West Virginia Glass Co., Martins Ferry, Ohio 1861; joined National Glass in 1899.

BIBLIOGRAPHY

Bones, Frances, *The Book of Duncan Glass,* Wallace-Homestead Book Co., (Des-Moines, Iowa), 1973.

Brown, Clark W., *A Supplement to Salt Dishes,* Wallace-Homestead Book Co. (Des Moines, Iowa), 1970.

Dreppard, Carl W. *ABC's of Old Glass,* Universal Publishing Co., (New York, N.Y.), 1949.

Florence, Gene, *The Collector's Encyclopedia of Depression Glass,* Collector Books (Paducah, Ky.), 1977.

Hartley, Julia M. and Cobb, Mary M., *The States Series, Early American Pattern Glass,* Craftsman Printers (Lubbock, Texas), 1976.

Hartung, Marion T., *Carnival Glass In Color* (by author), 1967.

Hartung, Marion T., *Northwood Pattern Glass in Color* (by author), 1969.

Heacock, William, *Encyclopedia of Victorian Colored Pattern Glass,* Books I, III and V, Antique Publications (Marietta, Ohio).

Heacock, William, *1000 Toothpick Holders — A Collector's Guide* (by author), 1977.

Heacock, William, *Pattern Glass Preview,* Issues 1-5 (by author), 1981.

Kamm, Minnie Watson, *Pattern Glass Books, Volumes 1-8,* Kamm Publications (Grosse Point, Mich.), 1939-1954.

Kovel, Ralph and Terry, *The Kovel's Complete Antiques Price List,* 7th, 10th, and 13th editions, Crown Publishers (New York, N.Y.), 1977-1980.

Lee, Ruth Webb, *Handbook of Early American Pressed Glass Patterns,* Lee Publications (Framingham Centre, Mass.), 1936.

Lee, Ruth Webb, *Victorian Glass Handbook,* Lee Publications (Framingham Centre, Mass.), 1944.

McCain, Mollie Helen, *The Standard Pattern Glass Price Guide,* Collector Books (Paducah, KY.), 1980

Mebane, John, *Collecting Brides' Baskets and Other Glass Fancies,* Wallace-Homestead Book Co. (Des Moines, Iowa), 1976.

Millard, Dr. S. T., *Goblets II,* by author (Topeka, Kansas), 1940.

Miller, Robert W., Editor, *Wallace-Homestead Price Guide to Antiques and Pattern Glass,* Editions 4 and 7, Wallace-Homestead Book Co. (Des Moines, Iowa), 1977-1981.

Peterson, Arthur G. *Glass Salt Shakers,* Wallace-Homestead

Book Co., (Des Moines, Iowa), 1970.

Schwartz, Marvin D. and DiBartolomeo, Robert E., Editors, *American Glass, Volumes I and II,* Weathervane Books (New York, N.Y.), 1974.

Swan, Frank H. *Portland Glass,* Wallace-Homestead Book Co. (Des Moines, Iowa).

Warman, Edwin G., *Antiques and Their Prices,* 7th, 8th and 15th Editions, Warman Publishing Co. (Uniontown, Penn.), 1963, 1966, 1980.

Watkins, Laura W., *Cambridge Glass, 1818-1888,* Bramhill House, 1930.

ALPHABETICAL INDEX OF PATTERNS

Numbers refer to PLATE number, **not** page number.

A

519

MEPHISTOPHELES, 179
MERRIMAC, 76
MICHIGAN, 17, 214
MIDGET THUMBPRINT, 28
MIDWAY see Pillow Encircled, 66
MIDWESTERN POMONA see Flower and Pleat, 124
MIKADO see Daisy and Button Crossbar Thumbprint, 83
MIKADO see Late Butterfly, 6
MILLARD, 160
MILTON see Log and Star, 94
MILTON CUBE AND FAN see Pineapple and Fan, 44
MINERVA, 181
MINNESOTA, 105
MINOR BLOCK see Mascotte, 53
MIOTON, 166
MIOTON PLEAT BAND, 174
MIRROR, 27
MIRROR see Galloway, 62
MIRROR AND FAN, 31
MIRROR AND LOOP, 18
MIRROR-KAMM'S, 22
MIRROR STAR, 49
MIRROR-THE, 182
MISS AMERICA, 52
MISSOURI, 192
MITRED BARS see Zig-Zag, 173
MITRED DIAMOND, 74
MITRED DIAMOND see Sunken Buttons, 85
MITRED DIAMOND POINT see Zig-Zag, 173
MITRED PRISMS, 173
MODEL PEERLESS, 70
MODISTE see New Hampshire, 96
MOESSER, 224
MONKEY, 3
MONKEY UNDER TREE see Monkey, 3
MONROE, 23
MONTANA, 182
MOON AND STAR, 40, 232
MOON AND STAR VARIATION see Jewelled Moon and Star, 29, 135, 232
MOON AND STAR WITH WAFFLE STEM see Jewelled Moon and Star, 29, 135, 232
MOON AND STORK, 9
MORNING GLORY, 130
MOSAIC-THE, 139
MOSAIC SCROLL, 38
MT. VERNON, 74
MULTIPLE CIRCLE, 176
MULTIPLE SCROLL, 37
MURANO, 193

N

NAIL, 22
NAIL CITY, 161
NAILHEAD, 51
NAOMI see Rib and Bead, 207
NAPOLEON, 75
NARCISSUS SPRAY, 133
NARROW SWIRL, 236
NATIONAL'S EUREKA, 73
NATIONAL #681 see Wellsburg, 152
NAUTILUS see Argonaut Shell, 217
NEAR CUT, 99, 108
NEAR CUT COLONIAL see Cambridge Colonial, 160
NEAR CUT #2508 see Eyelet, 16
NEAR CUT #2651 see Inverted Feather, 98
NEAR CUT #2660, 117
NEARCUT #2692, 164
NEAR CUT #2697, 101
NEBRASKA STAR see Bismarc Star, 103
NELLY, 213
NEMESIS see Tepee, 75
NEPTUNE see Queen Anne, 180
NESTOR, 171
NET AND SCROLL, 37
NETTED OAK, 198
NETTED ROYAL OAK see Netted Oak, 198
NEVADA, 184
NEW CENTURY see Delaware, 129
NEW ENGLAND FLUTE, 156
NEW ENGLAND PINEAPPLE, 43
NEW ERA, 93
NEW GRAND see Grand, 54
NEW HAMPSHIRE, 96, 111
NEW JERSEY, 92
NEW MARTINSVILLE CARNATION, 126
NEW MEXICO see Aztec, 101
NEWPORT, 190
NEW YORK HONEYCOMB, 30
NEW YORK see Manhattan, 17, 92
NIAGARA, 29
NIAGARA-U.S., 159
NICKEL PLATE #26, 236
NICKEL PLATE'S RICHMOND, 51, 91, 226
NICKEL PLATE'S ROYAL, 176
NONPARIEL, 55
NORTH POLE see Polar Bear, 5
NORTHWOOD-DUGAN BEADED CIRCLE, 22
NORTHWOOD NEARCUT, 108
NORTHWOOD PEACH, 141
NORTHWOOD'S SUNFLOWER, 131

530

531

538

TWIN LADDERS, 33
TWIN LEAVES, 195
TWIN PANELS, 219
TWIN PEAR see Baltimore Pear, 140
TWIN SNOWSHOES, 115
TWIN SUNBURSTS, 113
TWIN TEARDROPS, 66
TWO BAND, 34
TWO HANDLE, 25
TWO FLOWER, 123
TWO PANEL, 93
TWO-PLY SWIRL, 238
TYCOON see Long Optic, 27

U

UMBILICATED HOBNAIL see Button Band, 26
UNION, 85
UNIQUE, 56
UNITED STATES-THE, 184
URN, 186
U.S. BLOSSOM, 184
U.S. COLONIAL see Plain Scalloped Panel, 159
U.S. Comet, 82
U.S. CRYSTAL ROCK, 130
U.S. GEORGIAN, 158, 162
U.S. NIAGARA, 159
U.S. PEACOCK see Slewed Horseshoe, 106
U.S. PURITAN, 158
U.S. REGAL, 110
U.S. RIB, 205
U.S. SHELL, 55
U.S. SHERATON, 228
U.S. THUMBPRINT, 15
U.S. VICTORIA see Daisy and Scroll, 104
U.S. #156, 26
U.S. #341, 30
U.S. #5701, 165
U.S. #5705, 164
UTAH see Twinkle Star, 229

V

VALENCIA see Artichoke, 51, 199
VALENCIA WAFFLE, 88
VALENTINE, 179
VENICE, 176
VERA see Fagot, 79
VERMONT see Honeycomb with Flower Rim, 135
VERMONT HONEYCOMB see Honeycomb with Flower Rim, 146
VERNON see Honeycomb, 30
VERONA see Waffle and Star Band, 218
VESTA, 238

V-BAND, 190
VICTOR see Shoshone, 71
VICTOR see Shell and Jewel, 217
VICTORIA, 29, 58
VICTORIAN JUBILEE, 37
VIGILANT, 183
VIKING see Bearded Head, 180
VIKING see Panama, 75
VIKING see Queen Anne, 180
VINCENT'S VALENTINE see Heart in Sand, 31
V-IN-HEART, 115
VIRGINIA, 202
VIRGINIA see Galloway, 62
VULCAN, 205

W

WADING HERON, 9
WAFFLE, 220
WAFFLE AND BAR, 222
WAFFLE AND FINE CUT, 227
WAFFLE AND STAR BAND, 218
WAFFLE AND THUMBPRINT, 33, 226
WAFFLE BLOCK see Duncan's Late Block, 222
WAFFLE KEG, 225
WAFFLE OCTAGON, 222
WAFFLE VARIANT, 222
WAFFLE WINDOW, 221
WAFFLE WITH POINTS, 220
WARD'S NEW ERA, 51
WASHBOARD, 172
WASHINGTON CENTENNIAL, 34, 179
WASHINGTON-EARLY, 21
WASHINGTON-LATE, 16
WATERFALL, 88
WATERLILY see Magnolia, 125
WATERLILY see Rose Point Band, 131
WATERLILY AND CATTAILS, 125
WAVE, 207
WAVE see Wavey, 240
WAVERLY, 62
WAVEY, 240
WEDDING BELLS, 242
WEDDING RING, 35
WELLINGTON, 174, 208
WELLSBURG, 152
WESTERN STAR see Georgia Belle, 102
WESTON, 74
WESTMORELAND, 57
WESTWARD HO!, 2, 180
WETZEL see Star of David, 112
WHEAT see Panelled Wheat, 201

540

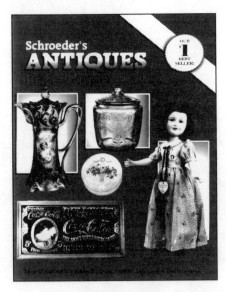